Defining Women's Scientific Enterprise

Defining Women's Scientific Enterprise

Mount Holyoke Faculty and the Rise of American Science

Miriam R. Levin

University Press of New England

Hanover and London

Published by University Press of New England,

One Court Street, Lebanon, NH 03766

www.upne.com

©2005 University Press of New England

Printed in the United States of America

5 4 3 2 1

Library of Congress Cataloging-in-Publication Data

Levin, Miriam R.

Defining women's scientific enterprise : Mount Holyoke faculty and
the rise of American science / Miriam R. Levin

Gift ³/₀⁵   p. cm.

Includes bibliographical references and index.

ISBN 1–58465–419–8 (alk. paper)

1. Mount Holyoke College.   2. Science—Study and teaching (Higher)—United States—
History—19th century.   3. Science—Study and teaching (Higher)—United States—
History—20th century.   I. Title.

Q183.3.U63M685 2004 2005

507′.11744′23—dc22   2004017360

For my children and my parents

Contents

Preface

Framing of This History

Readers may find the themes and conclusions of this book veer radically away from earlier books on the subjects of women in science, religion and science, and the rise of professional science in the United States. This book is not focused on the careers of individual women, nor on measures of success in terms of male academics at research universities, although these features of professional science do figure in the narrative. It weaves religion in, rather than out of, the story of Mount Holyoke to help explain the persistence of certain points of view about gender, remaining single, and scientific practice at the college level. I have tried to let the material speak for itself, setting myself down among the faculty members to see the situation from the perspective of what concerned them most: their position as single women faculty, their religious identity, and their role as participants in the periodic changes that affected higher education in science.

America is a nation where women have found opportunities to participate in the scientific enterprise. Historically, the most important source of possibilities for single women lay in posts as faculty in women's colleges and the seminaries that preceded them. As teachers and administrators in a network of single-sex and coeducational colleges and seminaries, the faculty of Mount Holyoke contributed to shaping and disseminating science from the time Mary Lyon founded the seminary in 1837.

Mount Holyoke provides an exemplar of the important role liberal arts colleges have played in the education of American scientists, one they continue to perform as preparators of individuals who go on to advanced training in the sciences and medicine. They are also significant employers of scientists, supporters of scientific research, and educators of science teachers and technicians. What Ernest L. Boyer, head of the Carnegie Foundation for the Advancement of Teaching, wrote about the pivotal role of colleges in general is also true of the science program of Mount Holyoke from its very beginnings: "The uniqueness of American higher education is rooted in preparation for the baccalaureate degree. The vitality of undergraduate education affects, I believe, all the others."[1] Boyer's affirmation of the American college's essential situation within the system of American education at all levels is made palpable and exemplified in the history of Mount Holyoke's long-standing commitment to science education.

This book is an exploration of the ongoing efforts of ambitious women faculty at Mount Holyoke who have been actively engaged in the development of American science since the early decades of the nineteenth century. It is a history in which changing mores of American society and shifting possibilities for work in science together shaped and encouraged their personal commitment to living useful lives as teachers. Within this dynamic circuit of national growth, Mount Holyoke provided these women a geographic place and physical space to actualize their efforts, framed by teaching science, by membership in a community of colleges, and by New England Protestant leaders' values and customs—including those regarding gender. The relationship between institution and faculty was reciprocal. The faculty members jointly contributed to raising the stature of Mount Holyoke in the process of adapting their own teaching and research at critical moments, thus maintaining a niche within the continually reequilibrating ecology of American institutions engaged in science. For over a century, the female faculty was single. A few men were added to the faculty at the turn of the twentieth century and between the world wars. Only after 1970 did married women, some with families, appear on the faculty roster.

Sources

This book draws on archival, primary and secondary materials from the fields of women's studies, history of science, sociology, and the history of American higher education, of the professions, and of religion and gender. Embedded as it is in the great upheaval and forging of an industrial capitalist nation, the narrative of the Mount Holyoke faculty's efforts also relies on several national histories of the United States to provide the framework. It is important to say something about the types and uses made of archival materials from the Mount Holyoke college archives. Two unfortunate and disastrous fires (1896 and 1917) destroyed large amounts of information that would probably have been useful for this project. In addition, the culture of the institution did not encourage and did not leave time for self-reflection. Few journals exist recording students' impressions, and I have located none for faculty, save for the journal letters (a collection of letters about events on campus written by faculty, copied and sent to graduates in missions and distant schools), a few pages with jottings that biology professor Cornelia Clapp kept in a notebook, and notes for a biography of Clapp that Ann Haven Morgan made based on interviews with her teacher and mentor.

Other forms of information supplement the personal data. They proved to be more helpful in determining the ways in which the seminary and then the college adapted to economic change and in turn tried to shape the scientific community and the market for women with scientific education. These sources include published pamphlets, personal letters, administrative correspondence, records of trustees meetings, college catalogues, the student newspaper and alumnae bulletin, and departmental records for the post-1917 period. In order to build a picture of the larger collegiate community with which Mount Holyoke was connected, the archives of Amherst College, Oberlin, Williams, and Harvard provided useful information for comparison. A limited number of interviews with faculty were conducted—limited primarily because only a few remained from the pre-1940 faculty. There are also various prints and photographs, mostly formal ones made for publicity purposes, documenting the campus, laboratory space, equipment and specimen collections, and faculty and students at work and play, as well as portraits of the faculty.

Especially important in regard to secondary sources are a number of studies treating religion and national industrial expansion. These books and articles provided the framework that could integrate the development of an institution and its faculty with that of the higher education work force. Among them Daniel Boorstin's *The American Experience* proved exceptionally suggestive. It combines a large view of the economic and ideological factors that inspired the population of the country to commit its energies to ordering the territory with an explanation of the role science and technology played in the national vision and the means to attain it. Moreover, despite the fact that Boorstin tends to conflate the experiences of men and women, or rather has little to say specifically about women, his conception of booster colleges and his recognition of the dynamic established by research and development activities during the late nineteenth and twentieth centuries are exceedingly useful. Although the chronology deviates a bit from that established by Margaret Rossiter, her path-breaking e-book *Women Scientists in America* was always a source of ideas and a map whose edges implied the tantalizing existence of a larger world to which women in science were connected—leaving the character of those social relations and motivations to be explored.

Acknowledgments

I owe deep thanks to the many people who have helped me along the way with this book. I want to thank Pamela Mack, colleague and friend, who shared the work on an earlier, uncompleted study of the history of Mount Holyoke in the professionalization of science. Professor Mack has generously made available her material from that manuscript, and I have cited it in the notes whenever relevant. That study was funded by a grant from the National Science Foundation, to which we are both grateful. Jill Norgren, Alan Rocke, Marjorie Senechal, Rosalind Williams, Robert Kargon, Catherine Kelley, James Morris, Paul Mattingly, Helen Horowitz, Jill Ker Conway, Laura Crawley, and Grey Osterud have read all or parts of the manuscript in its many versions and offered their suggestions for improvement. I have also benefited from discussions with Mary Frank Fox, Hugh Hawkins, Margaret Rossiter, Darhl Foreman, Toby Appel, Lorraine Nadelman, and my daughter, Petra Levin, who became a professor of biology while this book was being written.

Thanks are also due to Richard Lewontin, Sigrid Metz-Goeckle, Doris Jansen, Boël Berner, André Grelon, Cathérine Marry, Patricia Del Rey, Elizabeth Fox-Genovese, Arthur Molella, Gail Hornstein, all of whom invited me to present portions of this material in seminars where I received valuable comments and criticisms from colleagues and students. Semester leaves spent at the Five College Women's Center, the STS Program at MIT, and the Program in History of Science and Technology at the Royal Institute of Technology in Stockholm gave me the precious time needed for research and writing. Richard Lewontin welcomed me for a semester in his laboratory at Harvard as a visiting historian of science—and I am grateful to him and other lab members for insights and suggestions to focus on the institution as much as its faculty. Roe Smith at MIT was equally gracious. Public lectures at the Marine Biological Laboratory in Woods Hole, Massachusetts, Lakeland Community College, and the Lewis NASA Space Center allowed me to talk with women working in scientific fields about their educations and their attitudes toward religion. My friends Barbara and Bo Heald have been unstintingly enthusiastic and helpful in numerous ways. Deans Joseph Ellis and Donal O'Shea at Mount Holyoke have been supportive of this book while scrupulously respecting it as an independent study.

At Case Western Reserve University, my department and the deans of my college generously granted leaves that allowed me to finish the manuscript, while a grant from the W. P. Jones Foundation and a sabbatical helped fund them. At Mount Holyoke, Elaine Trehub and Particia Albright were unfailingly helpful over the years in searching out documents from the archives, providing invaluable information about the college. Robert Gross at the Amherst College Archives and Roland Bauman at Oberlin College archives are also to be thanked. Margaret Hepler and James Clapp provided family information on Cornelia Clapp. I owe a debt to Paula Hassett, Gillian Sexsmith, Rosalind Cuomo, and Gretchen Osgood, all research assistants on this book. Joshua Palmer merits special thanks for his Herculean efforts to help edit the manuscript when my eyesight failed. Katheryn Knuth was an excellent proof reader.

If this book meets with approval, these people deserve much of the credit for their many contributions. As with all such efforts, the failings are the author's responsibility.

One final point, a small claim to objectivity in this study: I spent my college and graduate school years in large, coeducational public universities, places with very different characters and histories from those of Mount Holyoke. It is perhaps because of these differences in my education and in my religious background that I have found these women and their institution so compelling a subject for understanding larger questions of women's role in science and in American higher education.

chapter 1

Introduction

When Mary Lyon opened the gates of Mount Holyoke Female Seminary in 1837, she hitched the fortunes of this evangelical New England institution to the rising star of science, in a young nation enamored of progress. The forward-looking union of the institution with science persisted long after Mount Holyoke became a more secularly oriented liberal arts college a half-century later. Until the Depression of the 1930s, the science faculty, composed almost entirely of single Protestant women, continuously led the institution's adjustments to shifting markets for scientifically trained college graduates. They enabled it to expand, participate in research, and produce large numbers of women majors who went on to obtain medical degrees and doctorates in the sciences and mathematics. In the process, four generations of women faculty who had graduated from Mount Holyoke improved their own status and authority, participating in the professionalization of American science that fueled the growth of higher education. Then, after almost a century, the conjunction of hard economic times in the 1930s, a sea change in American science, and shifts in social mores broke apart the female culture that had nurtured—and been nurtured by—science at Mount Holyoke.

This book is a history of science's remarkable century at Mount Holyoke, extending from the college's founding by Lyon, an unmarried woman who taught chemistry and botany, to the trustees appointing a married English professor from Yale, Dr. Roswell Ham, as the college's first male president, in 1937. In the interim, science and the science faculty moved from dominating the policies and culture of the institution to becoming a predominant subculture within a more cosmopolitan college setting. The decision to hire Ham to succeed Mary Woolley as president was symbolic of deeper shifts in American society during the Great Depression, ones with negative consequences for professional—especially single—women, within the scientific community.

The institutionalized alliance of faculty members with science benefited them—and the institution and its graduates—even as it limited them to certain self-defined activities and subjects and to ways of doing science that accommodated the prevailing social mores with respect to gender differences. Among the clear benefits were opportunities to cooperate with male scientists in disseminating and increasing scientific knowledge and to place the college's graduates in various new posts for women with this expertise. As they supplied trained women for a demanding market, Mount Holyoke science faculty members were even able to claim and define emerging positions that had not yet been identified as belonging to women, thereby enlarging the fields of action over which women had some control.

Mount Holyoke produced large numbers of graduates who disseminated scientific knowledge. They founded new institutions for women modeled on Mount Holyoke, they taught on college faculties, and they became researchers and technicians in academe and private industry. Those graduates who married and had families applied their knowledge in a multitude of ways, while others, including Emily Dickinson (who did not graduate), drew on their knowledge of the natural world to create artistic works.[1]

But there were constraints on what the science faculty was able to accomplish. Its members were limited, variously, by social customs, religious values, and the self-designated "female" character traits that privileged an elite of unmarried Protestant women. The limitations kept them focused on making advances that privileged the biological sciences and chemistry, laboratory-based teaching, technical expertise, and empirical rather than theoretical approaches to nature. In effect, they accepted a narrowing of possibilities for themselves in negotiating their role—and Mount Holyoke's role—in advancing science. In so doing, they helped define what came to be known as "women's work in science." Not surprisingly, the science faculty's aspirations sometimes met resistance from trustees, male scientists, and even from alumnae.

This book recounts the history of science at Mount Holyoke through a focus on the interconnected fortunes of the institution and its women science faculty, both locked together in the ambitious mission Lyon set for them. It is a trajectory marked by struggles to develop special fields of science instruction and personal expertise that kept abreast of progress taking place in male-dominated higher education. The book considers this history in light of three major topics that link local events and individuals to the unfolding national panorama of science in higher education: women's arrangements for teaching science at the college level, the relationship of science to religion, and the New England character of the Mount Holyoke faculty's approach to science.

Teaching Science at the College Level

Teaching science was a source of power and a means of advancement for Mount Holyoke faculty and graduates, and for the institution as well, in a nation where the demand for professionals with scientific knowledge grew faster than supply. Through teaching they participated in the expansion and structuring of the American scientific community and helped define the course of national progress to which science was linked. Lyon set the precedent with her commitment to dignify women teachers by creating a "castle of science," as their base. From 1837 onward, faculty teaching responsibilities mediated between filling positions available to women with advanced scientific education and attracting students ambitious for useful work that brought moral and social stature and a respectable income. To maintain an equilibrium between the push and pull of these evolving and interconnected constituencies, faculty members worked to keep pedagogy, curricula, and classrooms and laboratories up to date. Through their efforts they defined and claimed for themselves and their graduates particular areas of scientific work.

Fundamental to their success was the complicated and multilayered quid pro quo relationship they established with male faculty members at other institutions. The male scientists provided Mount Holyoke faculty with access to advanced scientific knowledge and with opportunities to benefit from the growing market for science. In return, the men were able to extend their influence over the formation of scientific personnel, gain support for their agendas, and disseminate their ideas through their Mount Holyoke connections. This reciprocal relationship was based on gender distinctions Lyon formalized to keep teaching at Mount Holyoke under the control of women faculty, even as they worked to find common ground with male faculty at other institutions. The distinctions included hiring women as faculty and having them select students on the basis of academic abilities and certain moral and intellectual traits. Students were then prepared for work that pushed the envelope but did not reject women's customary social roles; that respected women's biological differences from men, but did not yield on the issue of women's capacity for rational thinking and action.

Teaching at Mount Holyoke stressed the use of reasoning abilities and systematic procedures applied to gathering and recording detailed information based on empirical evidence. The programs emphasized laboratory teaching, manipulation of equipment, and the collection and classification of specimens from the wild, practices which differed in emphasis from those at male colleges where scientific theories received greater attention. The value of this pedagogy and the graduates it produced derived from Lyon's claim to women's special feeling for nature and to their superior self-denying character—a claim that took accepted biological, moral, and social constraints on women and turned them into marketable virtues uniquely possessed by Mount Holyoke women. The women faculty were not helpless in their struggle for advancement through science teaching. Historical contingency aided their ambitions. The self-conscious, Protestant-led educational movement to provide leadership in transforming the country from a rural to an industrial economy opened opportunities in science for Lyon and her academic descendants.

In the beginning, the all-female resident faculty members, who held the title of "teacher" at Mount Holyoke, were recitation leaders assisting visiting male professors from nearby colleges who offered courses of lectures in chemistry, botany, and geology and helped set the curriculum. Until 1900, these visiting men helped the women gain facility with new equipment, privilege laboratory teaching, in some cases integrate research programs, and set agendas for an increasing number of specialized departments. In the 1880s, however, women faculty members began to assume regular responsibility for lecturing and for the new laboratory-based teaching of science. After 1900, men were hired as permanent faculty members in a limited number of fields. The relationship with men, based on a common commitment to forming leaders of American society, was marked by tensions, sometimes to the point of crisis, stemming from differences in the aspirations each group had for teaching science. In the early 1840s, the 1860s, the 1870s, and again in the late 1920s and 1930s at Mount Holyoke, there were struggles between women faculty members and male scientists for control over teaching (especially lecturing), the curriculum, and the hiring of faculty.

Science and Religion

Religion was an important factor in the reciprocal development of science and institutional advancement at Mount Holyoke, as well as at other New England colleges during the period covered by this book. Mount Holyoke science faculty were participants in a community that remained almost exclusively Protestant and that stood at the head of an effort to assume the leadership of American society by dominating education. Moral and economic aspirations mingled with a commitment to service. Faculty members who taught science in higher education took up the charge to form the leaders of the society by keeping abreast of new knowledge, developing the pedagogical means of communicating it, and training a select group of students to be the next generation of faculty. The late-nineteenth-century struggles between church leaders and academics that focused on evolution were in part conflicts over the diverging objectives of churches and colleges, as industrial wealth and power steered scientific activity toward greater specialization within a secular context.

Lyon came to science teaching through her membership in a church-centered community of evangelical Protestants active in college and seminary founding. While the momentum of the Second Great Awakening and the influence of Calvinist churches on Mount Holyoke died out in the decades after the Civil War, the faculty, like the American scientific community, remained Protestant throughout the period covered in this book. The emphases at Mount Holyoke on teaching, laboratory work, the systematic collection of empirical evidence, and the practical preparation of students for paid employment, rather than on theoretical investigation and natural theology, allowed faculty and administrators there to avoid the acrimonious conflicts that occurred elsewhere between their male peers and churchmen for control over the purpose of scientific investigation. In fact, by respecting certain gender-defined parameters, these same emphases opened possibilities within the missionary movement, the academic system, and industry for Mount Holyoke graduates to expand the influence of the institution's commitment to science and to women's role in science.[2]

Religion defined Mount Holyoke faculty's commitment to science over this entire period in two ways. First, there was the evangelizing spirit shared with Protestant missionaries and churchmen. The language and ethos of missionizing was common coin. However, Mount Holyoke science faculty increasingly focused on their own special calling in a nation whose marketplace had its own exigencies and opportunities. Like male science faculty in the colleges, Mount Holyoke faculty members understood progress in terms of the value increasing knowledge held for their own professional standing, for the future of their institution, and for the good their work brought to secular life. Even those who dropped religious disclaimers altogether defined their professional identity in terms taken from the Protestant vocabulary of vocation. They supported science in the curriculum for the way it integrated students' thinking processes with the systematic quest for empirical evidence, requiring self-discipline and providing positive reinforcement for responsible behavior in the form of an ever-improved vision of the great design of nature. This vision gave students the model for a moral society whose members lived in harmony with nature and strove to make the material world conform to the scientific order. At the same time, tensions arose when faculties focused their attention on scientific practice.

The other way science was informed by religious belief at Mount Holyoke centered on the question of who should control subject matter, course content, and teaching in the classroom and laboratory: visiting male faculty and the trustees, or the women faculty. Gender divisions within church practices, Protestant theology, and the Protestant community itself faced the contradictions between a secularly oriented faith that gave equal stature to all believers in the eyes of God and a marketplace that constantly threatened the existence of the institutions that spread Protestant influence.

The liberating connection between Protestantism and science at Mount Holyoke, then, was threefold. First it was institutional. The relationship Lyon established with the evangelical movement opened the way for faculty members to contribute to the workforce by educating women teachers with scientific knowledge who might fill the demands of the market. She provided seminary and primary school teachers when college-educated men were going into the potentially more lucrative and respected professions of law, medicine, the ministry, and college teaching. But her faculty also prepared students for missionary work alongside men, putting their scientific knowledge and skills to work in founding schools and seminaries, teaching missionary children and converts, and avid building of collections. Through the Protestant networks linking colleges and seminaries, and later universities, Mount Holyoke faculty made common cause with male academics, with whom they developed relationships that respected the customs of separate spheres.

The second connection between religion and science was intellectual. It recognized women's rational ability, while distinguishing between the uses men and women made of their common capacity for reason. And the third connection was theological. Theology offered a religiously based ethical standard for the approach to the work of science, derived from notions of individual perfection attained through the study of nature. Thus, religion gave Mount Holyoke faculty members a moral claim to gaining full control over science teaching in their classrooms. But their reliance on theology also trapped the women in an adaptive strategy that limited their sphere of influence and their ways of doing science by establishing different activities and standards of excellence for measuring the achievements of men and women.

New England Location

Geography, although not destiny, was a powerful factor shaping the history of science at Mount Holyoke. Until 1940, the teaching of science there drew sustenance from the college's location in New England—and, more particularly, in western Massachusetts, where a cluster of colleges served both the ambitions of an aspiring population and the ideals and interests of Protestant leaders in education and business. New England was a geographic center of American higher education during this period of the nation's industrial development. The region boasted a number of men active in the creation of a professional American scientific community who were also engaged in promoting the higher education of women in science.

Lyon and her successors identified with the colleges of New England in a relationship marked by the sort of emulation, competition, and cooperation one finds among brothers and sisters in an extended family. They set male colleges as the measure of their institution's excellence and established cooperative relationships with them and with technical institutes. The emphasis on science was a direct result of emulation and the exchange of influence. After the Civil War, Mount Holyoke's primary rivals were the newly founded women's colleges in the region—especially Smith College, only 10 miles distant, and Wellesley College, whose president had worked hard to prevent Mount Holyoke from obtaining a collegiate charter from the state legislature in the 1880s. In the twentieth century, Holyoke science faculty developed programs and expanded their networks to hold their own among the single-sex New England colleges, which were caught in the dynamic of a market that by then included coeducational and research universities located across the country.

In New England society, the middle classes lived in a sex-segregated environment, both within the churches and in the public and domestic realms. At the same time, the society encouraged the sexes to work in tandem for the common good, and there were strong moral incentives for individuals to follow their own inner feelings of vocation. New England, moreover, had a surplus of unmarried women from poor or modest backgrounds who constituted a potential source of faculty and students for Mount Holyoke and who saw the college as a conduit to good jobs in a nation with an increasingly global reach. Like Lyon, many of these women came initially from rural backgrounds. Having to work for a living, they aspired to positions with intellectual status, moral authority, and security. Their numbers, in conjunction with economic demand for scientifically educated personnel, the social prestige of science, and the moral weight of Protestant women agitating for women's right to education at the highest levels at the best institutions, lent compelling force to the efforts of Mount Holyoke faculty members.

This book is not the history of liberal feminism, however, much as it focuses on women who embraced the professionalization of scientific work during a long period of women's efforts for political emancipation. While these women were well aware of the women's rights movement, the Mount Holyoke faculty did not seek, nor was the Mount Holyoke community geared, to support individual self-expression outside the context of the group. Lyon created a situation in which the institution and its faculty were to be synonymous. Mount Holyoke was a communitarian society where the women found meaning and rewards through a life of the chosen devoted to works. Science teaching was a vocation associated with a greater good. Lyon used the term "family" to describe this community. Beginning in the twentieth century, fault lines appeared in the family as the competitive individualism that marked the careers of male scientists in the new research universities was carried to Mount Holyoke through faculty members armed with doctorates received within these institutions. At the college, Protestant family solidarity weakened in the face of mounting faculty concerns to establish research programs, to publish, to compete for jobs and entrée to graduate programs for their students, and to pursue the lifestyle of their male peers. In the push and pull of maintaining equilibrium between external and internal pressures to keep in the running, President Woolley encouraged and rewarded faculty efforts by insisting on doctorates, supporting departmental expansion, and recognizing individual achievements in academic specialties in ways that emulated those of the men. It was this trend that left faculty unable to mount a common defense in the face of the Depression, and opened the way for the appointment of a male president. It was also this trend that allowed the college to begin to restructure the science departments to keep abreast of fast-changing developments in science at the end of the 1930s, through World War II, and after.

The history of Mount Holyoke science faculty sets its course within the current study of the history of science, a field of organized scholarly activity that emerged in the second decade of the twentieth century.[3] George Sarton, a Belgian scientist and mathematician, founded the history of science as a modern academic discipline when in 1913 he began publishing *Isis,* a journal dedicated to the history of science. During the First World War, Sarton immigrated to the United States where he took up a nonprofessorial position at Harvard and founded the History of Science Society in 1924. From his post at Harvard, Sarton used his institution-building skills and bibliographical knowledge to define the field as the story of the progressive accumulation of knowledge about the natural world accomplished through the efforts of a series of great thinkers, each building upon his predecessors' discoveries. Sarton, like all his generation, unself-consciously limited these contributors to men.

Following Sarton's lead, until the 1950s most historians of science focused on "internalist" descriptions of the evolution of scientific theories. Their primary interest was the physical sciences, and they sought to chart the emergence of the triumphant Scientific Revolution of the seventeenth century. In sociology departments some scholars such as Robert K. Merton gave attention to the constitution of scientific communities and norms, with special attention to the role of protestant religious beliefs in supporting scientific communities.[4] For most historians of science at that time studies of social or political context were considered outside or "external" to science and treated as largely irrelevant to the development of scientific ideas.

In the wake of World War II and the onset of Cold War policies supporting science, historians of science began to give serious attention to the relationship between the "internal" and the "external" histories of science. Princeton professor Thomas Kuhn's book *The Structure of Scientific Revolutions* in 1962 marked the first important step in this direction. Kuhn worked in the Sartonian tradition, and, thus, continued to focus on the history of scientific ideas, notably the Copernican revolution. However, in writing about Copernicus, Kuhn began to question the rational, evolutionary nature of scientific activity. He proposed the idea of the "paradigm shift" in which science operates differently in "normal" and "revolutionary" phases.[5]

While Kuhn's concept of a "paradigm shift" has been adopted into common parlance—often in ways Kuhn himself would neither recognize nor appreciate—his role in altering the discipline of the history of science is inarguable. There has been a paradigm shift in the field, opening its almost exclusive focus on scientific discoveries about how nature operates, to embrace the study of how science itself operates. Since Kuhn, the history of science has been increasingly dominated by scholarship exploring the social roots of science, its social organization, the rise of the profession, its embedded values, and other social and cultural dimensions of this vast enterprise. Taking up Robert Merton's thread, the effort has been to understand science from the historian's perspective: as a complex set of human activities and institutional arrangements, having their own dynamic, responsive to economic and social change, and shaped by a variety of values and attitudes.

A good deal of the most recent literature in the history of science takes a close look at the sites in which research was carried out. Bruno Latour and Steve Woolgar's examination of "laboratory life" has been highly influential in focusing the attention of historians of science on what goes on in the spaces where science is practiced—that is, on the process and practice of science by human beings informed by their everyday concerns, as opposed to its results.[6] Other scholars have recently begun to show how the practice of science also includes teaching and how the pedagogy and findings of science are mutually interactive.[7]

Thus, from the 1960s onward, historians of science have been formulating a much wider range of questions that do not reject the Sartonian internalist focus out of hand, but certainly have forced the field to consider a broader range of subjects and perspectives as relevant. They have reached a general (though by no means unanimous) consensus that they should consider both "external" as well as "internal" developments in the co-production of science.

The history of the scientific profession has been one of the most significant areas of research activity by those interested in external developments in science. From the 1970s onward, a number of historians drew on the sociology of the professions to study the community of trained scientific specialists that formed in tandem with America's arrival as an international power. They delineated the creation of the profession as an upward trajectory jointly fueled by scientists' quest to advance knowledge and the nation's demand for it. In the late 1970s, Daniel Kevles established a norm for these studies in an influential book tracing physicists' rise to prominence within the research universities during the early 20th century.[8] Also by that decade scholars had begun to publish challenging studies on the relationship between gender and science. Encouraged by the women's movement and federal legislation, they sought to explain the liminal status of women in the emergent profession and to identify those who had succeeded.[9]

The history of science at Mount Holyoke presented herein is set within these post-Sartonian trends. It expands and deepens our understanding of professional activity by seriously considering the role religion and women played in collegiate level science. This book proposes that colleges as well as universities were sites of great activity and continuous engagement with the forces placing science at the forefront of American society between the 1830s and 1940. Protestant values and ideals of service at the collegiate level, for example, opened opportunities for women to participate with men in higher education to form the scientific community and to weave that community into the larger national fabric.

This view challenges the model devised by Daniel Kevles to explain the progressive professionalization of American science, with its marginalization of both women and college-based science faculty and its denigration of religion in the name of objectivity. In brief, Kevles presents a trajectory of success that rises out of late-nineteenth-century struggles within research universities for academic freedom from religious bias. Male scientists dominated the graduate schools of the research universities as they came to prominence in twentieth-century America. These men devoted their lives to the pursuit of new truths through research in specialized scientific disciplines—the evolving field of physics, in particular. The colleges stood in opposition to this system. The religious beliefs to which the colleges were committed and their emphasis on teaching made them old fashioned by blocking the development of objective scientific research. Within the secular, male-dominated, university-based Kevles model, women were outsiders, isolated individuals trying to get into the system, who for the most part accepted the few niches men made available to them. They were ghettoized in the natural sciences, in teaching, technical and research associate posts, or in women's colleges considered uncompetitive.

Such is the model that has strongly influenced the history of women in American science. Writers seeking to explain and rectify the record have focused on the heroic struggles of singular women who succeeded against the odds in getting doctorates, doing significant research, and, in too few cases, gaining recognition for their work. Their efforts have borne important fruit. Margaret Rossiter's research drew important attention to women's colleges as worthy of researchers' attention, and pointed to Mount Holyoke as an important institution in the history of women in American science. Yet, feminist historians' measures of women's success in the professional hierarchy have tended to be those set by men, often including the characterization of women's colleges as second-rate science institutions where women could find employment as teachers and might do research on a very limited scale, but always in the shadow of the universities.[10] Religion, too, has been overlooked.

I intend to provide new answers to two major questions that trouble the history of women in American science as it is now written, based on the current professionalization model: Why did women enter science in the first place, when it seems to have been so hostile an environment for them? And how did the division of scientific work take the sex-based forms it has?

In answer to the first question, I seek to establish that women were welcome within science education almost from the moment higher education began to expand in this country—but customary divisions between men and women in evangelical circles and women's own sense of their capabilities circumscribed that welcome. The market and the moral imperative of evangelical Protestantism supported their participation and turned possibilities into opportunities for women teachers. Men and women lived embedded within a common value system that brought both into scientific work within a common culture. Rather than viewing the women as outsiders trying to break into a male preserve, adherents of that culture placed great value on the formation of a male and female elite capable of understanding nature. If men and women had unequal or different functions, they were all part of the same elite core with a common notion of service.

The struggles by women to work within accepted divisions of labor (or to push the envelope) were struggles to readjust power relationships within a social world whose members held some goals and values in common but contested others. This was the world of the American colleges—single-sex, Christian institutions, for the most part, that had set the standards for the American education system downward and then, after the emergence of graduate schools in the late nineteenth century, upward—to accommodate graduate programs, the doctoral degree, and new disciplines, theories, and research activity. The upward adjustment responded to pressures from faculty members, administrators, and students within the colleges and, externally, from professional scientific organizations, government, business, industry, and, not least, changing cultural mores.

Rather than being phased out by research universities as science professionalized, the colleges remained a vital part of American science education throughout this period, even if they became part of a larger ecology of competing institutions engaged in forming a scientific work force. If college faculty members spent a great deal of time teaching, some of them also did research and offered master's degree programs in an effort to integrate themselves into the expanded system of higher education and employment possibilities. Teaching and research were often combined. Both the hostility toward women and the increasing difficulty women had in gaining access to graduate education and research jobs in science can be understood in terms of the growing competition for niches in that environment.[11] When science faculty members at single-sex colleges began to compete with one another and with coeducational undergraduate schools for access to graduate schools and employment for their graduates, the Protestant consensus based on an ideal of complementarity between the sexes broke down.

In answer to the second question (How did the division of labor take sex-based forms?), which is, in fact, related to the first, the history makes plain that Mount Holyoke women helped define women's work in science by self-selecting for certain styles of teaching and subject matter that they identified with useful, gender-specific character traits complementing those of men. The menu from which they selected these traits, however, was not one they had helped draw up. To determine the qualifications women needed to succeed in the market place for scientific knowledge, they used as standards a set of customs and values that circumscribed the roles and capacities of educated men and women in American middle-class society. Lyon established the precedent that her select group of women were preordained to be superior to men in their capacity for self-denial and perfection in the rational exercise of their vocation as natural teachers—that they were better at inventing ways to attend to details and hands-on work in science than men, whose forte lay in conceptualizing the big picture of nature. If men introduced students to the laws of nature—the organization of the physical and biological world and the principles on which natural phenomena operated—women taught them the details of the processes of organization by engaging them in hands-on experience.

Mary Woolley would expand that fundamental self-definition in an audacious effort to break through the boundary into the male scientists' traditional purview by adding Mount Holyoke women's capacity for invention and creative research to their talent for empirical and technical accuracy. She gave teeth to her claim by requiring that faculty have doctoral degrees. The combination presented a new hybrid identity for Mount Holyoke women in science: They were, like men, true scientists—and even, by nature, more competent. They were, therefore, competitive with male and female colleagues from other single-sex and coeducational colleges striving to gain access to university graduate programs devoted to research. In the 1920s and, especially, the economically hard-pressed 1930s, Mount Holyoke science faculty came under increasing attack for espousing this new identity.

There is additional historical and theoretical support for these answers. They recall German sociologist Max Weber's study of the connections between Protestant beliefs and culture and the development of capitalism, as well as Robert Merton's study on Puritans and the scientific revolution of the seventeenth century. As Merton observed in the preface to the 1970 edition of his study, the question about what are the modes of interplay between society, culture, and science are germane to every historical epoch in which "men are at work in science."[12] If we read men and women for the nineteenth and twentieth centuries in the United States, then we can begin to see how the socially patterned interests and motivations in the social sphere of science have been intertwined and interdependent with those in other social spheres in this later period. To do so broadens the sphere of science to consider professionalization as the product of contingencies in which individuals within a religiously defined social group responded to what they perceived as opportunities in a variety of ways that meshed with one another.

Closer to the history of Mount Holyoke is the work of Max Weber: *The Protestant Ethic and the Spirit of Capitalism* (1904–1905)—one of the most influential essays on the subject of the relationship between religious values and economic change. Weber wrote it after a trip to the united States in 1904, where he was deeply impressed by the capitalist wonders on view at the Saint Louis Worlds Fair and by the evangelical protestant colleges he visited. He drew on this experience to propose the Puritan notion of the calling (*"Beruf"*) as the point of departure for the creation of the secular work of the professions. He also argued that the idea of predestination—of each person having a special calling that cultivated rationality as a form of proof of self-worth—provided a rationale for the scientific character assumed by the professions. Although criticized by recent scholars for his treatment of rationality and science as norms rather than biases, culturally and chronologically bounded descriptions of certain values and notions of reason, Weber's analysis is quite solid when applied to the motivations of American Protestants from this period based on his personal observations and discussions with educators.[13] This self-worth was reflected in asceticism, self-control, and profitability, while science was celebrated as the rationality of ascertaining the best course of action, or method for attaining desired results. Here lay the origins of the modern division of labor into distinct professions serving social needs and into a hierarchical ranking of tasks based on intellectual criteria. The development of the professions in the American nineteenth-century context was the result of Protestants from the middling classes, ambitious, seeking to maximize their chances by claiming certain parts of the market for services as their own. Education was very important to them, as a source of knowledge and of certification of their special claims to status and fees.

Fresh in Weber's mind were American enterprises, including universities and colleges, that were merging horizontally and vertically into large, interlocking systems. His study looked back to find the source of the human energies that had driven these enterprises from their scattered, small-scale isolation toward this complex arrangement. He found the answer to this re-

structuring in the peculiar asceticism of the Protestant work ethic. He identified science as second only to the ministry as the highest form of work approved by Calvinist movements. For those who studied nature in this systematic way were directly affirming God's works while their own efforts
brought divine order into the world.[14] Weber allows us to understand how
the evangelical movement's spate of college and seminary founding during
the nineteenth century gave aid and comfort to capitalist forces by encouraging scientific work. And how that very work ethic embodied contradictions that gave male scientists the conviction to break with churchmen and
women faculty to push male scientists for higher status and more power as
industrial growth proceeded.

Scientific work became the personally transforming activity par excellence, for it brought order into the conduct of its adherents and proved their
faith in worldly activity. Because it was a very intimate, personalized experience of nature and relied on empirical evidence to support or modify its suppositions, scientific work spoke to the practitioner's own sensibilities in a vis-
ceral way that affirmed self-worth at the same time it seemed to bring one
closer to the divine spirit in nature. Paradoxically, the insistence on parsi-
monious reasoning and emotional constraints it imposed on those who did
such work produced the psychologically liberating reward of greater understanding and a feeling of power over nature. To paraphrase Weber, this way
of working and thinking "can only be the product of a long and arduous
process of economic education."[15] Writing of women workers, especially
unmarried ones, Weber cited the example of

girls having a specifically religious, especially a Pietistic, background. One often
hears, and statistical investigation confirms it, that by far the best chances of economic education are found among this group. The ability of mental concentration, as well as the absolutely essential feeling of obligation to one's job, are here
most often combined with a strict economy which calculates the possibility of
high earnings, and a cool self-control and frugality which enormously increase
performance.[16]

This particular conception of labor as a calling essential to capitalism
was alive and well in the ranks of Mount Holyoke faculty. Mary Lyon had
recognized these traits would be positive factors in claiming and developing
a place for Mount Holyoke in the emerging scientific community. It gave faculty the rationale on which they entered into scientific work in a complementary position to men, while the self-affirming experience of doing science en-

couraged them to push for greater intellectual autonomy and recognition in the field, as they participated in specialization, research, preparation for new career fields, formed new networks, and met new standards of credentialing.

Five chapters follow this introduction to the fundamental theme that drives the narrative: how Mary Lyon's being called by the Protestant community to educate women in the study of nature set her faculty on a path of professionalization that defined a portion of the market for science as their own. The chapters are so divided as to emphasize the connections between significant moments in the professional development of Mount Holyoke's science faculty and events of national import affecting the market for scientific knowledge and the structure of higher education. The chapters explore the faculty's process of accommodation—sometimes successful, and sometimes not—to the metamorphosing organism of American society. A final chapter describes briefly the continuities and changes at Mount Holyoke since 1940, in light of the decline of single-sex colleges and the post-1970 women's movement.

Chapter 2, "Sanctified Scientific Teachers—Teachers of Science (1837–1859)," covers the period from the founding of Mount Holyoke in 1837 to the watershed of the Civil War. These were years of growing enthusiasm for science, higher education, and women's education, during which the population grappled with the complexities of the first industrial revolution and state and federal governments promoted exploration and called for a trained workforce. They were also years when the missionary movement provided colleges and seminaries with a set of higher goals and ambitions closely tied to national progress. The chapter recounts how Lyon brought her female faculty into an emerging professional scientific community through an educational mission that complemented the work of male science faculty at colleges closely identified with the movement. The chapter describes as well the arrangements she brokered with these men to divide the market. The arrangements established gender-based fault lines and interdependencies in scientific work that for the next eighty years would guide the Mount Holyoke faculty's relationships with male scientists, their choice of subject matter, as well as their methods of teaching, and would set the standards they used to define their market and their professional image.

The next chapter, "Taking the Academic Science Path in an Era of Collegiate Innovation (1860–1888)," is an account of the second and third generations' efforts to take advantage of opportunities the Civil War opened to those with scientific knowledge—and to women. It examines how the heirs to Lyon's legacy (including Lydia Shattuck, Cornelia Clapp, and, to some extent, Henrietta Hooker) found an outlet for their own sense of calling as science teachers by establishing Mount Holyoke as a viable competitor to the new women's colleges that rejected evangelicalism. Their efforts were crowned by the award of collegiate status to the institution, despite strong opposition from Wellesley and Harvard. The chapter also looks at the colleagueships they inaugurated with a younger generation of ambitious male scientists through their participation in Louis Agassiz's summer school on Penikese Island off the coast of Cape Cod, and the gendered character of the professional opportunities these new colleagueships opened to women faculty. Of special interest is the ease with which the female science faculty were able to introduce Darwinian evolution and dissections of marine organisms without the protest that occurred at Amherst College.

Chapter 4, "Redefining Scientific Labor in the Age of Specialization (1889–1900)," covers the twelve years when Mount Holyoke women participated with other American science faculty in the institutionalization of new discipline-based networks and the organization of colleges and universities along the same rational (read *scientific*) bureaucratic lines being drawn by industrial corporations and government. It explores how Mount Holyoke expanded into a full-fledged liberal arts college and how the change reduced the power of science faculty members in governance but encouraged them to develop their specialties by exploiting opportunities within the expansive new system. Of particular significance is Cornelia Clapp's participation in the founding and development of a private research center, the Marine Biological Laboratory at Woods Hole; her role was an influential model for the new gendered connections among college science faculty, university researchers, and research institutions.

The fifth chapter, "Apogee and Defeat of the Female Science Mission (1901–1937)," follows the trajectory of the period during which industrial consolidation, supporting new, often coeducational research universities, and social progressivism, promoting women's political and intellectual equality, together reframed the context for women's higher education in science. Beginning in 1901, President Mary Woolley, taking advantage of the expansive atmosphere for women, radically reworked Protestant views of women's intellectual abilities into a more exalted idea of vocation that would make her faculty competitive with male colleges in the university-dominated system. The chapter explores how the focus of the fourth generation of science faculty, imbued with this revised sense of vocation, negotiated changes in the organization of science at Mount Holyoke. They produced a hybrid institution and hybrid professional identities, functionally linking faculty to research universities and industry, but on condition that they not compete with men for positions. Their focus on empirical laboratory research, on teaching technical skills and practical rather than theoretical subjects, and on building up the traditional strongholds of chemistry, zoology, botany, physiology, and, to some extent, geology led in several cases to rapid program development and mutually profitable networking with universities, industry, and research centers. In the 1920s, their success coupled with Woolley's expansionist program left the way open for trustees to hire men (some of them married, with families) in regular faculty positions for the first time in the new departments of physics and laboratory psychology, for which there were few qualified women available.

The last section of chapter 5, "The Decline of the Professional Family in Hard Times," discusses the subject of Woolley's successor. The economic and cultural crises of the Depression exacerbated antifeminist feelings in the society, which took the form of increasing pressures to hire men and educate women for domestic life. Those sentiments were at work at Mount Holyoke during the 1930s. They played a role in the struggle over the choice of the next president that ended with a shift away from Lyon's primary mission to educate women for paid employment and from the commitment to a faculty composed of single women. During this period members of the science faculty alienated some trustees and alumnae, and there was a successful move to hire a male president, and with him curtail the political power the women science faculty had exercised in their departments.

The final chapter, "Conclusion," summarizes the changing nature of Mount Holyoke women science faculty's activities from 1837 to 1940 in light of their shaping this scientific enterprise and women's place within the wider field of science. It ends with a brief look at the past six decades, during which scientific educational settings and workplaces in the United States turned more coeducational and large numbers of women moved to gain equality with men in what has become the most pervasive, expensive, and highly regarded national enterprise. These decades at Mount Holyoke belong to a continuum in which past traditions and policies for transforming women's scientific work in relation to that of men continued to come into play. From 1970 on, in particular, women science faculty there took advantage of federal legislation on Affirmative Action and opportunities to push for equality in the workplace, advancing themselves and keeping their institution at the forefront of collegiate-level science education for women in a very different world. The book ends with the question of whether these new forms of adaptation have produced real equality, simply opened novel paths to another configuration of women's work in science, or made possible a variety of choices that allow for women's roles as wives, mothers, and professionals.

chapter 2

Sanctified Scientific Teachers— Teachers of Science (1837–1859)

Mary Lyon founded Mount Holyoke Female Seminary in South Hadley, Massachusetts, to "do something for women teachers" that would help them find steady, well-paying work in respectable posts where they could change the world for the better. To this end she structured the new seminary to give scale and scope to her ambition by forming alliances with churchmen and college men in the missionary movement and by introducing science into the curriculum, the religious culture, and the daily life of the institution. Seeking to extend to prospective students benefits gained from her association with evangelizing educators enamored of science, Lyon opened possibilities for the women she employed as teachers to advance their own prospects through teaching science in the Protestant community. In antebellum America where single women had few economic recourses, she integrated the welfare of her women faculty with the fortunes of the seminary and united them with nascent forces of progress.[1]

There was no more propitious time and place for her efforts to take root. It was a moment of dramatic transition from an agrarian to a capitalist and manufacturing economy in a region caught up in the energies of national expansion.[2] Here, amidst the rocky hills and fertile valley carved by the Connecticut River, ambitions met and joined forces. The aspirations of men engaged in scientific activities, the missionizing enthusiasm of church officials for establishing God's plan on earth, and the hopes and needs of a surplus of single women were wedded in Protestant church-affiliated efforts to produce pious leaders by expanding higher education for men and women. Within the numerous colleges and seminaries founded by these congregations during this period, faculty members and administrators hoped to organize a national leadership qualified on both sacred and secular terms. Science education, which cultivated common habits of thinking, behavior, and standards of truth through self-correcting empirical observation of natural phenomena, presented all these constituencies an attractive combination of moral, intellectual, and vocational possibilities for realizing their ambitious goals.[3] As each had a different perspective on their role in realizing these mutual goals and hence on the uses of science, there was a great deal of pushing and jostling for places, and conflicts arose between churchmen and college science faculty, each seeking to draw Mount Holyoke women to their cause.

Social customs buttressed by theology, however, narrowed the range of women's participation in scientific work to that circumscribed by separate spheres for men and women engaged in a common mission. Lyon, taking these limitations into account, set out certain parameters for Mount Holyoke and its women faculty. She thus established traditions of teaching and methods of doing science that enabled her and her faculty to take advantage of competition between church and academic men to capitalize on the growing demand for teachers and for scientific knowledge. In so doing, she institutionalized certain gender-based divisions of labor, styles of teaching science, and subject fields within a larger communitarian vision that subordinated the individual self to a complementary, cooperative venture.

In a two-phase process stimulated by general economic development in the region, she first established the institution with the assistance of these constituencies. In the 1840s facing the threat of failure, she then expanded and reorganized its operation to further embrace science teaching as American society lurched ahead rapidly. Together over the following decades, continuing after Lyon's death in 1849 to the Civil War, the seminary and the women teachers of science struggled to prosper from this tension-filled yet optimistic tripartite alliance. By 1860 they found themselves at a crossroads regarding which of two paths toward specialization they should take.

Foundations

Lyon's decision to situate the large white seminary building on a hill in the small village of South Hadley placed Mount Holyoke in the midst of a society encouraging science, higher education, and religious missionizing. In surrounding towns and villages in Massachusetts and New England, capitalist investors built manufactories that harnessed the power of rivers and streams, stimulated middle class expansion, and left many farmers struggling to adapt to a cash economy. Economic interests, nostalgia for a passing agrarian society, and scientific curiosity combined in a growing passion for the study of nature and for state-funded studies of the region's natural resources.

The men who conducted these studies formed the kernel out of which the academic base of the American scientific community began to organize and grow. Among them Edward Hitchcock, the geologist from Amherst College, was a formidable figure.[4] The Calvinist churches whose clergy and elders had ruled the old Massachusetts theocracy adapted to the secularized polity by turning their ambitions on colleges and theological and female seminaries to educate pious leaders for entry into a range of emerging professions. Their wedding of science to religious training in New England higher education brought the study of nature into the curriculum along with ambitious faculty with expert knowledge and scholarly interests to pursue.

Lyon's strategy was to strike a balance among all these constituencies in favor of Mount Holyoke's commitment to advance its own. To ambitious single women like herself who saw no futures on the hard-pressed farms of the region, the seminary promised employment to some and education to others in the field of teaching. To churchmen within the Calvinist congregations of Franklin County (pastors and church officials) it offered an organized means of forming pious and hardworking teachers who would educate prospective wives and children for the men they were preparing for national leadership in colleges and theological seminaries. To male faculty members from nearby Amherst College, with its strong commitment to science, Mount Holyoke offered several opportunities. It opened controlled avenues that personnel could use to disseminate their scholarly knowledge to a wider audience, and it prepared graduates who would make companionable wives for Amherst men—among whom would be the next generation of college faculty, businessmen, doctors, and lawyers.

Lyon's connections with teachers who had worked with her at Ipswich Female Seminary and with women from the region were a source of funds she used to leverage equity in dealings with men and male dominated groups.[5] Armed with these funds and exercising moral suasion through publicly circulated prospectuses and letters to officials, she laid out a set of working principles defining where equality with and recognized differences between her seminary and male theological seminaries and colleges' constituencies lay. Her strategy was to avoid publicly condemned competition with men, while pushing the envelope of possibilities open to unmarried women. It was an effort she characterized as getting her way by making men feel that the original idea was theirs.[6] These principles would open the way to a gender-based division of scientific labor.

A good example of how Lyon used this strategy is an 1836 letter to Hitchcock in which she fuses the radical proposal to raise her women's moral and functional stature with the energetic and unassailable language of evangelism. Claiming Mount Holyoke teachers were the moral equals and working helpmates of male faculty at the theological seminaries, Lyon wrote:

> Fill the country with ministers and they could no more conquer the whole land and secure their victories, without the aid of many times their number of self-denying teachers.[7]

Here she balanced her equation of the sexes by forging a reciprocal relationship between economic worth and worthiness in the battle for Americans' minds and souls to which she was joining Mount Holyoke teachers.

Her second line of argument established a basis for equity in the relationship between Mount Holyoke and male colleges, proposing that the systematic education offered by Mount Holyoke faculty was as valuable to the goals of the church as that provided by the male colleges. And she was quite self-assured in saying that she expected church officials to monetarily reward these institutions equally for the services they rendered to each sex. Conflating religious with eleemosynary objectives, Mount Holyoke education constituted several forms of profitability to all concerned for the investment of the teachers' time and energy. An 1837 circular advertising the seminary declared:

> It designs to fit young women to be educators rather than mere teachers . . . and also to establish the principle that the education of the daughters of the church calls as rightfully for the free gifts of the church as does that of her sons.[8]

Lyon also worked to see the appointment for the seminary of a board of trustees who would provide necessary links with promoters of science to make these aspirations practicable. These men included six ordained ministers, four of whom headed congregations; the other two were Amherst College men—of whom the Reverend Edward Hitchcock, a fast-rising geologist, was deeply involved in the promotion of science on a national scale and in academic circles. The laymen on the board were church officials, and included wealthy farmers, an iron maker, a mill owner, a manufacturer, a businessman, and a lawyer. They came from towns in the region and from around Ipswich and Boston in the eastern part of the state. They were linked to other congregations, missionary organizations, businesses, and manufacturers across the state; to governmental and quasi-governmental organizations engaged in establishing public education and running state geological surveys; and even to the state legislature—which voted crucial subsidies to the new seminary. By virtue of their various fields of expertise and connections, these men saw to the seminary's investments, to its chartering and endowment, as well as to its victualing and construction. All held office in the regional churches; all were devout and devoutly committed to educating women for useful Christian work. And together they represented a collection of people whose lives and fortunes were deeply affected by economic and technological changes afoot. They also saw scientific education as producing graduates equipped to order the future, and the study of nature as providing them the harmonious vision of heaven on earth to be realized bit by bit.

Hitchcock, of course, was the member with the most prestigious scientific standing. Others were actively interested in astronomy, in agricultural improvement, and in invention for profit. Their support for science at the seminary was enthusiastic and evident in the proposal of Board President the Rev. William Tyler to place an astronomical observatory atop the roof at the center of the seminary building. Hitchcock especially provided links to men with scientific knowledge who were on the faculties of local institutions or who worked for state and national governments and who were members of the new scientific societies then forming in Boston and later nationally. Others had connections with churches and colleges in Massachusetts, Ohio, and Pennsylvania, and with the emergent academic and missionary organizations that placed faculty in colleges and seminaries being founded across the country and abroad. By the time Lyon opened the doors of the seminary, she had enmeshed it in a web of relationships that commingled evangelical and scientific interest with her ambitions for educating cadres of women teachers drawn from the hard-pressed agricultural communities in the region. Science was central to making their work useful.[9]

In fact, through the trustees' connections and some fund raising of her own, Lyon made science central to the entire program. In her prospectus for the new seminary, Lyon wrote, "The grand features of this Institution are to be an elevated standard of science, literature, and refinement, and a moderate standard of expense; all to be guided and modified by the spirit of the gospel."[10] Not just science, but a highly precise and organized approach to nature in all facets of seminary life would set standards that lifted faculty and students alike above the ordinary.

The original building with its symmetrical design, Spartan classical style, and pure white exterior encompassed all the activities of the seminary—save for church worship which took place in the South Hadley Congregational Church on the town common. Here teachers and students found efficiently

arranged living spaces, student and faculty rooms, kitchen, refectory, classrooms, offices, and meeting spaces. The design helped integrate all facets of
teachers and students' lives into a coherent educational program aimed at
producing sancitified teachers. It was an institutionalized structuring of space
and action that the ever-enthusiastic trustee Edward Hitchcock described as
"Pangynaskean" or whole woman forming.[11] Ambitious novitiates with mixed
experience and knowledge would be transformed within its walls through the
study of nature and the discipline of a divinely inspired rationally ordered
life, to emerge as perfect educators able to impose that natural order elsewhere.

Within the seminary, Lyon, with the aid and advice of her trustees, especially geologist Hitchcock, configured the scientific curriculum, divided the
labor of teaching, styled teaching practice, and made science integral to the
entire Mount Holyoke culture on a highly gendered basis. As discussed later,
Lyon thus bound their fortunes up with that of Mount Holyoke and hitched
them all to the rising star of science married to religion.

Teaching

The curriculum is the most obvious place to look for signs of how science
figured in the faculty's teaching program. It is as much a source of information on questions of what the women faculty taught and how they taught it,
as it is on how they divided the labor of instruction into different tasks and
how these were shared between visiting male science lecturers and Mount
Holyoke faculty. From the answer to these questions, we can begin to understand how Lyon simultaneously cooperated with college men in inaugurating a hierarchical and gendered division of intellectual work and disciplinary
subject matter while opening opportunities for women faculty to advance
themselves through teaching science.

In accordance with church interests, natural theology was the most
prominent among the religious subjects that capped a curriculum dominated
by science. The Natural Theology course, based on Bishop Paley's *Natural
Theology, or Evidences of the Existence of the Deity Collected from the Appearances of Nature*, made clear the connections between religious belief, scientific methods,
and natural phenomena.[12]

In science, the subject matter covered was impressive. Its range suggests the
extent to which Lyon was able to move into and shape this relatively new and
undefined field of academic study. Subjects offered in the first years included
natural philosophy, astronomy, geology, chemistry, and botany. By the sec-

ond year there were seven science courses offered, which all students had to take. All these courses were taught through a highly structured combination of lectures and recitations. In some cases the written and spoken word was supplemented by female faculty-conducted demonstrations—or "experiments," as teachers called them. Only in one course, Botany, did faculty have students personally utilize an empirically based system to collect, analyze, classify, and preserve specimens they had gathered on their own.[13]

Recitations or "classes"—as the teachers termed the formal gathering of students where lecture material was discussed—were the women teachers' responsibility. These periods were devoted to systematically querying students about the material presented in lectures by men and in their readings. However, in these early years, as a kind of bridge over the gender divide, Botany depended on a text written by a woman that adopted the male college lecture format and style of discussing the theological implications of nature study. The text was that Lyon had used at Ipswich: Elmira Phelps's *Familiar Lectures on Botany* (4th ed., 1835). Popular in seminary and common school classes, Phelps's book was organized as a series of lectures on special topics. She devoted the first lecture to discussing the importance of systems in science and in practical life, for they enable "us to gain a knowledge of these laws and relations [of nature]. The Deity has not only placed before us an almost infinite variety of objects, but has given our minds the power of reducing them into classes, so as to form beautiful and regular systems."[14] Only in Botany were students fully engaged in an interactive process of learning science. Faculty members not only used books to teach students in recitation classes how to gather evidence and identify plants, but they also took students outside to collect specimens, which students organized into herbaria. Whether they added to the existing body of catalogued plants is not known.

There were also occasions when a few faculty, notably Mary Lyon herself, performed demonstrations for the edification of the entire female community. Teachers' demonstrations in chemistry, for example, made the relationship between natural phenomena and their causes more palpable to observers. Lyon's wish that her faculty make these demonstrations smooth and efficient impelled her to provide them from the very beginning with the best equipment she could afford. She spent $100 for the original chemistry apparatus, a collection assembled after considerable research and travel to inform herself about what was available on the market. In fact, her commitment to the demonstration method of teaching was so strong that this equipment was one of the earliest purchases she made. It was a pedagogical strategy she had acquired during her tenure at Ipswich Female Seminary, where she had taken personal responsibility for selecting equipment. In March 1837, just months before the new seminary opened, she wrote to Zilpah Grant requesting a list of the chemical apparatus Lyon had purchased in her previous post.[15]

There was a crisscrossing of logistical, gendered, and economic rationales for these arrangements within the customs of church propriety. Such was the case with the useful, and apparently innovative, strategy of dividing the work of teaching between men who visited the seminary for short periods of time, during which they offered a series of lectures, and the resident women faculty who led the recitations, performed demonstrations, and supervised collecting over the course of each semester. In establishing these partially gender-based divisions in the work of teaching science, Lyon gave a substantial nod to practical necessities. Men from the colleges and institutes in the region presented lectures, often to the assembled student body and faculty, devoted to each of the major sciences. They spent as much as several months a year at the seminary, laying out the fundamental ideas, general laws, and latest discoveries in their sciences. They also discussed the moral, social, and scientific significance of this subject matter. For example, at various times Hitchcock presented lectures and lecture series at the seminary to an assembly of teachers and students on the subjects of anatomy, physiology, and geology, as well as natural theology.[16] These presentations often repeated those given at Amherst College, but at times could be more radical and tailored to the female audience—as was the case with his lectures on human physiology and reproductive anatomy. The women teachers then had the responsibility of leading recitations based on the lectures to small groups of students. It appears these recitations were held just after the lectures.

Three exceptions to these hierarchical, gendered divisions in modes of instruction occurred in classes devoted to the physical sciences, save for chemistry and the natural science of botany. First, Lyon relinquished to men full control over the physical sciences, chemistry excepted. Second, in that subject, the women offered demonstrations and recitations, and later on in the 1840s would tentatively try their hand at lecturing. Judging from the catalogues, botany seems to have been a subject almost wholly in the women's hands, taught through recitations and the interactive method of collecting, identifying, and preserving specimens.

Why these divisions? And variations from field to field? The answer is complex and to some extent speculative, but extremely important for understanding women's role in originating gendered divisions in types of work and fields of specialization that developed in American science. It is also significant in establishing the contribution women made to the foundations of laboratory teaching in higher education. Lyon worked out these divisions with the male visitors and trustees, we can assume, without too much stress. It was a pragmatic approach that took into account a number of factors: first, that men who taught science in the colleges had lecturing experience and were sanctioned to speak in public; second, that they had more knowledge of science than either Lyon or her teachers; and third, that they were more interested in adding to the body of scientific knowledge than were the Mount Holyoke faculty members, whose main interest lay in improving their science teaching. A fourth consideration is that, as shown later, the Mount Holyoke women had little time for the extra study and preparation lecturing required. The men neatly introduced women teachers and students to general information about the particular science, its laws, the type of phenomena it considered, and the methods for identifying, categorizing, and explaining these phenomena. Thus, lectures by men such as Hitchcock with connections to both colleges and scientific societies served a variety of purposes—not least of which was increasing the time women teachers had for the multitude of other responsibilities needed to maintain the community of women.

This is not to say that the work of demonstrating chemical experiments and collecting and organizing specimens was without benefit to the women teachers. For example, the method of teaching that included demonstrations or collecting and handling of specimens was in fact an effort by Lyon and some of her faculty to upgrade their status and to try to make more scholarly methods well established in primary school teaching by associating them with the elevated study of nature. This was a strategy used by science faculty in the colleges as well. Paul Mattingly has shown that during the 1830s and 1840s distinctions arose between college, seminary, common school, and academy teachers, and intellectual achievement was the measure used by college men who set the standards. College presidents in the early 1830s, including the Rev. Herman Humphrey, Hitchcock's predecessor at Amherst College, had fought to counteract what they defined as an antischolarly stress on "a more direct procedure of instruction" as a way to distinguish college teaching from the pedagogical methods being taught to future teachers at the seminaries and normal schools.[17] Science instruction with its use of technical equipment, its reliance on specimens and hands-on, interactive learning in laboratory teaching, aimed at an empirical understanding of natural laws, was a step above and beyond the manual arts and buttressed scholarly integrity by Christian ideals of personal witness rather than simple moral discipline.

As for gendered divisions in control over subject matter, at that time the physical sciences, especially geology, astronomy, and natural philosophy (later known as physics), were the sciences most closely associated with the theological uncovering of the divine design, and therefore with male activities of interpretation, preaching, and professing. Moreover, geology and astronomy both had ties to practical, economic interests of the state and nation as governments became interested in identifying and exploiting natural resources and trade possibilities. Custom, law, and vested interests kept them in the hands of knowledgeable and well-connected men. Chemistry, on the other hand, was not yet well developed as a science, nor was it yet important to industry, but it offered a means of understanding simple processes observable in the everyday activities of women—soapmaking, dyeing and so on. It was thus an opportunity for the women who taught it to empower themselves. Botany, too, was not economically significant, and its foundation in an old-fashioned systematics, its general popularity among women, and the abundant flowers, trees, and grasses growing in surrounding fields made it a perfect teaching resource for these women.[18]

Expense may also have been a determining factor accounting for the difference between chemistry and botany teaching methods. There were not enough funds to provide the necessary equipment, supplies, space and assistants for the seventy enrolled students to do chemical experiments on their own. In contrast, resourceful botany teachers took advantage of the fact that local fields were filled with a wide variety of plants that could be gathered for free. Lyon's herbarium with 300 specimens served as a standard of excellence that teachers encouraged students to emulate. As a consequence, Botany became extremely popular. Students competed with one another in the effort to find and identify the largest number of species, to such an extent that Lyon feared the extinction of the very things they honored.[19]

It is possible to argue that there was nothing foreordained about this intellectually and sexually based division of teaching labor. It certainly reflects shrewdness on Lyon's part. Simply from a practical standpoint, the designation of lecturing and interpretation as men's purview and recitation drills as women's respected certain evangelical customs in church where the ministers preached and women prayed and led children's Sunday school classes. This distinction also respected customs regarding what was proper behavior for men and women in public spaces—that is, places outside the home where men and women met together. At Mount Holyoke, visiting male faculty and clergy spoke to a mixed assembly, for there were often men as well as women visitors to the seminary; however, women faculty never did so. They saved their pedagogical efforts for the classroom, and only spoke before all-female assemblies at the seminary. (Lyon never spoke at the trustees meetings, for example.)[20]

If Lyon respected these customs, she also turned them to her and her faculty's advantage as she made the radical claim to a new public sphere of action for women, opening access to higher knowledge and the resources needed to teach it. However, she shared with these men a deep belief that encompassed and validated these arrangements. As Amanda Porterfield has pointed out, the communitarian theology to which Lyon and her supporters subscribed established women's right to participate in the missionary endeavor.[21] Much has been made of the democratic potential of Protestantism, particularly of evangelical Protestantism. Maintaining that both men and women could be saved, it opened the way to the belief that a select group of men and women in its leadership might be equally capable of studying nature to understand God's laws and, thus, intellectually equal. As David Noble has noted, within Protestant circles the way was opened for women to study and teach science because of the role that nature played in salvation. Certainly, descriptions of this experience emphasize the degree to which the young women felt themselves drawn into a higher level of consciousness, often achieved through the agency of communion with the landscape.[22]

But if the process of salvation through the agency of nature served to certify membership of men and women in this elect group of social leaders, the ministry had established unequal gender-based divisions of intellectual labor. Most important among them was the theological view that men were by nature different and superior to women. Biological differences dictated differences in social functions—women were designed to bear children and, hence, to teach. Men were endowed with the ability to reason widely and interpret "the word," women to disseminate it. Both possessed the capacity for systematic thought and behavior necessary to their tasks. These divisions were carried over into the way male and female faculty taught science in the schools. Within the church, men did the public speaking to mixed audiences. They discussed, wrote, and published their interpretations of biblical subjects within a public realm that included women and children who were expected to listen to, but not to engage in, these forms of intellectual activity themselves. Women, however, did have an intellectual, but not an interpretive or public, role. They were teachers, communicating these ideas to other women and children. The fact that women were a majority in the churches elevated the pedagogical function ministers' wives performed as Sunday school teachers and prayer group leaders, and it focused women's attention on perfecting their knowledge of how to communicate information. It also gave them a special area of subject matter to master in addition to the standard topics: women's reproductive physiology.

In order to have the sort of companions they desired, churchmen sup-

ported the employment of women teachers and the establishment of institutions to train them. They also held the line at what was seemly to teach—
that is, not treading on men's right to define the larger picture and interpret
it. They thus helped bring into being a type of professional helpmate: the
unmarried female seminary teacher endowed with the knowledge, skills,
habits, and religious credentials necessary to acculturate the ministers' future
wives and the mothers of their children. In so doing, the ministers opened
up possibilities for Protestant women teachers to advance and extend their
own sphere of influence in higher education among women and children of
both sexes. The physical sciences and botany especially were recognized as
necessary areas of teachers' competence.

However, if the ministers sanctioned women teachers' right to assign scientific subject matter—making them equal to male teachers in this regard—
religious custom also restricted women from engaging in either discovery of
new information, interpretation and criticism of existing ideas, or participation in public forms of discourse. All of these circumscribed women
teachers' sphere of action within a narrower field than that allowed to college men, but gave them potentially greater power over the dissemination of
scientific knowledge. In the coming years, Mary Lyon would use her connections with members of the evangelical community and its theology and
customs to launch Mount Holyoke on a scientific basis in order to make the
most of this power, and to begin in a small way to test its limits.

Lyon's resulting solution was an arrangement to share the work of teaching with men in ways that served these multiple purposes. At the same time,
she kept women focused on pedagogical skills, laboratory teaching, expanding specialized knowledge, and disseminating scientific knowledge, rather than
aspiring to engage in nascent research efforts, publishing, or other activities
related to the development of science on a national scale. It was also an arrangement that respected the need for economic restraints in order to be able
to support the curriculum. Here in the encompassing realm of seminary life,
Lyon extended the reach of science into the daily running of the seminary.

Religion and Science

In this educational effort that made faculty servants of the institution's goal
to produce qualified Christian teachers, Lyon additionally charged them
with supervising the lives of the students outside the classroom. Supervising
students' behavior and systematically cultivating their physical, emotional,

and spiritual well-being entailed aligning their charges' existence with certain standards that Lyon termed "natural" (or fundamental, uncorrupted).[23] These standards were the source of good health and spiritual salvation if properly respected. Within each man and woman's spirit and body lay the potential for engaging with this divine order, bringing it to expression in a well-ordered secular activity. It was the teachers' responsibility to see that this natural state was cultivated through the application of scientific knowledge to all facets of daily life. For teachers this effort at systematization was directed toward their own quest for scholarly knowledge about the natural world, their pedagogical methods, and their nonteaching activities.

One facet of science that is generally ignored because scholars tend to consider it "unscientific" is what can be termed "the science of religious credentialing." More a science of psychology or human nature than of physical matter, it played an important role in the teachers' identity formation. For any system of the sort they were building to prosper, they felt it necessary that members of the community work with concentrated enthusiasm. Here in the systematic cultivation of this seemingly unscientific feeling lay Lyon's teachers' claim to special status.

What was enthusiasm? Mary Lyon made it clear that this feeling of intensely pleasurable energy was a guarantee that one's own nature and that of the divinity were joined in harmony.[24] It gave teachers and students' actions integrity. It also made the teachers' work easier to carry out. Such energy fueled the engine of the seminary so that it ran smoothly and in a way that could be claimed to be entirely natural. The rules were intended to be guides steering female energy into the proper channels, instilling a self-monitoring sense of prudence, efficiency, economy, and order. To embrace one's work in the seminary with such rationally canalized energy was a sign that the spirit of God was at work in the person, just as it was in the formation of the natural landscape.

It is not surprising then to find that enthusiasm lay at the heart of the experience of salvation that was a sine qua non at the seminary.[25] In the early nineteenth century women provided the greatest number of converts in the evangelical churches. It was an experience that gave them "great, and sometimes unspeakable happiness."[26] Teachers, who counted increasing numbers of women in their ranks, came to consider salvation a certificate of membership in a special cadre of those chosen to lead the nation.[27] This combination of administrative requirement with personal commitment was the case at Mount Holyoke from the beginning. All the faculty members at the seminary were required to show that they had undergone conversion, and every year the principal's report began with an accounting of how many souls had been saved at the seminary during the previous twelve months as one of the major signs of the system's success in advancing the numbers of Christian teachers they were forming. During the first twenty years, 739 conversions took place out of less than a thousand women graduated.[28]

Enthusiasm for nature had a special status in the salvation experience primarily because it was the context in which Mary Lyon remembered she had come to feel redeemed. Her story of standing on the summit of a hill in Buckland, Massachusetts, on a beautiful Sabbath afternoon in the spring of 1816, was well known within the Mount Holyoke community and revered as a kind of myth about the founder. There, transfixed by the glorious, light-filled landscape, she was filled with a sense of compassion for "a perishing world" and a desire to work to save it.[29]

Moreover, while by the late 1830s evangelical educators had come to require that teachers have a certificate of salvation to qualify for employment, the fact that some Mount Holyoke teachers had experienced redemption through communion with nature, as had Lyon herself, may have provided Lyon with an incentive for choosing these individuals to teach the science courses or helped the teachers self-select for this subject area. In any case, the experience of salvation, the triumph of the moral and outward-focused self over the indulgent self, moved Lyon and her faculty one step farther along in their quest for a publicly recognized, marketable sign of the superior education they offered at affordable prices.

Domestic System

Faculty were also responsible for Mount Holyoke's domestic system, a task that required teachers to develop rational organizational skills and pedagogical methods to economically manage running the seminary. The system essentially required that teachers aided by the students do the cooking, cleaning, laundry, and other chores necessary to maintain the extensive family household in which the work of teaching and learning took place. In the first years of Mary Lyon's principalship, the seminary had no internal source of running water, wood had to be carried in daily to provide fuel to heat the main rooms, food had to be prepared, laundry and cleaning done, and money was short for hired help. There is strong evidence that Lyon and her trustees justified the system as a way to demonstrate that work without monetary compensation would produce other forms of reward for the women and for the seminary. Among the most important was the hope of some guarantee the seminary and the faculty jobs would survive. In this case, Lyon's claim to a scientific and natural program rested on the fact that the seminary was run by human energy operating as efficiently and economically as possible.

In order to do this, teachers put into practice the scientific information and organizational methods they used in the classroom and in daily life. They also drew on the rules and regulations regarding cleanliness, diet, personal behavior, and exercise, based on that knowledge. If faculty and students ate natural foods, faculty members guided students to prepare and serve them in an orderly manner. If they lived in well-washed clothes, slept in clean sheets, and walked on well-scrubbed floors, faculty members arranged and oversaw the washing and cleaning. If faculty members taught botany and chemistry recitations, they worked with students to care for the small botanical garden and the storage rooms for equipment and supplies. If they celebrated the vision of a community based on a natural economy, they worked together in pie-making circles and water brigades where the ideal became reality. Through their various understandings of science and its idealistic and practical dimensions, the teachers tried to bring into being a highly controlled environment that they viewed as the type of natural society they were educating their students to go out and make of the nation and the world.

The system attempted to resolve the problem of how to get this precariously funded enterprise started by enlisting teachers' and students' energies to the cause. It enabled the students and faculty as well, most without significant economic resources, to pay their way. And in these first years, the type of work it entailed was not unknown to these women who came almost exclusively from the hard-pressed New England farms in the region. While it enabled impoverished students to gain an education at very modest cost, and thus entrée into an emerging and more socially prestigious profession, the domestic system set the women faculty in a paradoxical and difficult situation. Even though this duty helped the teachers retain their jobs, raise their standard of living, and gain higher social standing, it also exploited their ambitions and their bodies, by turning a substantial amount of energy and time away from improving their teaching. Whether or not students took this experience with them when they organized their own households, responsibility for it fell on the shoulders of the teachers, who had to allocate some of their time and energy to these duties, rather than to teaching.

Lyon insisted that all these systematic efforts be further disciplined through the imposition of specific traits she identified with women's character: perfection in performance; manual dexterity; a high degree of emotional energy;

and a self-denying, economically rational spirit. Here was the foundation for steering her teachers and the students into defining women's scientific work and endowing it with economic value. Her views on self-denial, referred to earlier in this chapter, turned it into a mode of projecting economical constraints onto the organization of the material world in their purview. This was the case, whether it be the handling of equipment in the classroom for demonstrations, the information they communicated, the lives of the students, or the daily chores within the spaces of the seminary. Lyon also insisted that all work be done "perfectly." She herself was driven by a profound concern to take care of even the most minor details in setting up the seminary, from buying scientific equipment to furnishing the rooms. In what would amount to an obsession with detail in the last years of her life, she turned her energies into setting an example for the other teachers in the classroom by teaching chemistry recitations and mastering the demonstrations for chemistry.[30] Moreover, she felt it possible for these teachers who came from backgrounds similar to hers to adapt the practical skills women practiced in their rural households (the handling of tools for weaving, cooking, raising vegetables, animal care) to classroom and seminary needs.[31]

In its first three years, Lyon's effort to define teachers' scientific work and to make teachers' work scientific intertwined to give women who taught science a footing on the highest educational level within the evangelical Christian movement. Moreover, she helped women teachers develop a desire for expertise in teaching science—although neither the definition of science as research nor the figure known as a "scientist" yet existed in America. Her plan had the character of the little factories and utopian experiments springing up in western Massachusetts during this period, and like them it was presented as if designed in accordance with nature's laws. But like the Brook Farm experiment and all the failing underfunded enterprises dependent on and exploiting the labor of participants to make up the difference, it was impossible to keep the seminary running as an almost self-sufficient enterprise, no matter how "natural" its system when the more appealing alternatives of industrial society presented themselves. Although there was a budget surplus due to the teachers' economies, the fact was that the rate of student retention was low. Despite Lyon's effort to be very selective about admissions and to increase the total number of students enrolled at any one time, "seldom did more than one third of the old pupils return and scarcely more than one in ten of those who enrolled received graduation certificates."[32] The opening of state normal schools, combined with the vigorous public primary school system inaugurated by the state that took root in the 1840s, opened a formidable competitor for Lyon's source of students. Moreover, the growing number of middle-class families living in thriving towns across New England desired a more comfortable way of life for their daughters.

One additional factor in Lyon's equation was the need to retain her faculty. While the teachers did not openly complain, or at least the record does not show this, there is no doubt that the pressures on them were enormous, while possibilities for more exciting and rewarding employment elsewhere were growing. Some of the original teachers had left because they were worn out by the work required of them. Several others died from disease that was no fault of the seminary or left to care for ailing relatives. Others were drawn away by the promise of opportunities in the West, some to work in the new seminaries and others to marry New England clergymen and doctors or missionaries at home and abroad. The possession of a measure of job security, room, board, and perhaps a small salary and the opportunity to professionalize their status in exchange for the crushing physical and administrative labor required of them were not enough to outweigh these other factors in some of the faculty's minds. Their situation had to be made more attractive if the seminary was to have some stability.

Crisis came in the spring of 1840 when an epidemic of typhoid fever raged at the seminary. The infection struck forty individuals and at least nine women died. According to Cole, the number of women registering the next fall dropped and the epidemic hurt efforts to raise funds.[33] Lyon would have to ease nonacademic burdens on teachers and students alike, while making the seminary attractive once again to Christian women through modernizing reforms that appealed to a wider swath of the middling classes.

The Castle of Science

Renewed and more extensive commitment to science and the missionary societies provided the answers. A way out was to expand and reform the seminary and its program by joining Mount Holyoke up with the energetic forces driving both the missionary movement and academic science. By the 1840s missionary societies aimed at founding missionary schools and seminaries at home and abroad were organizing extensive networks that sought to make common cause with eastern colleges and seminaries. During these same years college science faculty, under the leadership of men including Edward Hitchcock, became participants in a growing national network of professional associations aimed at increasing and disseminating scientific knowledge. American expansionism, government support for developing national resources, and a tractable citizenry fueled both these male-directed efforts. In tandem, these forces external to higher education stimulated demand for able, religiously sanctioned teachers and for scientific education. Together they unleashed a dynamic that increased enthusiasm for women's higher education in science from both quarters, even as it opened a power struggle between churchmen and college science faculty for control over higher education. Many male science faculty, encouraged by their growing stature in the secular world and drawn by the excitement of identifying, organizing, and interpreting the newly opened continent, sought their own converts and disciples to spread the word. Without throwing over their commitment to Protestantism, they challenged pastors' authority over the curriculum by creating a new persona of the "scientist," a man imbued with equivalent moral integrity and zeal now placed behind the mission of interpreting nature in light of newly gathered empirical evidence.[34]

Lyon's genius was to recognize that Mount Holyoke's concentration on forming teachers could serve the interests of both college men and churchmen without taking sides in their theological and institutional controversies. Enlisting the aid and advice of trustees, Lyon sought to benefit from the access Hitchcock and men in his professionalizing network offered to the latest scientific knowledge and from the access missionary societies offered to potential students and posts for graduates. The result was a reformation of the institution that allowed women teachers to narrow their work responsibilities to focus on classroom teaching, especially on teaching science, and the organized dissemination of science teaching on the Mount Holyoke model through the missionary network.

These complex developments in both her market and her network encouraged Lyon and her trustees to expand the seminary, improve its facilities, and upgrade its offerings in science without fundamentally altering either the gendered division of scientific labor, nor the identification of science with the formation of women teachers rather than with research. The economies of Mount Holyoke teachers in the first years produced budget surpluses, encouraging trustees and donors to increase their investment in the seminary so as to take advantage of the market. They voted to enlarge the physical plant, to increase the amount and quality of scientific equipment for teaching, and to make improvements that eased domestic work and made life for faculty and students more comfortable. With the approval of the trustees, Lyon now realized her original plan of adding a southern wing completed in 1841, and planned a northern wing, completed in 1853, as well

as a two-story piazza across the front of the main building in 1845. Her desire to cap the main building with an observatory, "though authorized in 1853,
took form as a separate structure, leaving the 'cupola' to be erected in 1860
as a purely ornamental superstructure."[35] In 1847 Lucy Curtis, with Lyon's
approval, had seen to it that the seminary's flower gardens were improved in
order to meet the botany classes' enthusiastic demand for specimens.

The faculty members who taught science reaped the largest number of
benefits from the improvements. These benefits enhanced their status and
authority on campus, while allowing them to keep pace with changes in scientific knowledge and practice. These women, aided by Professor Ebenezer
Snell of Amherst College, used newly available funds to purchase equipment
for teaching natural philosophy, natural history, and chemistry. The trustees,
former students, and friends of the seminary donated funds to buy books
and journals for the library, intended to enrich the minds of young women
"by scientific, & [sic] literary knowledge."[36] Faculty members who taught
science classes were also able to claim a significant portion of the new space
for academic purposes, particularly for instruction in science. While the South
Wing contained rooms for students, allowing for the expansion of the student body, the North Wing design contained additional classrooms, some of
which were to be used for science recitations, and a lecture hall where teachers
and invited male faculty could present scientific demonstrations and lectures.
The North Wing plan also contained a large amount of space specifically
designed for scientific purposes: a chemical lecture room and laboratory in
the basement.[37] By the 1840s, the botanical gardens were already managed by
a teacher and under the regular care of four students assigned this as their
domestic task. Thus, faculty who taught science gained control of additional
space and a cadre of students for their special teaching purposes.[38]

With improvements came changes in teaching science that had implications for the social status of women science teachers, as well as the division
of labor between men and women. Textbooks are one indication of this
shift. As college science faculty members began publishing books with more
recent information for the academic market, Mount Holyoke faculty members kept pace by adopting new texts. The teachers updated the botany lessons in 1846, by replacing Phelps's text, inspired by her teacher Amos Eton
and geared to academy-level education, with the new edition of Wood's
Botany. Faculty member Susan Tolman explained she preferred this text because it provided her with a more logical system for understanding plants: "I
have examined it & think I shall like it much better than the old edition.... He
drops the artificial system entirely & makes use only of the natural. This is

a great improvement."[39] The appeal of the natural embedded in the text carried with it the gloss of new and better knowledge made accessible to teachers.

Men continued to present the lectures for science courses during this period, and Hitchcock's presence and influence increased enormously. The
teachers continued to be responsible for demonstrations; however, Lyon did
not rule out the possibility that sometime in the near future faculty might
have to develop ways to teach students to do experiments themselves in order
to meet changing job requirements. Always planning ahead to ensure that her
seminary remained competitive without offending notions of female propriety, Lyon carefully questioned a male correspondent who sought to hire
one of her graduates as to "whether you consider it important that the candidate should have had any experience in giving experiments."[40]

The amorphous nature of divisions in scientific labor in the seminary at
this time left leeway for the women faculty to attempt moving into more intellectually adventurous areas of science teaching being defined by men while
working to distance themselves from a lower class of teachers in primary
schools and from less scholarly finishing-school faculty. They were also anxious to make it clear they were not from the laboring classes.

This was a precarious business that the teachers attempted to sort out
within their sense of what might be socially possible and personally desirable for women in their position. Lyon did lecture on chemistry at this time,
as did other teachers, but gentility was an issue. Thus, Susan Tolman wrote
of her colleague Miss Whitman, "she gives . . . very interesting lectures. She
calls it talking. She became most discouraged to day [sic] with the Galvanic
Battery, & said she believed it was not for a lady to manage."[41]

This jockeying for a place, gingerly pushing upward into male elites' intellectual company while aggressively pushing back the working classes, was
a process that filled some of the women faculty with mixed emotions, for it
meant that moving up socially through science actually separated them from
other socially ambitious middle-class women even as it attached them more
closely to certain men.

The presence of men and male authority increased in the science classes
during these decades. In the 1850s Professors Paul Chadbourne and Albert
Hopkins, both from Williams College, came and lectured. Chadbourne
would give annual lectures in chemistry at Mount Holyoke from 1854 to
1865.[42] A number of science lecturers also led the school in morning devotions during their visits. An 1852 journal letter reports that the lecturer on
natural philosophy, Professor Hopkins, attended the religious meetings of
the school on Thursday and Sunday evenings and led the students in morning devotions.[43]

Decisions on subject matter for lectures and pedagogical formats seem to have been made by the men in consultation with the teachers. With the advantage of greater specialized knowledge gained through experience working outside academe, men certainly felt fewer social constraints than did the women teachers as far as taking the floor to lecture or to inaugurate innovative subject matter and teaching methods. It is not easy, therefore, to determine whether Mary Lyon or Edward Hitchcock was first to propose a course on human physiology specially tailored to women. It was Hitchcock, however, who delivered the lectures and demonstrated his points to the women faculty and students using a mannequin of his own devising. In his assumption of this activity, he not only took responsibility for and control over information concerning women and their bodies, but also helped establish formal conventions for its presentation and dissemination in the name of efficiency.

The result was a complex sociological and psychological readjustment of working relationships. As Miss Whitman recounted:

> To make the lectures more profitable, the school is to be divided into classes to recite the lectures. All the teachers will hear classes. The Manikin [sic] is exhibited to us. How clear an idea it does give us of the human system. . . . He [Hitchcock] is so perfectly modest in all his descriptions of the human frame, that one cannot possibly *fear* he will say any thing undesirable.[44]

There was a certain thrilled anxiety women teachers experienced concerning their new working personalities and the boundaries and filters on communication they were helping establish with male college faculty to give shape and order to their working relationships. Distancing themselves from their own bodies required an objectification of themselves, of their very sexuality, even as they raised their social status as teachers. The terms they chose to describe this process reveal a strong affinity with emerging capitalist ways of viewing the world in terms of cost and profit.

In 1845 Hitchcock offered a compelling image of nature within which the women could formulate their professionalizing identity changes. He articulated the ideas in a major sermon, rather than in a lecture, he delivered at both Amherst and Mount Holyoke in the winter of 1845—the year he became president of Amherst College. Speaking as both a minister and a man of science, he entitled his discourse "The Coronation of Winter" and infused it with his knowledge of chemistry and optics, as well as observations of a recent meteorological event.[45] The important point is that he proposed that those who could embrace a certain broad, economically conservative explanation of nature were God-chosen leaders of the nation. In it he offered these faculty and students a compelling vision of stewardship that would overcome their fears of breaking with conventional values and give them a means of building a different road to social advancement.

His words transformed the phenomena of that winter, of alternating snow and rain, thaw and deep freeze, clouds and sunlight culminating in a dazzling colored landscape of jeweled effects, into a stunning example of nature's God-given economical character. Human beings' sensitivity to the beauty of this event and their ability to explain it were a sign that their own bodies were made on the same principles. As a contrast, Hitchcock connected the newly prosperous middle-class desire for showy finery to their enthusiasm for diverting the Niagara River from its natural bed. These were understandably people "whose attitude towards the land is wholly utilitarian and exploitive."[46] Both represented the corruption of God's natural law.

Hitchcock's additional lesson for his audience was offered in answer to the question of how the divine presence in nature would arm them for the task of saving the nation. If the flicker of colored light that met the eyes as one walked through ice-covered fields rewarded certain individuals with an intensely personal feeling of pleasure, it was because these phenomena were modes of communication through which God made contact and singled out the individuals whose materially uncorrupted sensibilities were unself-consciously in tune with his laws. When combined with a knowledge of scientific laws and a lifestyle based on the economical character of nature, this special response guaranteed these individuals would know how to treat themselves and the land properly, and how to lead others to do the same.

Of course, Hitchcock set himself as the intellectual leader and spiritual guide of this group of men and women. Lyon, for her part, adapted his ideas about God-given nature into a practicable system for running the seminary in the 1840s, making it not only scientific but "natural" in principle. Having her faculty and students live in accordance with this ideal of the natural became her objective as she drove herself to systematically control the feeding and maintenance of their bodies. Of the menu with its emphasis on unprocessed foods, she wrote: "I prefer that you should have nothing but fresh fruit—rather have nothing but in its Eden-like state, from trees or bushes."[47] Of physical exercise, she expressed concern that the "younger generation had less physical stamina and endurance than their elders," and thus less moral fiber. "Those who enjoy bodily idleness enjoy sin," she charged, and saw to it that at Mount Holyoke "free, unconstrained natural exercise be taught."[48] It is likely that Lyon would have agreed with Hitchcock's later statements made in his lectures on physiology that a properly functioning body was proof of Divine Benevolence rewarded by a sense of happiness and well-being.[49]

As for the rules, they embodied her own, female version of Hitchcock's moral indictment of commercial capitalist culture. By banning the use of tea and processed foods, novels, and magazines purchased from stores, the teachers attempted to keep out materialistic, consumer-oriented stimulants of the commercial market that would disturb the natural moral economy of life within.[50] The fact that many of these were produced outside the region and transported into the area also made them undesirable. In this additional way, teachers who practiced these constraints and enforced them over others validated Lyon's claim that self-denying teachers were an unmatchable force for social good.

As a form of further resistance to these misguided artificial attractions, responsibility for one's clothing demonstrated to young women that husbanding their resources in ways that emulated nature's own economy had its rewards. Silence and submission to authority in lessons were seen as training women to conform to their proper nature; it was behavior that the teachers exhibited in the company of men, whose responsibility it was to delineate and interpret. These rules were also meant to keep any ideas and speculations the students might have on their own or have heard on visits home from circulating within the seminary.

The teachers' efforts also had their practical side, and because of it, the teachers had some concrete measure for believing that science made them successful. In an era before the discovery of the germ theory of disease, various theories existed to explain infections and their spread, and a number of methods were adopted to prevent and control them. Cleanliness, proper exercise, natural foods, and simple living were often believed to be ways of maintaining good health, because they brought the individual's body into harmony with the divine perfection of nature. Or as Hitchcock would sum up the rationale, "Pain is a sign of imperfection."[51] If the teachers strove to develop a moral economy that operated in accordance with natural law, they also believed they were enhancing the chances that their community of women would be a healthy one by adopting this course. Thus, for example, those who were sick were immediately isolated from the well, for many of the same reasons that the teachers isolated themselves and their students from the morally corrupt.

While teachers of science benefited from improvements in classrooms, equipment, and space more than faculty who did not, their classroom responsibilities also increased. This call on their time and energy was offset by funds that made it possible to ease the domestic work responsibilities of all the teachers. In the 1840s Lyon bureaucratized the seminary by hiring people to do special types of work under her direction. She was able to hire a woman to take charge of the kitchen, so that teachers no longer had to concern themselves with planning and purchasing food or with directing students who prepared and served it. She also brought in technological innovations that reduced manual labor. Indoor plumbing alleviated the need to carry water for personal washing and laundry from the well into the building and up the stairs. If it still remained to the teachers to oversee the running of the domestic system and of the family system, they had hired help and a set of written rules to make the domestic work load and family responsibilities less labor-intensive. In a shift of responsibilities toward those of the classroom where a wealth of material now surrounded them, they standardized their modest dress and self-denying ways. Moreover, they continued with great success to encourage their charges to follow their example, accepting Christ and a life of material self-restraint, even as the national market economy boomed.[52]

The reforms Lyon instituted opened opportunities for teachers of science at the seminary to become more influential on campus and more specialized in their teaching. The new space allocated to classrooms, increasing amounts of scientific equipment, new books with the latest ideas, the botanical garden managed by promising students, increased numbers of visiting scientists who lectured, all improved classroom conditions for teachers and encouraged them to participate in these improvements. As Susan Tolman's enthusiasm over the adoption of the more up-to-date botanical textbook attests, these reforms fed their intellectual curiosity and ambitions. They gave the women the means to improve their own knowledge in special fields, and the apparatus that identified them as specialists. Student assistants gave them more time to focus on their teaching, while the botanical garden provided all the teachers with a specialized space on campus devoted to scientific endeavor. These students, selected for their special interest in botany, would also be a means of replenishing the faculty with women they had trained once they had graduated. The plan for the chemistry laboratory in the North Wing promised to place even more specialized space devoted to teaching science under their control. Their ties with men could open opportunities for communication with the wider community of scientists, helping them to maintain a clear sense of collegiate standards, as well as to continuously redefine and expand their power and influence as teachers of women within the scientific enterprise. Lyon's decision to issue certificates to all students who had completed the seminary course, regardless of whether they had been saved, tended to encourage the faculty to develop their intellectual and pedagogical, as much as their spiritual interests. The decision to have the students examined publicly and to add a separate seminary certificate to the religious certification challenged the teachers to improve their own scholarly standards and to take pride in their own academic accomplishments.

Other reforms eased the lives of all the faculty members outside the classroom, allowing them to focus more attention on the work of teaching and still feel they were maintaining a natural system. Lyon also invested them with a bureaucratic structure and written set of rules that released them from personally supervising the lives of the students. The reorganized domestic system relieved them from supervising the laundry and kitchen. Having students monitor those who were ill also helped. Moreover, the more varied diet made daily life more comfortable. The plans to give them private living space in the North Wing, as well as better heating and water supply, must also have been an incentive to stay. While salaries do not seem to have risen, and in fact teachers may have followed Lyon's custom of tithing a fair percentage of her salary to the church, they did have some money on hand to use during vacations for their own travel. These were the years in which she reiterated her desire for students and faculty to "Be perfect in all requirements here." And by 1847, she felt her new system was well established.[53] It was something to write home about, and one student's letter enthusiastically expressed her admiration for the integrated environment in the phrase "a castle of science."[54]

The image of a girded fortress conjured up by the term "castle" is misleading, for Lyon's reforms also integrated Mount Holyoke into two growing networks that offered opportunities to women teachers in higher education at the time: that of missionary societies, specifically the American Board of Commissioners of Foreign Missions (ABCFM), and that of male science faculty in the colleges. Through her faculty and trustees she established working relationships with the ABCFM and the Society for the Promotion of Collegiate and Theological Education in the West. She was able to place her graduates in positions where they could disseminate the study of nature and her scientific system within an emerging educational network. Moreover, the college men and ministers who ran these societies looked to Mount Holyoke as a model for the women's seminaries they wished to found and as a source of principals and faculty members whose scientific knowledge, teaching, and organizational skills were valued assets. Already in 1838, the Reverend

Milo P. Jewett, who would later be Vassar College's first president, had relied on Mary Lyon's advice in planning a new building for the Judson Female Seminary in Marion, Alabama, which he then headed. In the 1850s, the Western Female Seminary at Oxford, Ohio, and the Willoughby Seminary (later the Lake Erie Seminary) in Painsville, Ohio, not only copied Mount Holyoke's family and domestic systems, but often were partially staffed by Mount Holyoke graduates who served as teachers and administrators under the direction of male ministers. Each of them offered courses in sciences and adopted versions of Lyon's Mount Holyoke system. These two were among a number of institutions founded during these and later years that were known as sister and daughter seminaries.[55] They included Mills Seminary in California; the Huguenot Seminary and College, Cape Province, S.A.; and the International Institute for Girls, Santander, Spain.[56]

Mount Holyoke graduates in some cases desired to follow Mary Lyon's more independent path, striking out in the new geographic frontiers to found seminaries of their own over which they had some autonomy from male control. Fidelia Fiske ('42) was one case in point, establishing a missionary seminary in Turkey for the education of native teachers at which science was taught.

Through their graduates the faculty members created conduits for the dissemination of science education among women engaged in teaching in this country and abroad, and placed professionally oriented women in a position to encourage women's continuing participation in the scientific enterprise. Mount Holyoke graduates as well as faculty members entered the missionary field beginning in 1839, and their numbers grew steadily after that. Six teachers in 1843 left for missions, five of whom married male missionaries. Under the impetus of Fidelia Fiske, Mount Holyoke seminary furnished the principal and founder of one of the seven seminaries and three female seminaries through which the American Board of Missions sought to extend its influence by educating native teachers and preachers.[57]

Another was Susan Tolman who, after teaching at her South Hadley alma mater where she was active in modernizing the botany course, left to marry a minister and serve as a missionary teacher with her husband in Ceylon and the Sandwich Islands. Eventually with the aid of her husband she founded Mills Seminary in California, a territory newly opened and thriving after the 1849 gold rush. Susan Tolman had studied science under Mary Lyon and was deeply influenced by her mentor both intellectually and spiritually. She had taught science courses at Punahu College during her missionary work in Hawaii, often under difficult circumstances—although things were perhaps not much better at Mount Holyoke during the 1840s. Her reminiscence about this experience bespeaks a sense of the energy, adaptability, and common sense with which she approached the duty of teaching chemistry to young women converts from the islands.

> I procured an old retort, made oxygen gas in the kitchen stove, with a washtub for a pneumatic cistern, fruit bottles for receivers, and these with the help of students, I carried on soup plates from the kitchen to the farther room in the college building.[58]

Results

The differences between the path pursued by Mount Holyoke science teachers and that of faculty at the colleges in these years make clear how the reforms of the 1840s began to distinguish professional complementarity in academic science. While a full study of science at the male colleges still needs to be done, it is possible to sketch a picture that shows both similarities and differences. Of course, the most obvious difference is that there were no divisions of labor based on sex. However, unlike Mount Holyoke, the male colleges were presided over by ordained ministers. These men exercised direct control over the curriculum, teaching methods, and lives of faculty and students through the creation of an all-encompassing collegiate culture. Intellectually, as at the Mount Holyoke Seminary, theology capped the course of studies in the colleges. Students took courses in secular subjects, but these were always infused with moral significance, while classes in Bible study, Christian ethics, and natural theology made explicit the hierarchical relationship between the Christian world order and the secular subjects that served to support it.[59]

Other differences help us understand the divisions of labor that male science faculty who lectured at Mount Holyoke established with the women. On their own campuses they presented lectures and supervised recitations, although it seems there were fewer recitations than at the seminary, and mechanics often took care of the demonstrations and equipment.[60] As at Mount Holyoke, college presidents used rules and regulations to bring students' behavior into line with religious ideals of Christian character. Faculty members took charge of monitoring them. At Bowdoin College, for example, there were strict fines for nodding one's head at prayer and public reprimands for more egregious slips such as smoking, tardiness, or working on the Sabbath.[61] Finally, by holding frequent revivals on campus and counseling students to come forward and be saved, the presidents tried to win their emotional allegiance to the collegiate mission, making them members of a company of the elect in whom the old values and traditions had taken on new career-oriented meaning and social purpose.[62] However, in all these areas, male faculty members had less responsibility outside the classroom and were less rigorous in their policing than their Mount Holyoke counterparts. This was primarily because male students often did not live on campus and were difficult to control.[63]

The big intellectual and cultural difference between the genders among faculties was in what male faculty members emphasized. Within the classroom at the male colleges, faculty members who taught science stressed lectures, and in their lectures they concentrated on large ideas and theories. The course listings for Amherst and Williams colleges during these years show fewer science courses than at Mount Holyoke, but more theological and natural philosophy topics. In their desire to raise their own social status through claims to scholarship and discovery, the college faculty members who taught science were careful to keep their focus on the nonutilitarian aspects of their subject.[64] And they were anxious to distinguish themselves from men of the church and from academy and seminary teachers (whether male or female) in these years by adopting the newly coined term "scientist," with its connotations of discovering new knowledge, rather than passing it on. As Hitchcock defined the ideal man of science in a talk delivered at Andover Theological Seminary in 1852:

> He is a man who loves Nature, and with untiring industry endeavors to penetrate her mysteries. With a mind too large for narrow views, too generous and frank for distorting prejudice, and too pure to be the slave of appetite and passion, he calmly surveys the phenomena of nature, to learn from thence the great plan of the universe as it lay originally in the divine mind . . . and we may be sure that whatever goes by the name of science, which contradicts a fair and enlightened exhibition of revealed truth, is only false philosophy.[65]

He makes the scientist a special kind of worker whose sanctified masculinity is identified with the possession of both intellectual power and moral integrity over information about nature. Unlike Mount Holyoke women, who were terribly concerned about adhering to orthodoxy and focused on doing things correctly, men who taught science in the colleges were divided over how to interpret the meaning of the information they gathered, but not about the righteousness of their mission to do so.

After Lyon's death, these two directions in teaching held equal, primarily through a balance struck between the power wielded by Edward Hitchcock and that by the Reverend Roswell Hawks on campus and on the flow of graduates into other positions. With weak female principals and the trustees each marshaled to his side, these two men struggled for influence over the faculty and students. While Hitchcock became the champion of science in the interest of spiritual liberation, physical health, and intellectual progress, Hawks supported systematic order and discipline of the spirit, mind, and body in the name of moral growth. Although Hawks foiled Hitchcock's bid to bring the seminary under direct control of college science men by undermining the geologist's move to appoint the Rev. Albert Hopkins from Williams College as Lyon's successor, Hitchcock continued to be active in seminary life until his death in 1864.[66]

Hawks focused his attention on family life, seeing to it that teachers enforced the systematic rules governing students' behavior, dress, and participation in the domestic system and religious life of Mount Holyoke. He even set himself up in living quarters on campus. Hitchcock, on the other hand, made his presence known by giving an annual course of lectures and arranging for male colleagues from other colleges and institutes in the region to do the same. In this way he saw that the teachers were exposed to the newest ideas of some of the best men in American science and links were formed that reinforced common interests and dependencies. He always took care, however, that these men of science made their religious commitments known. For example, Hitchcock himself presented lectures at Mount Holyoke on such subjects as "The Religion of Geology," in which he made references to the work of Asa Gray and Louis Agassiz.[67] Hitchcock cemented ties between seminary faculty and others from Williams College by inviting Professors Lassell and Chadbourne to lecture on chemistry. Chadbourne would continue to lecture annually for eleven years. And he drew on his involvement with the professional organizations being formed in these years and adapted the knowledge published in their journals to his teaching at the seminary. The American Geological Society and the American Association for the Advancement of Sciences were especially important.

The result is that we can see the tide of some teachers' enthusiasm focus in on improving their knowledge of scientific subjects and their ability to teach them in the classroom. In the spirit of interdependency with men that Lyon had been so careful to define and cultivate until the day she died, in 1851 teacher Helen Peabody wrote about Professor Lassell of Williams College, whose lectures on chemistry she found a model of inspiration:

> He enters farther into the subject than we have ever had any one before and is intensely interesting. . . . He presents his subject in such a manner as to awaken

an interest where none had previously existed & to elevate our views even to sub-
limity of the power that willed matter into existence & of that science which
teaches the intimate and invisible constitution of bodies and reveals to us the
compounds which may be formed from simple substances & the laws which gov-
ern their combination.[68]

Hawks and Hitchcock also laid claim to the legacy of Mary Lyon, each
interpreting it in his own way. Hitchcock published an enormously popular
biography of Lyon within two years of her death, while Hawks established
the tradition of Mountain Day, in which students and faculty climbed
Mount Holyoke each spring for a service in honor of her birthday.[69] The
significance of Mountain Day was not lost on Hitchcock. It is the source of
the one image that best encapsulates the divergent character of these interpretations and of the paths the faculty found open to them in the decade
and a half after the principal's demise. Two years in a row on Mountain Day,
as the Reverend Hawks led the circle of women seated on a grassy knoll in
their meditations, a group of Amherst College students and their professor
enthusiastically scoured the same area for flowers and grasses to add to their
botanical collections.[70] While some Mount Holyoke students complained
that the young men disturbed their tranquility, there were no doubt some
faculty members and students who wanted to get up and join the young men
for a variety of reasons. For faculty members, it may have struck them as a
fitting way to honor Lyon's own achievements as a botanizer. Whether or not
the teachers found the tactic too crude, Hitchcock had used the occasion to
dramatize the opposition between the choices open to them: either vigorous
engagement in a coeducational group led by men working to find the order
in nature, or docile subordination to men who sought to discipline women's
natures into order.

Changes in the seminary culture during these years produced a highly
gender-conscious proto-professional identity among the science faculty members that they passed on to the next generations. They came to regard a high
degree of competence in certain pedagogical activities performed by male
college faculty as the measure of their own status as teachers. Handling
equipment and performing demonstrations, as much as lecturing, drew their
attention when time and funding allowed, rather than what passed for research in the 1840s and 1850s (save for botanical systematics) and writing for
publication. Moreover, they looked to men from the colleges to educate
them in what they needed to know for teaching. In the pre-Civil War era, this
meant primarily either men who came to the seminary to lecture or who

wrote books ordered for teaching purposes, although in a few instances teachers with special authority took time for study outside the seminary. In 1845 Mary Lyon and another Mount Holyoke teacher, Mary Whitman, accompanied Hitchcock, his wife and son, and Professor Adams from Middlebury College on a two- or three-week geological tour of Vermont.[71]

Ironically, for the women teachers, the gendered division of labor made it possible for them to take advantage of the struggle between male science faculty and churchmen for adherents who would disseminate their views. Because of their concentration on the mission of teaching and on the formation of women teachers, the women were able to move toward focusing their energies on teaching and even on science teaching without compromising evangelical orthodoxy. During the late 1840s until the Civil War, the women faculty who taught science had been able to forge a synthesis between the two options and to produce a generation of graduates who imbibed that synthesis, carrying it beyond the seminary's walls, primarily but not entirely through the agency of the missionary movement in higher education.

In terms of Mary Lyon's goal of forming teachers with a strong commitment to science, the faculty members made her scientific system a success. In fact, they produced graduates who found employment or took advantage of economic opportunities that opened for three categories of teachers: graduates who went directly into teaching positions either in seminaries for training teachers or in common schools, particularly in the territories to the west; graduates who went into missionary teaching posts in seminaries and schools out West and abroad; and graduates who used intellectual and administrative skills learned at Mount Holyoke to found sister and daughter seminaries modeled on Mount Holyoke in which they hired other graduates from their alma mater.[72]

In point of fact, however, changes she made within Mount Holyoke compromised the original syncretic culture that once unified all aspects of the teachers' activities into a religiously defined goal because they confused the definitions of what was natural to women's character and lifestyle. For example, judging by the teachers' response to working with demonstration equipment, being a science teacher committed them to activities that even they felt turned them into peculiar women. The galvanic battery was after all "not for a lady to manage." Depending on Hitchcock to inform them about women's physiology through demonstration also seemed to blur the biological divisions that should have maintained women's control over the subject.

If these changes opened opportunities for those teachers interested in science to pursue their specialty with greater zeal in the classroom, they did the same for faculty more interested in teaching as a specialized profession based on pedagogical expertise. Even more than the colleges, the seminary became a stagecoach pulled by two horses trying to go in two different directions but kept moving in parallel by an ill-fitting harness of imposed "scientific" rules and regulations. Unlike the struggle between churchmen and college men on male campuses, however, that at the seminary was an extension of the men into women's territory. This fact left the women at one remove from shaping the course of their professional fates.

Before the end of the Civil War, the expanding economy and growing demand for teachers of good Christian character created a situation in which trustees could support both paths and faculty members could choose to be drawn to one or another of them. After the Civil War, the economic downturn combined with competition for students from newly founded women's colleges in New England altered Mount Holyoke's circumstances in the marketplace and the entire network of relationships her faculty had with churchmen and with college men. A new generation of women faculty and trustees at Mount Holyoke chose to reform the seminary into a college favoring scientific specialization and more liberal lifestyles compatible with industrial capitalism, in order to assure their own and their institution's continuing high status.

chapter 3

Taking the Academic Science Path in an Era of Collegiate Innovation (1860–1888)

Introduction

Mount Holyoke science teachers took advantage of the liberalized climate the Civil War created for women to participate in the energetic expansion of science that created a more complex academic universe.[1] In the decades after war's end, these women advanced their ambitions for greater autonomy from men in a successful struggle to use science to meet the challenges new women's colleges posed to the seminary's continued existence. They avidly adapted new theories about evolution and developments in specialized scientific inquiry to this end. Moreover they capitalized on the growing popularity of laboratory teaching learned from colleagues at male colleges, technical institutes, and universities to create a distinctive niche for Mount Holyoke as an institution with the revised mission of producing Christian graduates for specialized, secularly oriented scientific work. As a result, they were able to strengthen the position of science education while marginalizing that of missionary teaching.

By 1888 their efforts would transform the Mount Holyoke community into a college with a seminary program, staffed by an increasingly specialized faculty and granting a bachelor of science degree to all its graduates. Their success drew institutional support away from the old primary goal of providing missionary teachers, releasing faculty to concentrate on developing expanding work spaces, modernizing the curriculum and their own knowledge base, and reforming classroom teaching. They would alter the religious culture and responsibilities of the faculty, transforming their professional identity and transferring religious sanctions and the enthusiasm of personal calling to women's intellectual pursuits. There would be both beneficial and limiting consequences for the gendered division of labor they renegotiated with a new generation of men enthusiastically engaged in the national passion for getting ahead by participating in scientific progress.

In addition to Mary Homer, the seminary physician who was an early catalyst for modernizing the seminary, two women from the second and third generations of Mount Holyoke teachers took the major initiative in these reforms: Lydia Shattuck, an impressive botanist and chemistry teacher who had studied under Mary Lyon, and her young protégé Cornelia Clapp, who established the first zoology courses at the seminary. One of the pivotal events linking their lives to the fate of the seminary was their enrollment in the summer courses for teachers at Louis Agassiz's Anderson School of Natural History on Penikese Island off Cape Cod in the early 1870s. The liberation they experienced living among men and women exposed to Darwin's radical theories and to Agassiz's invigorating study of living marine organisms catapulted Shattuck and Clapp into a whole new way of thinking about teaching science as part of a growing network of ambitious Christian academics just in the process of forming.

The impress on them of an environment remarkably different from that which had existed in Lyon's day was profound. Around the seminary were spaces marked by the industrial wealth that now overtly identified itself with science. The Civil War had stimulated the growth of manufacturing and with it the increase of populations in towns and cities where factory buildings, mills, and workers' houses abounded. Extended roads, canals, railroad lines, and telegraph poles now provided civilian's with paths of transport and communication that had served the war effort and its industrial base. Increasingly the buildings sported innovations such as steam heat, elevators, gas lighting, and internal plumbing, promising an easier and more comfortable working life. Advances in chemistry and physics underpinned these technological developments.

New campuses, universities, land grant colleges, colleges for women, and the established male colleges identified themselves with science and technology as they jostled for position. The industrial wealth and government investments swelled by the North's success in the war supported these endeavors. Among such institutions were the Massachusetts Institute of Technology, Worcester Institute of Technology, Massachusetts Agricultural College, Johns Hopkins University, and expanded colleges such as Amherst and Williams, Harvard and Yale Universities, as well as Wellesley, Vassar, and Smith colleges for women. Mount Holyoke Female Seminary with its plans for a new science and art building and library counted itself among them.

Less visible were changes the war had made in the cultural landscape that enfolded higher education. The focus of the North on saving the Republic had confirmed science as a religiously sanctioned, virtuous, and socially significant activity in its own right, demoting evangelical missionizing to second place in the minds of many middle class families. Public enthusiasm for science and technology focused on the secular progress its practitioners could bring about through research and its application. Still Protestant in character and personnel, this community was now highly competitive and beginning to use doctorates in science from American and foreign universities, college degrees, and laboratory research to measure interinstitutional status and rank in a quest to appeal to prospective students. Darwin's theory of evolution drew the attention of ministers, scientists, and educators as they struggled to make sense of the changes that surrounded them through an intense study of the biological and geological record.[2]

The war also opened possibilities within and outside academe for middle-class Protestant women to enter into the life of the nation more fully and directly. With that opportunity came struggles and new coalitions with men and among women for power over theoretical and empirical knowledge and the award of credentials certifying its possession. Mount Holyoke's scientific culture, with all its values of thrift, devotion to perfect performance, and division of labor, prepared faculty members to tailor these opportunities to their own needs.[3]

The chapter is divided into five sections, all of which consider the changing definitions of the women faculty's scientific work within the context of broader social and institutional transformations that made specialization of scientific knowledge, doctorates, and college degrees desirable measures of faculty status. These were associated with the professionalization of science between 1860 and 1888.

The Liberating Path of Science (1860–1873)

The Civil War relaxed the cultural atmosphere in the nation to the extent that it weakened barriers to women's engagement in intellectual and public life. This freedom had its effect on the seminary teachers as well as on the old scientific program and the dual goals it had served. At Mount Holyoke during the war, as the manufacturing economy around South Hadley boomed and aging trustees and male college professors turned their attention to the war effort, the women teachers were relatively freed from male constraints to pursue their intellectual inclinations. The last years of the decade and the first years of the 1870s, however, brought teachers led by Shattuck into tension with a new cadre of trustees working to reassert the board's authority over the affairs of the seminary. The teachers responded by contributing to the economic growth of the seminary as a way to exercise leverage over the definition of their scientific work. The economic depression that began in 1872 gave them added authority as they gained trustees' support in competing with women's colleges for a place in the academic market.

The emergence of a more self-assertive female presence in seminary affairs dates from 1860, when a woman physician, Mary Homer, was hired instead of a male—no doubt because the war drew the men away and Hitchcock was in his declining years. Homer and her successors (many Mount Holyoke Seminary graduates with medical training) then took over teaching physiology—a shift that in itself signifies the increased control women teachers had gained over even the most intimate sort of knowledge that Hitchcock had presumed to hold. Homer seems to have done so with Hitchcock's blessing, modeling her lectures and demonstrations on his methods, for one of her first requests to the trustees was a new mannequin to use in physiology classes.[4]

In addition to taking over teaching the science of women's health, Homer assumed responsibility for seeing that her expertise was used to improve the general health of women faculty and students. Her requests for a number of substantial changes in the physical plant, which increased the comfort of residents, always referred to the latest public health research findings. On the basis of her reports to the board's Sanitation Committee, trustees voted funds to install steam heating and internal plumbing with running water, and to open walls for windows to improve ventilation. This woman physician not only increased women's power over their own bodies and their environment further than previously in a period when such efforts were highly controversial. She extended women faculty members' control of specialized knowledge and hence their status and influence over the running of the seminary.[5]

Lydia Shattuck's activities during the 1860s and early 1870s show her to have been even bolder and more effective than Homer in making seminary policy, while equally oriented toward secular concerns in her intellectual activities. Her status as a senior teacher who had studied with Mary Lyon carried great authority with teachers and trustees. She was an avid botanist, amassing a large collection that included rare ferns coveted by Asa Gray for the Harvard collections. She was also well versed in chemistry and the developments that were changing its scientific foundations. Her accomplishments and knowledge in both fields were well known and respected by her male contemporaries, perhaps through Paul Chadbourne, who had taught botany and chemistry at Williams while lecturing at the seminary. Her personality, the serious interest she had in the latest research and methods reported in the scientific literature to which she subscribed, and her avid interest in forming collegial relations with prominent male scientists make her the most significant figure among the faculty in these years. That she took over lecturing in chemistry for three years and was invited to attend the celebration that launched the American Chemical Society in 1874 confirm her importance.[6]

In the more relaxed circumstances of the early 1860s, Shattuck's self-reliant approach had freer reign. It energized the intellectual atmosphere in the seminary. Her personal qualities surface in an anecdote Cornelia Clapp later related about Shattuck. It seems that Shattuck and another student were bathing nude in a stream near the seminary when some men approached. Shattuck, seeing that the solution to a potentially demeaning situation lay in avoiding recognition, counseled the student to quickly hide her face, their bodies being unfamiliar to the intruders.[7] In the 1860s she put some of this shrewdness to use, gaining teachers' support in raising funds for an elevator to ease work of all kinds and also for a new science building.

This mixture of self-confidence, quick intelligence, ironic distance, and common sense was apparent in the ease with which she moved to assess for herself the relationship between religion and the very human activity of scientific work. This was a much discussed topic in these years among churchmen and men of science writing in popular and professional journals at a time when Darwin's ideas pushed to the fore the question of the deity's role in directing the course of change in nature. Sometime between 1860 and 1866 she advanced an opinion on this subject, which she recorded in her notebook: "Never suppose that a *law* is *inflexible*. It is the human way of looking at Divine actions. It is the way in which a thing *does* happen, not the way in which it *must* happen. Then prayer may be effectual to change even a law."[8] In 1872, on her 50th birthday, she made an informal presentation of Darwin's theory of evolution to teachers and students. At that time she may have come out in favor of his ideas as wholly appropriate to scientific study, if not to the goals of faith.[9]

In developing such opinions she moved into that male realm of intellectual endeavor and interpretation of nature that Lyon had not broached. The curious harmonization of scientific pragmatism and moral conviction shows her to have been acutely aware not only that the focus of scientific inquiry was now on change and the processes or mechanisms of change. It also indicates that she favored the collection and study of empirical evidence and had a resistance to accepting theoretical constructs as immutable. Science is a process of discovery and correction in which the evidence of nature constantly amends human error, but the ultimate causal reasons are not knowable to us. In the context of American Protestant society and of the major figures in science in these years, her reference to the posssibility that prayer could change the course of events is not so amazing, for its assertion of the power of human faith bespeaks her compliance with a common conviction that individuals had the potential to make a difference in this world through their religious commitment. In this way, she separated the objects of her scientific inquiry and its internalist concerns from those that were unknowable.

She also reached out beyond the confines of the old intellectual circle in western Massachusetts to correspond with two major scientists at Harvard on the subject of botany: the opponents in the controversy over Darwin's ideas, Asa Gray and Louis Agassiz. And she brought her knowledge to bear as she became the major figure in developing science teaching into a specialty at Mount Holyoke in this decade. These relationships took on a different character from the old helpmate one. This was so partly because the relationships seemed more intellectually egalitarian as laboratory work became more important, but also because they were entered into by men and women with agendas that placed gathering, organizing, and explaining new information for personal and institutional advancement as conditions to be met before the goal of saving the nation could be accomplished.

In the 1860s, motivated by a desire to classify her extensive botanical collections as accurately as possible, Shattuck began corresponding with America's foremost supporter of Darwin's theory of evolution: the botanist Asa Gray at Harvard. Gray was also known for defending and disseminating a system for classifying plants compatible with Darwin's ideas on descent, which he termed the "natural system."[10] Perhaps with the encouragement of Edward Hitchcock, who had spoken about Gray and Agassiz in a popular lecture on "The Religion of Geology," Shattuck first wrote to Gray in 1862 asking him to identify some plants she had collected. Sometime during the early 1860s, she also visited the Harvard herbarium he had created. This massive collection organized by Gray and his assistants in accordance with Gray's new system made Lyon's older collection of 300 examples seem very provincial. Although there is no record of Shattuck's meeting him then, there followed a series of letters from Gray and his assistants to Shattuck that reach into the 1880s, the highlight of their relationship being Gray's visit to Mount Holyoke in 1876 as an invited speaker at the meeting Shattuck hosted of the Connecticut Valley Botanical Society.[11]

The correspondence between Shattuck and Gray is significant for a number of reasons. First, it reveals that Shattuck was working to build an exchange of information between herself and a figure responsible for far-reaching changes in American science. Her initial letter to Gray, dated June 30, 1864, requested that he identify a specimen for her. She asks, "Will Dr. Gray pardon a student in Botany for intruding upon his very precious time." The tone is less obsequious and self-deprecating than it is a reflection of a strategy that one would take to elicit the desired response from someone who had hundreds of such requests to answer. Indeed, Gray only took the time to scribble his brief reply at the bottom of her letter and returned it.[12]

Gray's letters to Shattuck, and those of his student Joseph Trimbull Rothrock to her, are friendly and direct, showing great respect for her with no hint of condescension. Gray not only identified specimens for her, but was obviously beholden to her for sending some of her finds to him. He also seems to have been a bit cowed in the face of her erudition. She, on the other hand, sought to establish her authority on the subjects of botany and chemistry. She did so as a researcher engaged in naming and placing specimens she had found and in revising existing constructs by pointing out weaknesses in Gray's classification system, and also as a teacher concerned with having the most up-to-date and accurate information to impart to her students.

One letter from Gray indicates that he had consulted Shattuck about revising his botany text and taken her suggestions to heart.[13] He wrote her about his *Structural Botany* and *Lessons in Botany* texts in 1873, after she had paid a visit to the Botanic Garden in Cambridge. In what seems to be a reply to suggestions she made for bringing the text up to date, he wrote, "but I suppose I might bring up the Chemistry of the latter [the Lessons] to the modern style. A slight change would do it." To her implied criticism that he underestimates the intelligence and knowledge of the seminary teachers who use his text, he adds in lame defense, "Remember it was written in the days of 'H.O.' not of 'H.O$_2$.'" He also admits to her that there were some "*sad* omissions."[14] This exchange suggests that Shattuck was well aware of the "quiet revolution" that had recently taken place in the field of chemistry and the need to respect readers' intelligence.[15] These letters also reveal Shattuck to have been an independent thinker, becoming what Hitchcock would have considered a clear-headed scientist who understood what it meant to use empirical evidence to test hypotheses based on theory.

Her long correspondence with Gray and her use of his system, however, suggest a pragmatic willingness to ignore focusing on Darwinian mechanisms which raised the specter of materialism, while enjoying the benefits of Gray's superior system for classifying living plants. Gray himself shrewdly sidestepped this topic in the many editions of textbooks he wrote and marketed to teachers in seminaries, colleges, common schools, and academies, smoothly concluding that "the Creator established a definite number of species at the beginning, which have continued by propagation, each after its own kind."[16] Much of his success in this vein rested on his ability to show teachers how to explain his system and to use it as a tool for identifying species of plants, their development, and their logical relationships as links in a reproductive chain, while making certain to assuage any fears they might have that he was a gross materialist.

By the late 1860s Shattuck may have come to believe, as did Asa Gray himself, in the "innocence of science of theological bearing." As Gray's biographer Hunter Dupree expressed it, assuming this position meant that "a scientist could adopt the new theory without destroying his previous religious orientations."[17] Equally pragmatic, Shattuck's similar reasoning would enable her to disregard any objections that Louis Agassiz had to Gray's system and to Darwin's theories, and to take advantage of what Agassiz had to offer in the method of basing conclusions on empirical observation.[18]

As Shattuck's correspondence with Gray indicates, she had established a new form of complementary relationship between herself and contemporary male scientists at other institutions—one based on an exchange of information regarding research and teaching. In this new quid pro quo, she used his work in her teaching and in her botanical research. For example, in 1867 the acting Principal Sophia Stoddard happily accepted her recommendation that Gray's *Botany* be substituted for Wood's.[19] Gray's text made it possible for her to formally introduce his ideas into the classroom and thus to identify herself as a teacher with expert knowledge of this special field.[20] On his side, Gray, eager to see his classification system become a universal standard, was anxious to reach the burgeoning number of students in colleges, seminaries, and even academies and common schools through the sale and use of his textbooks. Seeking the advice of experienced teachers such as Shattuck, who was interested in the chemistry of plants as much as their development and morphology, was one way to keep his texts up-to-date and usable in the classroom. Shattuck made the most of this sort of exchange and the mutual enhancement of professional status it brought through her activities in founding the Natural History Society. In 1868 she invited geologist James Dwight Dana to speak in South Hadley, and in 1873 Asa Gray came to do the same at a meeting of the Connecticut Valley Botanical Society at her invitation.[21]

In one other way Shattuck's activities and exchanges created room for women teachers to revise their job definition and raise the stature of their position in the twelve years before Penikese. Not only did she engage in the standard form of botanical research of her day, but she did what Lyon had attempted and failed to do for lack of time. She presented "with much acceptance" the course of twenty lectures in chemistry in 1870 and again in 1871 and 1872. Although whatever record she may have made of her lectures cannot be located, their significance is profound. Not since Mary Lyon's attempt over thirty years before had a teacher taken on this responsibility, and never had a woman assumed such authority at the seminary for so prolonged a time. Just why she ceased lecturing in chemistry after 1872 and how this decision was related to events at the centennial celebration of Joseph Priestly's birth in the late summer of 1874 when the American Chemical Society was founded are discussed later in this chapter.[22]

The teachers enthusiastically acknowledged the political significance of Shattuck's accomplishments. Commenting on her course of lectures in chemistry, teacher Esther Thompson wrote in a March 1870 journal letter, "You see we believe in 'Woman's rights', . . . in her right to know as much as man, and knowing it, to tell it in just as agreeable and effective a way."[23]

The references, the tone with its note of self-satisfied achievement and excitement, reveal the teachers' identification with the more public efforts of women like Elizabeth Cady Stanton and Susan B. Anthony to win the right to vote for women in these years. After all 1872 was the year that a woman first ran for President. At the same time, there is righteousness about the different, more intellectual path of equality with men into which Shattuck had led Mount Holyoke women faculty within her own institution. In this effort she joined a small number of women faculty at the new women's colleges who were making an assault on male claims to intellectual superiority in science during the early 1870s. Astronomer Maria Mitchell not only developed an impressive program in astronomy and physics at newly founded Vassar College, but she supported her students' efforts to enter into doctoral programs at the new Johns Hopkins University and Massachusetts Institute of Technology.[24] While Mitchell's struggle was buttressed by the fact that her institution awarded college degrees, Shattuck, following along an analogous tack, was at a disadvantage here. As discussed later, the Mount Holyoke faculty members were well aware of the emergence on their horizon of these women's colleges and of women science faculty who were setting new standards of scientific achievement and competition for women that undermined the status of female seminary education.

The note of defensiveness should not be overlooked, however. The

women teachers' efforts to raise their status by specializing in science teaching, lecturing, and engaging in research did not go unchallenged nor their
course undeterred by men in these years. Beginning slowly in 1860, picking
up after 1868, and coming to a head in 1872, challenges to the teachers' authority from men grew in intensity within and outside the seminary. They
were in fact interconnected and fed one another, as new trustees established
or renewed networks with colleagues at colleges, new technical institutes,
and universities. Events at the Priestly Centennial in 1874 to which Shattuck
was invited exemplify the predicament that ambitious men in the physical
sciences were creating for women science faculty members in these years.

To begin with trustees came in with a strong paternalistic set of ideas that
shaped their views of women's higher education. In the early 1860s this paternalism was rather meek, limited to a few members and easily overridden. The
major example of it dates from 1860, when several trustees had questioned
Homer's request for a new mannequin on the grounds that the public might
not think it seemly for seminary women to study physiology in this way. Although objectors eventually acquiesced in favor of Hitchcock's Sanitary
Committee recommendation that the requested funds be granted, by the last
half of the 1860s circumstances changed.

After 1867, younger men ambitious for themselves as Protestant leaders of
higher education appeared on the board. Their influence was extensive, including Mount Holyoke in a network of institutions for the higher education of men and women that they were anxious to promote. Whether businessmen, college faculty members, or divines, they shared a missionary zeal
for expanding the number of educational enterprises and placing women
teachers under the tutelage of men. Heavily weighted toward businessmen,
lawyers, and college faculty with connections to industry, and a number of
old and new colleges and institutes, the board favored secularly oriented reforms at the seminary identified with the emerging physical sciences. All had
impeccable religious backgrounds, and more than two-thirds held college or
professional degrees.[25]

Among them were six who held L.L.D.'s; six with D.D.'s; three who held
both; one with an L.L.D. and an M.A.; and one with an L.L.D., an M.D., and
an M.A. Not only were they better educated than former members, but they
formed an interlocking directorate through dual appointments, business,
banking, and professional connections, and family ties that stretched across
the state and reached into the U.S. Congress. One was a Boston merchant
who served as a congressman and head of the Republican National Execu-

tive committee. Three were on the Amherst College faculty, one was president of Amherst College, and one was a graduate of Amherst. Their connections with women's higher education linked them to Smith and Wellesley colleges. One of them was the founder of Wellesley College, and two others sat on Smith College's board of trustees—one elected president of that board in 1874. One had a brother who was president of Smith. Two were sons of former Mount Holyoke trustees. The president of the Mount Holyoke board was an avid advocate of both Smith and Wellesley colleges.

While they supported women's higher education, and indeed saw themselves as its champions, they regarded the institutions that furnished it as businesses which produced a product for which demand was growing and increasingly diversified. For trustee Henry Durant, who would found Wellesley College, "There could never be too many Mount Holyokes."[26] For others, there was no need to fear competition from the other women's colleges being planned, for they considered Mount Holyoke Seminary a preparatory school. For others, too, it seemed Mount Holyoke would always flourish because no other institution could offer an education at so low a price. "Where else," one asked, could one receive "the best education that the country or the world affords for $150 a year."[27]

Yet in what was a salute to conserve an older definition of science, they continued to see scientific instruction as the source of Mount Holyoke's prestige in preparing teachers and missionaries. With their sights set on limiting the teachers' aspirations, the trustees inaugurated plans for modernizing and expanding the physical plant and scientific instruction with an eye on making economies, rather than on raising standards of knowledge, credentials, or tentative efforts to participate in research, even at its most simple. The most significant item in their construction program was to be a building for teaching science and art. In 1870 A. Lyman Williston, among the wealthiest trustees, pushed this plan forward by donating part of the funds needed, with the understanding that additional funds for the building would come from other sources.[28]

As for scientific instruction, the most efficient and economical way to bring it up to date and add new luster to the seminary's image was the well-worn tradition of bringing in knowledgeable male faculty from other institutions for periodic lectures. This policy enabled men to dominate the intellectual life of the seminary once again, bringing their prestige to it and drawing prestige from their affiliation as they passed on in diluted form the latest information to teachers and through them to students.

Between 1867 and 1872 Mount Holyoke hired a number of ambitious male science faculty from several institutions to lecture. These men had begun to form an academic network of individuals who promoted one another and moved from post to post. This network drew Mount Holyoke into an orbit that once again included Williams, Bowdoin, and Amherst, but also Dartmouth and the new Worcester Free Institute. Probably through Paul Chadbourne, then at Williams College, or through Edward Hitchcock Jr.'s brother Charles, the board hired Charles Young in 1867 to lecture on astronomy, replacing Snell's course on natural philosophy. Through the agency of his brother, Edward Hitchcock, Jr., who sat on the Mount Holyoke board, Charles Hitchcock of Dartmouth College was then hired in 1868 to lecture annually on geology. In 1873 Chadbourne, who had exchanged lecturing in chemistry at the seminary for a series of college presidencies, probably recommended President Charles O. Thompson from Worcester Free Institute to take over that topic. By 1875, just two years later, the male presence on campus had increased dramatically, although not all of the men presented full courses of lectures.

The renewed presence of active men on the seminary's board of trustees after 1867 helps explain the circumstances under which Shattuck came to teach the course of chemistry lectures for three years. Between Chadbourne's relinquishing the post and the time he could find a qualified male replacement, she filled in. Or at least that was the perspective the board had on it. As a result of their policies, by 1873, women science faculty were being relegated once again to handling recitations and doing demonstrations. Lecturing still separated them from male faculty, but not in all fields. In the fields of astronomy, chemistry, geology, and physics they were under the direct tutelage of male lecturers with degrees who were on the faculties of degree-granting institutions and engaged in publishing and research.[29] Botany and physiology were left to the women to develop, and, as will be seen, so was the emerging field of zoology, not yet inaugurated in the curriculum.

This masculinization of postwar science at the seminary was part of a larger movement in the American scientific community to professionalize the standing of its practitioners and enhance their authority. Despite the secular focus of this movement, the presence of evangelical Protestant rationales against women's participation in intellectual and interpretive activities remained, now reinvigorated with a competitive spirit born of wartime experience, industrial practice, and economic uncertainty as women entering into colleges and universities threatened to take places reserved for men. The physicist Henry A. Rowland offers a typical example of those male scientists who resisted women's entrée into the hard sciences. Rowland, on the faculty of the newly founded Johns Hopkins University (1862), made no bones about where he felt the boundary line between men and women's work in chemistry lay; nor did he hesitate to see that this view, which many of his colleagues shared, became university policy. Underpinning his attitude was a view of research that equaled Hitchcock Sr.'s in its claim to be a religiously sanctioned activity of the highest moral import. However, Rowland, reflecting the postwar generation's more individualistic attitudes, countered Hitchcock Sr.'s image of the scientist as a truth-seeking male social leader with a more overtly self-promoting definition of a self-improving, intellectually superior individual.[30]

Shattuck, because of her intellectual stature and daring challenge to evangelical custom, experienced the full force of this trend toward masculinized professionalization at both the national and local level. After 1872, as already noted, she no longer lectured in chemistry, a change that returned her to a more acceptable female role, for this responsibility was assumed by Charles Thompson from Worcester Institute of Technology, who resumed the evangelical Protestant-based tradition of male lecturers in chemistry that had been broken in 1869. In 1874, when she attended the celebration that marked the founding of the American Chemical Society, she came face to face with more organized and formally expressed rejection of women teachers as fully recognized contributors to the field.

The Priestly centennial signified the kind of opposition women, and in this instance Shattuck was an example, were facing as a new generation of ambitious men put their energies into the development of specialized fields of research. Although she and several other women attended, the photograph commemorating the event is without women. It is a symbolic statement reflecting the course of the chemical profession whose new national association was given birth at the centennial. In a rationale replete with circular reasoning, the new society eliminated women from full membership status based on their insufficient credentials as much as their sex.[31]

There is no doubt that Shattuck's stature as a well-known teacher of chemistry, emerging as a field of graduate study at the time she attended Penikese, was such that she had been one of the few women present at the "Centennial of Chemistry." Despite her knowledge, her contacts, and her reputation, Shattuck hadn't the post, the degrees, or the time for research to qualify because she had been limited as a woman. But, as at the seminary, she may also have been excluded by men who felt she threatened to cross the boundaries that evangelical Protestant custom and belief had set on women's intellectual work.

This is not to say that the Mount Holyoke science teachers were helpless or passively acquiesced to these efforts to put them back in their place. They lobbied the board successfully to have their domestic duties eliminated in order to devote their time solely to teaching, improving their knowledge and work on curricular affairs.[32] Indeed, probably under Shattuck's leadership, they followed Lyon's example and sought economic leverage to promote their objectives and retain a say in seminary affairs. Shattuck raised funds from the teachers and students to pay for the elevator that would alleviate their physical labor. More significantly, she managed to gain a stake in the new building for art and science by getting the teachers to agree to forgo large raises so that that money could be used to furbish a major portion of the spaces they would use for scientific instruction. She may also have raised funds from alumnae for this purpose as well. Shattuck's student Susan Bowen pursued the idea of establishing a natural history cabinet, sending out a call to alumnae and friends for specimens of minerals, stuffed birds, ferns, and seashells, which was enthusiastically answered.[33] This focus furthered teachers' enthusiasm for developing the possibilities open to them to establish their intellectual authority in the newer biological sciences, while being educated by the male lecturers to teach the latest discoveries in the physical sciences.

In characteristic form, the trustees recognized the teachers' claim on the space by thanking the "self-denying teachers" for helping make the new building a reality. The end result was that the teachers still divided the labor with male lecturers in the old manner in the fields of chemistry, astronomy, physics, and geology—that is, the physical sciences most closely associated with industrial growth and national economy and traditionally with interpretations of natural law. They retained the right to have charge of botany and physiology, those biological sciences most identified with laboratory work, the manipulation of living organisms, systematics, and evolutionary theory and least with economic and industrial interests. Those fields, at least botany, in these years were becoming feminized.[34]

This situation unfavorable to the teachers would have prevailed, had not the deep depression of 1872–1876 caused a crisis in the market for women's higher education. With Wellesley and Smith colleges about to open and Vassar already open, the supply of students able to afford higher education was sorely limited. Applications to the seminary dropped, as did the size of the student body. The crisis opened an opportunity for the teachers to gain a greater say in seminary affairs, to formulate a vision of what the institution might become, and to see how they might obtain trustees' support for their efforts.

There is much in Mount Holyoke faculty members' focus on keeping up with scientific developments and expanding the presence of science on campus that places them among male faculty at institutions responding to calls for practical reforms in the 1860s and early 1870s. As Laurence Veysey has shown, "During the ten years after 1865, almost every visible change in the pattern of American higher education lay in the direction of concessions to the utilitarian type of demand for reform."[35] If educators during this period made a distinction between "utilities higher and utilities lower," Mount Holyoke teachers and trustees took the former road, as did a new generation of administrators at Harvard and Yale.[36] However, following this path, which was only a logical continuation of one of the seminary's original commitments, did not mean that faculty members at Mount Holyoke were simply pulling abreast of their colleagues at some of the male colleges. Rather, it signified that these faculty members were all conjointly changing the knowledge base and creating a professional context for scientific training, as younger men and women found themselves places in a few institutions congenial to establishing specialized teaching and perhaps research. Thus, Shattuck's and other teachers' reform efforts during the 1860s and first two years of the next decade carried with them an assumption that she and the teachers under her influence were reaching for a higher, as yet institutionally and curricularly undefined identity in a fashion similar to and for many of the same personal reasons as the men teaching in the colleges with whom they had interactions. The seminary was both an instrument and a beneficiary of their ambitions. The effect of these ambitions on the missionary goals and evangelical culture of their institution they had yet to consider. Penikese, where she, Bowen, and then Clapp would live and work with some of these men, would give the women a clearer idea of where it was they could go and the possible means to get there, as well as the enthusiasm for the task.

The Importance of Penikese (1873–1874)

During the school year 1872–1873, just before the decision to allow Shattuck and Bowen to attend Penikese, the Reverend Edward Kirk of Boston, then president of Mount Holyoke's Board of Trustees, pressed then principal Miss Julie E. Ward for evidence that the seminary had remained in the fore-front of higher education. Having made a study of the seminary, comparing its curriculum to "those of Vassar, Cornell, and other colleges; asking what changes might seem desirable . . . in the curriculum, in the lecture system by scientific men," he sought ways to enlist the trustees in the "great work of keeping our seminary in the front rank of educational institutions" but left open the question of how the teachers would contribute to the seminary's survival.[37]

Ward, an extremely conscientious woman who felt quite threatened by the uncertain situation, defensively reported that the seminary's position had not slipped at all. It is instructive to note that in her annual report she used both Amherst and Vassar colleges as her measures, indicative of the teachers' con-tinuing belief that collegiate status was gender neutral and remained the measure for their institution.[38] Yet despite the fact that male colleges also suffered from increasing competition in these years, the new women's col-leges, not the men's colleges, were really the issue. Not only did they have fairly strong public support, they had the advantage over Mount Holyoke of the name "college" with its secular and modern connotations and promise of degrees rather than certificates.

Shattuck and the other teachers could not ignore this situation. As Shat-tuck later wrote to a friend in 1875, the year Wellesley and Smith colleges opened after years of planning:

> I suppose you are so far from Wellesley and Smith colleges that you do not dream of a number less than usual, even by one, because of their opening. Some one has said that everybody thinks he can make a young ladies' school a success, but he had better not boast too loud in the beginning. . . . Some who would otherwise come here will of course be in those schools this year. . . . Please do not say anything to Miss Ward about my allusion to these schools for she is disposed to cry.[39]

In the arena of higher education, Mount Holyoke's one advantage over the women's colleges lay in its strong tradition of science education, allow-ing the institution to benefit from the enormous popularity science had come to enjoy in post-Civil War America. The commitment to science would distinguish Mount Holyoke from other women's colleges, enhance the pres-tige of its teachers and curriculum, and signify to the public that it was both modern and progressive. In order to exploit this advantage, however, Mount Holyoke teachers not only had to continue modernizing the science offerings and strengthening their connections with the scientific community; the sciences also had to become the basis for a profound cultural reform within the seminary that would bring Mount Holyoke into adjustment with indus- trial society's demands for more modern credentials. A significant move in this direction came from faculty pressing trustees for time and opportunity to learn more about their areas of special scientific interest and to integrate their new knowledge into their teaching.

Such thoughts must have been in Shattuck's mind when she received the prospectus for Penikese in the late spring of 1873. Here was an educational program designed to introduce science teachers to new knowledge and meth- ods for learning about the natural world. In addition, it was offered by a Harvard professor who was one of the leading naturalists in America, and arguably the most popular of his day. Agassiz also did not threaten the semi- nary's theological mission. He had taken the high road on the utility of sci- ence without giving up his belief in the presence of the divine in nature. At the same time, he garnered support for scientific activities like the Anderson School from men who had made their money in manufacturing and were in- terested in supporting science education.[40] In short, Agassiz offered Mount Holyoke's teachers the possibility of new networks, modern scientific knowl- edge and teaching methods, and status that might help them and their school retain their place among the leaders of higher education.

Although by no means an egalitarian on gender issues, Agassiz was toler- ant of women who wished to engage in science in positions less lofty than his. His wife Elizabeth was a staunch supporter of women's education her- self, as well as being extremely knowledgeable about science and an effective disseminator of her husband's ideas through the publication of his lec- tures.[41] The Agassizes had worked closely together in planning the Ander- son School, which their prospectus made clear was open to women as well as men. Finally, Agassiz in his final years wished to disseminate his scientific ideas and teaching methods among teachers as a strategy for influencing large numbers of people through educational networks. The Anderson School was designed with people like Shattuck in mind, and it drew primarily men and women teachers from seminaries, normal schools, and small colleges who educated young people to be teachers themselves.[42]

To Shattuck, who had tied her fortunes and those of Mount Holyoke to the comet of science, the Anderson School offered the opportunity to learn new ideas and ways of studying the natural world which she could introduce in the seminary as part of her efforts to save it.[43] As one of the senior teach- ers at the seminary who had some say over the curriculum, Shattuck was in a position to make radical changes in the seminary, not simply in her own classroom.[44] Her decision to take along a protégée each year would enhance her objectives and bring younger women's energies into the cause.

With this very clear objective in mind, in the summer of 1873 Shattuck and her younger colleague Susan Bowen joined thirteen other women and thirty-five men on Penikese Island. Almost all of the cohort were ambitious teachers like themselves, but attracted there for a variety of reasons and not necessarily committed to a particular institution.[45] The next summer, when she brought along Cornelia Clapp, there were about the same number of attendees. The Anderson School of Natural History, although it only lasted two seasons, attracted a surprising number of men who would become major figures in the first generation of American academic-based biologists, as well as part of Mount Holyoke's professional network. These men included David Starr Jordan, who in 1891 would become the first president of Stanford University and contribute much to the study of ichthyology; Charles Otis Whitman, who in 1888 would head the first marine biology laboratory in the United States at Woods Hole, Massachusetts, and in 1892 direct the Biology program at the new University of Chicago; Edmund Beecher Wilson, one of the founders of modern genetics; and William T. Sedgwick, who would become important in the development of the biology and sanitary science programs at MIT. In fact, Penikese set the stage for the development of the Woods Hole Marine Biological Laboratory (the MBL), which would also include significant numbers of women in its summer program.[46] Cornelia Clapp would become the first woman trustee of the MBL, as well an instructor in the summer school there and the first professor of zoology at Mount Holyoke. Thus, the Anderson School of Natural History was a co-educational crucible in which American biology began an important phase of its institutional, intellectual, and social formulation. But its influence on the development of science at Mount Holyoke reached beyond serving as a source of inspiration for biology courses.

Much has been made of the importance that Agassiz's dictum "Study Nature not books" had for the teachers *cum* students at Penikese.[47] It broke with the long tradition of memorizing texts and relying on them for guidance, substituting instead a method derived from Pestalozzian notions of human learning but focused on gathering and critically analyzing new information. Agassiz forced the teachers to rely on their own observations of plants and animals they had collected and to develop their own conclusions based on empirical evidence. While Mount Holyoke teachers had long practiced collecting in their botanical studies, the study of zoological organisms, particularly marine life, was one of several dramatic changes for them.

As the historian Jane Maienschein pointed out, the school experience was much more than simply roaming about collecting specimens to be categorized:

> It is true that the instruction was highly individualized, with each student spending a good part of each day exploring, collecting, observing, recording, and generally studying nature rather than books. . . . But good books, not mere repetitive textbooks, also had their place. So did lectures. Agassiz invited a number of important biologists to address the group on a range of natural history topics. In fact, each day began with structured lectures, followed by an hour or so of dissection. Afternoons often brought freedom to roam and collect, but the evenings were spent attending further lectures, dissecting by candlelight, and then writing up notes from the day's work into the late night hours. . . . Agassiz and his invited speakers also helped to articulate appropriate problems.[48]

Along with this rigorous schedule based on collecting and laboratory study of animals as well as plants, there was much conversation about the latest ideas. Cornelia Clapp recalled lively discussions about the latest biological theories, particularly those of Darwin. Penikese marked the first time that she had heard theories discussed in any detail and in a comparative way—an insight into her consciousness that the division of labor with college men had left her with a awareness of the very empirical thrust Mount Holyoke's science teachers had given to their offerings up until then. Indicative of the participants' struggle to deal with questions of the origin of species and inheritance was the open consideration of the idea of the Immaculate Conception.[49]

Another exceptional feature of the Penikese school was its coeducational character. The school did not respect the gendered institutional barriers that had created separate educational cultures for men and women who had similar intellectual interests and objectives. Despite some initial objections to admitting women at the time plans were being laid for the school, a remarkable degree of friendly exchange between the sexes marked the actual experience. Men and women, all highly dedicated to education, ate, worked, and socialized together. Here at the moment of true professionalization of American biology were established habits of free intellectual exchange and cooperation among men and women from similar backgrounds and with similar commitments, all of them Protestants. They soon bonded and developed a group identity that persisted through the years. Being a "Penikesian" had lifelong consequences for Cornelia Clapp, for example. It gave her entrée into the network of ambitious young male biologists then in the process of formation and would lead to a variety of opportunities to improve her stature, including an invitation to join the teaching faculty at the MBL in 1888 (discussed in the following chapter).[50]

Perhaps the most unusual among the Penikesians was David Starr Jordan, who had attended a female seminary near his home in upstate New York when no high school was nearby. Educated by women, he was not afraid to learn from them, nor to help them realize their ambitions. He would become a firm friend of Cornelia Clapp and later of Mary Woolley.[51] The relative degree of Jordan's egalitarianism towards women can also be measured by his willingness to hire women for the faculty of Stanford when he became its first president in 1891. C.O. Whitman also had a number of close friendships with women and actively worked to make research programs, lecturing and study at the doctoral level co-educational activities. He would become Cornelia Clapp's dissertation adviser and urge her to take a position as an instructor at the Marine Biological Laboratory. Among this group, Shattuck and Clapp not only fit in well, but Shattuck was strongly admired by both men and women. "Jordan . . . sat at the feet of Miss Shattuck," Clapp recalled.[52] Such exchanges laid the foundation for a sense of shared professional identity among male and female teachers of zoology from which both the men and Mount Holyoke faculty benefited greatly.

For Cornelia Clapp the experience of Penikese was profound and liberating. Intellectually, it changed her entire view of what science was, what she wanted to do, and how she could do it. Penikese was akin to a religious awakening for her. As she recounted in an interview in 1921 conducted by her protégée, professor of zoology Ann Haven Morgan:

> I had an opening of doors at Penikese. I looked and saw a thousand new doors. Everybody was talking. Discussions in every corner, history, the immaculate conception [*sic*]. I felt my mind going in every direction. I had never heard much theoretical discussion before. . . . I had a turn about face the next year after Penikese. I wanted to teach then.[53]

A stunning insight into the gendered nature of her experience occurs in a comment she made to Morgan: "all bent on one thing, then another, like a boy, first an entomologist, then a conchologist, and then a fish woman."[54] Two generations earlier Mary Lyon had identified her profoundly moving experience of nature with a feeling of drawing closer to God, whereas Clapp found it a liberating event that forged a connection between her sense of self and the possibilities of the subject she would teach. It was the moment when her professional identity as a science teacher began to be formed, strongly associated with what she saw as masculine personality traits in which an invigorating freedom to act unfettered figured large.

Penikese opened intellectual doors for those who attended, as they were introduced to laboratory methods of investigation using fresh specimens. It also inspired them to invent new career paths by taking advantage of the rising demand for science faculty in American higher education. But there was great variation in the nature of their professional aspirations and in the possibilities open to men and women. Hence the opportunities to be made of them by men and women differed. It is worth noting here what those paths were. Between 1873 and 1891, David Starr Jordan would realize Agassiz's hopes for disseminating his ideas through his Penikese disciples by holding positions in five different institutions in the Midwest, moving from college teacher to professor of natural history and then president of Indiana University. Inseparable from his climb up an institutional ladder he was helping to define was his struggle to establish himself as the dominant scholar in the field of descriptive ichthyology, to which Agassiz had introduced him. Through a series of major publications, Jordan named thousands of species of fish and contributed empirical evidence to support Darwin's theory of evolution.[55]

Susan Hallowell, a student at Penikese in 1874, also moved up the ranks in higher education after Penikese. As Joan Burstyn has recounted, Hallowell was chosen as Wellesley College's first professor of botany when it opened in 1875. But in contrast to Jordan, she does not seem to have held any desire to make her mark through research and publication, probably partly because they brought women science teachers little or no rewards so far as employment in women's colleges was concerned in these years. Instead, she focused on improving her career chances as a teacher with advanced training in biology by introducing Agassiz's methods of instruction to students, designing new courses and producing graduates who majored in biology.[56]

For Shattuck and Clapp at Mount Holyoke, their lot had already been cast with that of the seminary, and they returned there to continue the reforms. Both were armed with new knowledge, while Clapp came back with strengthened personal commitment, enthusiasm and ambition. If Susan Bowen preferred to devote what would remain of her life to being David Starr Jordan's wife and helpmate, Penikese pointed the way for Shattuck and

Clapp to continue to change the character of their home institution and to advance their own professional aspirations along the path of laboratory science teaching.

Clapp and the Penikese Effect (1874–1886)

After their return to the seminary in 1874, Shattuck and Clapp found the path of scientific instruction forked. Two groups with two different modes of organizing the work of teaching and two different kinds of relationships between men and women existed. Each had its own networks into a different set of sciences as well. One was that established by the trustees, which depended on visiting male faculty who gave courses of lectures and guided teachers in the physical sciences; the other was that established by the teachers, or Shattuck and Clapp to be exact, in the biological sciences. In it, women faculty heads, laboratory work, and occasional male lecturers were the norm. Additional education was gained by visits to other campuses for instruction.

On their return from Penikese, Shattuck and her protégées continued to take an active role in further reforms. Now, however, the reforms were more systematic and they focused on the development of laboratory work. Building on the long tradition of Mount Holyoke's science teachers' expertise in doing hands-on demonstrations that required equipment and their religious feeling for nature, collecting, and classification, they turned this intimate form of work into the basis for a program based on Agassiz's lessons and methods. In so doing, they moved into the realm of scientific discovery and technical work that brought the study of nature at the seminary into a laboratory setting. Through their efforts, they not only joined themselves with the general trend among American academic scientists toward building a culture defined by laboratory-based research, but they further weakened their ties with the old missionary-oriented objectives and evangelical culture of the seminary.

They gave momentum to efforts already begun when Susan Bowen returned from the 1873 summer session to inaugurate the natural history museum at the seminary. Her initiative emulated Agassiz's vast study collection at Harvard's Museum of Comparative Zoology. As a result, she helped place Mount Holyoke among a growing number of colleges that had or were forming their own natural history cabinets for local use and general study.[57] Although Bowen left the next year to marry Jordan, she had laid a foundation for a collection that was carried on by others.

In the years after Penikese, Shattuck ceased lecturing in chemistry and followed Agassiz's methods by extending botanical teaching to include training students to use equipment and do analysis with freshly gathered samples. She turned her energies toward developing the botany lectures and laboratory teaching and to identifying a protégée from among her students to carry on her efforts (Henrietta Hooker). This was not so much a retreat from the assertiveness the women teachers had championed when she assumed the traditional male work of lecturing, but a redirection of that energy and ambition into a field that was itself in the process of self-definition.[58]

She thus pushed trustees for money to purchase new equipment for the botany laboratory rooms she was setting up. The result was a set of microscopes for teachers and students to use, two of them Zeiss. In order to assure that fresh specimens of a wide variety of plants were always available, she started a new botanical garden in 1878 and supervised the building of the first plant house in 1882. These improvements enabled her and the other two botany teachers to teach the study of plant growth using both fresh and preserved materials for examination under the microscope.

She did not give up chemistry, however. Leaving the courses of lectures to visiting male faculty, such as Thompson, she continued to teach the laboratories, to develop the laboratory spaces, and to engage additional graduates in teaching the recitations and laboratories as well. She thus ensured that under the tutelage of the men, the women faculty would at least keep their knowledge of the field up to date, while devising ways to teach methods of analysis and technical skills to students.

It was the ebullient Clapp who plunged into laying the foundations for what might be considered a small empire. She took over Susan Bowen's natural history collection project when Bowen left to marry Jordan, and saw that the collection was continued and expanded by other professors, students and graduates as well as herself. She also recognized that the collection was not an end in itself, but engaged her in a network of specialists whose colleagueship she could cultivate. Clapp reported visiting Agassiz's Museum of Comparative Zoology, where she informally discussed with Harvard faculty the identification of certain specimens she wanted to include in the seminary collection.[59]

The collection itself was modest and contained a variety of specimens that reflected the categories established at the Museum of Comparative Zoology. It incorporated specimens gathered from local surroundings, such as plants and dinosaur fossils, as well as minerals, plants, and bird feathers collected in distant locales by former students on missions. There were also plaster casts of fossils purchased with seminary funds. Judging from illustrations in the 1882–1883 seminary catalogue—which are all that remain to document the collection destroyed by fire in 1917—Clapp was able to garner an impressive space for the collections. They took up a two-story room of some size and were organized in accordance with evolutionary stages of development.[60] They were used for both teaching and research purposes.

In establishing this collection, Mount Holyoke joined the ranks of a number of male colleges who were doing the same thing, including Williams and Amherst colleges, both of which had extensive botanical, geological, and dinosaur fossil holdings. As Sally Kohlstedt has discussed, natural history collections had become popular adjuncts to science on campus by the time of the Civil War, drawing together students, faculty, and local natural history enthusiasts. But in the postbellum era Clapp tended to emphasize their value for teaching and research, more than their value in building goodwill for the seminary by serving the scientific interests of local community members, a policy inaugurated by Williams about the same time.[61]

The most dramatic change Clapp made just after her return was no doubt the introduction of zoology into the curriculum. Not having marine organisms to dissect nor rooms fitted as laboratories in 1874, Clapp and the college physician settled on what was most handy. They captured and chloroformed one of the many cats kept on the still very rural campus to keep down the mouse population. Using the side porch of the seminary as their laboratory, they dissected the animal so that they and the students could study its anatomy. In the following years, frogs captured from the campus pond and earthworms and chick embryos purchased from local farmers were used for demonstrations in the zoology courses. There is no evidence to tell us whether or not students participated in the first dissection, but after 1876 when Williston Hall was built, students had laboratory space available to do so.

In the years from 1875 to 1888 Clapp worked out a program for teaching zoology that places her in the ranks of male Penikesians inventing the discipline at American colleges. In an age before laboratory manuals, these individuals created a classical laboratory-based zoology course by identifying the organisms and developing the protocols that would allow students to systematically explore anatomical structures and physiology at the same time that Johns Hopkins University professor Henry Martin was shifting science teaching from lectures and demonstrations to laboratory-based, process-oriented group activity in the new university research setting. At Williams College, for example, Edmund Wilson found the common earthworm a good organism to use for teaching and study in his zoology course and worked out procedures for dissecting it. William Thompson Sedgwick at MIT also welcomed Clapp into his zoology course there for a semester. At Clapp's invitation, both men came to lecture at the seminary in the mid-1880s.[62]

Clapp's zoology course might have been extremely provocative in an institution devoted to evangelical ideals of character formation, given the anti-modern climate that prevailed in some male colleges of the 1870s and 1880s—particularly Amherst, with which Mount Holyoke teachers had strong ties.[63] The contrast between the ease with which Clapp's innovation was introduced at Mount Holyoke and the reception dissection later received at Amherst College provides some idea of how well Mount Holyoke teachers with great influence in their institution were able to use Penikese ideas to finesse the relationship between science and modernization.

At Amherst College, where churchmen's influence remained strong, President Seelye forbade the dissection of living organisms by faculty and students on religious grounds, as part of his stand against what he saw as the materialism that modern science encouraged in students' ways of thinking.[64] Other presidents tried to have it both ways. At Princeton, James McCosh isolated science from the rest of the liberal arts curriculum in a compromise with churchmen to preserve religious orthodoxy and yet remain competitive with the more pragmatically oriented new land-grant colleges.[65]

One other direct result of Penikese for Clapp was the network of colleagueships it opened for her, particularly with men working to develop the discipline of biology as they moved from one post to another in academe. In the decade following her Anderson School experience, Clapp went on extensive walking and collecting tours organized by David Starr Jordan, tramping hundreds of miles through the White Mountains and North Carolina with him and a group composed of men, their wives, women science teachers, and male students. On these trips she also visited major institutions such as the Smithsonian. In the summer of 1879 she accompanied Jordan on a trip to Switzerland. A semester-long leave granted her by Mount Holyoke in 1883 allowed her to learn about the biology of the earthworm from Wilson at Williams College. Later she reminisced about attending the meetings of the British Association for the Advancement of Science in Montreal in the 1880s, where she noted the excitement both of dressing up for a gala evening reception with Jordan and of hearing a lecture entitled "Life and Electricity Identical" by Professor Barker from the University of Pennsylvania, probably a reiteration of ideas that Faraday had recently advanced.[66]

While such activities enriched her own teaching, they also helped to establish her and Mount Holyoke as important figures in the community of American biology during its formative period. In addition, Clapp initiated contacts with various men with whom she and her students would do work in the future, particularly at the Marine Biological Laboratory after 1888. Equally important, they provided her with the experience of a much freer, more sociable existence than that within the seminary. Other changes emanating from the Penikese experience include the expansion of the teaching of botany. By 1879 there were three faculty members responsible for this subject, including Lydia Shattuck and another of her young protégées, Henrietta Hooker, who would head the new Botany Department founded after 1888.

In fact, in the dozen years following Penikese there was a general expansion in the science offerings at Mount Holyoke. In part, this expansion was fueled by enthusiasm and ideas generated at Penikese. But as Charlotte Shea has argued, it reflected a much more ambitious strategy on the part of several senior teachers, Shattuck among them, who aimed at reforming Mount Holyoke into a college along scientific lines in order to save it.[67] Their tack was to introduce curricular reforms centered on science, improve the physical plant, assume responsibility for all aspects of the teaching, and gain the support of industrial capitalists. Their goal was to gradually reform the entire institution into a degree-granting college to ensure that Mount Holyoke would continue to be an effective educator of women for work after graduation. These efforts parallel reforms occurring in many men's colleges, which, like Mount Holyoke, were driven to adapt to changing middle-class mores and employment opportunities by rising competition in higher education.[68] Yet, as discussed later, the faith Mount Holyoke placed in science made the seminary distinctive.

In a climate in which religious enthusiasm if not American Protestantism was waning, the stature of missionary work declined in American society; at the same time, demand for teachers, the other occupation for which Mount Holyoke faculty had prepared students, remained high. Increasingly, however, the seminary certificate seemed insufficient to the public as a credential for employment, as it would for other careers opening for women in the coming decades.[69] A degree from what Shattuck had called a "scientific institution" was a dramatic declaration of modernity. Moreover, for those seeking jobs within higher education, academic degrees were more and more necessary, especially in the women's colleges so concerned about establishing their intellectual stature in the eyes of the public. In the battle over whether to grant collegiate status to Mount Holyoke, both supporters and detractors believed that a college degree gave women easier access to a wide variety of job opportunities; although, as Dr. Marianna (Mary) Holbrook, the seminary physician and a supporter, pointed out in 1888, it was not a guarantee of immediate success.[70] The teachers' sense of their own intellectual strengths, of the social climate and trends in American society, and the traditions of Mount Holyoke coalesced around science as central to their vision of what kind of college Mount Holyoke would be.

The sciences at Mount Holyoke benefited enormously from this broader effort at reform in ways that engaged the faculty in a professionalizing process. There was an increase in the number of women teaching science and in the number of science courses taught. The new prominence given to science accompanied an even more significant change: Teachers began to specialize during the 1870s. By the time the 1879 catalogue appeared, eleven of the twenty-eight women teaching faculty were listed as responsible for instruction in specific sciences, although most teachers were not limited to one area. Cornelia Clapp, for example, is listed as Zoology and Gymnastics, and Lydia Shattuck as Chemistry and Botany. In addition, a new generation of teachers was identified with areas of expertise: Lucy Holmes, Physics and Natural Theology; Frances Hazen, Latin and Botany; Sarah Melvin, Chemistry and Rhetoric; Elisabeth Bardwell, Mathematics and Astronomy; Louise Cowles, Geology and Mineralogy; Henrietta Hooker, Mathematics and Botany; Isabella Mack, Mathematics; Adeline Green, Latin and Mathematics; and A. Adelaide Richardson, the seminary physician, Physiology. By 1887 Mount Holyoke boasted that it had more offerings in science than any of the women's colleges.[71]

The significance of this listing is twofold. First, it is the first time that the teachers were designated by academic specialties. Before this, only their names were given, in contrast to the male lecturers. Second, the subjects for which they are responsible are limited to at most two and, save for Holmes, separated from theology. Thus, there seems to have been an effort to simultaneously give the teachers a professional identity and to publicize the modern character of Mount Holyoke's offerings, particularly in scientific disciplines.

In looking at the record, however, we should not assume that the teachers were already specialists in their areas, save in the case of Shattuck who had already been lecturing and doing research in botany, as well as lecturing in chemistry by this time. The evidence in catalogues suggests that they may have been assigned areas that the senior teachers felt important to curriculum reform and in which they had some talent or interest that could be cultivated. Elisabeth Bardwell spent some time in 1873 at Dartmouth College and went on to teach astronomy, as well as math and physics, until her death in 1899. Clapp, another case in point, will be discussed in more detail in the next section. Cowles spent time during this period at the Worcester School of Technology in 1880–1881 and taught mineralogy until she retired in 1904. Mack taught math and physics until 1886, when she left teaching to care for her invalid mother. Hooker persisted in the development of botany courses, taking advanced work at other institutions and in Germany after 1888, while Shattuck taught both botany and chemistry until her death in 1889. The seminary physician continued to have the additional responsibility of teaching physiology—although the seminary now hired its own graduates with medical degrees for the position, rather than retain a male physician. But not all these initial assignments were successful. Green left off teaching mathematics by 1886 to concentrate on Latin and U.S. history. Melvin had given up chemistry by 1887 to concentrate on rhetoric alone.

At the urging of the teachers, Mount Holyoke worked to meet the demand for faculty with specialized scientific knowledge in ways very similar to those pursued by the colleges. One solution was for college administrators and trustees to encourage those already employed to engage in advanced study and research in a specialized field. The case of Samuel F. Clarke, professor of natural history at Williams College, is a case where the desires of the institution and ambitions of a faculty member coincided. In 1883 Clarke, who had received his doctorate from Johns Hopkins, convinced the rapidly expanding college to support the rental of laboratory space at the premier marine biology laboratory in Europe, the Naples Biological Station in Italy. He also had the permission of college authorities to spend the winter and spring of 1883–1884 there.[72]

Leaves of absence, like that awarded to Clarke, could open opportunities for the colleges to bring men working at the cutting edge of science to teach on their campuses. Thus, at Clarke's suggestion, Williams hired his cousin Edmund Beecher Wilson, who had a newly minted doctorate from Johns Hopkins as well, to replace him for half the fall and for the spring term. Wilson, who had occupied the college's table at Naples the previous summer thanks to his cousin's support of his application, taught a laboratory course in biology that included a novel five-week study of the process of cell differentiation using the common earthworm as an exemplary organism. He also presented a series of nine lectures to the entire college community on "Aspects of Modern Zoological Research." These lectures encapsulated a well-organized picture of the value that modern scientific theory had both for the development of biological research and for the use of research in building a better society. Wilson began by critically detailing the implications Darwin's theory of evolution and Agassiz's vitalism held for defining current laboratory-based areas of research into the causes of living things. He then laid out the panoply of new subject matter in biology being drawn from the ideas of Darwin and Agassiz and the theoretical issues with which they dealt. His last lecture stressed the value of pursuing pure biological research and study for the advancement of moral, practical, and nationalistic goals. In a beautifully orchestrated way then and within a short span of time, Wilson set before members of the Williams College community the range of theoretical concerns, specializing trends, and moral and social rationales that were coming to characterize professional science in these years.[73]

In supportive conditions, an established faculty member could exploit organizational reforms to found a department devoted to a specialized field of study and create enough specialized courses to form a major. The adoption of the new elective system, for example, allowed them to make these reforms. Although usually attributed to Charles Eliot, who introduced the elective system in its most thorough-going form when he took the reigns of Harvard in 1869, Roger Geiger points out that:

> the importance of the elective system for the development of American higher education lies in what it allowed faculty to teach. Elective courses not only permitted new subjects to be taught but also freed traditional subjects like classics to be developed in more specialized and advanced forms ... the objective of a college education shifted imperceptibly ... to that of instilling increasingly specialized knowledge.[74]

Thus, at Oberlin College, which was still not a fully integrated coeducational institution in the 1880s, Professor Frank F. Jewett built a modern chemistry department with over eight specialized courses organized in a progressive sequence under the encouragement of President Fairchild's modified elective system, introduced in 1875. Jewett, who had done graduate study at Yale's Sheffield Scientific School and at Göttingen University in Germany, was hired by Oberlin in 1880.[75] At Amherst College, Benjamin K. Emerson returned to his alma mater after graduate studies in Berlin and Göttingen to teach biology. In subsequent years he introduced biology courses heavily weighted toward engaging students in meticulous laboratory work associated with research. Four to five weeks were spent on the study and dissection of the clam as an exemplary invertebrate animal on which research could be conducted. Afterward, students had to write a thesis based on their observations of its structure and development. The chemistry and physics professors soon followed his example.[76]

The colleges also backed their science faculties' efforts to develop professional specialties by providing the necessary resources, or agreeing to accept gifts designated for these purposes. New buildings were often funded by local manufacturers and businessmen interested in education, while former graduates who continued to practice habits of collecting learned in their college years sent specimens they had gathered while on missions to foreign posts. Williams was one of the most impressive in terms of the facilities built and furbished by gifts for scientific work, particularly in natural history subjects. Jackson Hall contained the Lyceum of Natural History, whose study collections were the fruits of periodic faculty-led expeditions to various regions of the country, financed through a gift to the Natural History Department. This institution served both interested amateurs in the local community and members of the college. Although it was an example of the natural history societies popular in the 1850s through the 1870s where colleges often functioned as centers for local science enthusiasts, it was also a vestige of the old ties between the colleges and the local communities they still partially served.[77] By 1883, Clark Hall housed expanding natural history collections gained through bequests, gifts from missionaries, and purchases. More modern laboratory methods gained a further stronghold when the college turned vacated spaces in Griffin Hall into a lecture room and laboratory, furnishing them with microscopes and other equipment for biological investigation. More advanced instruction in physics, chemistry, and astronomy became possible with purchases of the latest equipment and apparatus, including the gift of a refracting telescope and a new observatory to house it from David Dudley Field.[78] The result was that the science faculty had a very visible geographic stronghold on campus.

At Mount Holyoke specialization did not mean that the teachers had achieved equal status with men during the 1880s. While Mount Holyoke science faculty were moving toward specialization in their teaching at the seminary, they lacked the freedom open to men to pursue their interests further. Clapp's colleague from Penikese, Edmund Wilson, for example, when required to teach both moral philosophy and biology at Williams—a situation at which he balked—moved to increasingly research-oriented positions when opportunities arose. Thus, he went to MIT in 1884–1885, then Bryn Mawr when it opened in 1885, and later to Columbia University in 1891.[79] A comparison of the early careers of two Penikesians already briefly discussed in this chapter, David Starr Jordan and Cornelia Clapp, reveals the degree to which the careers went in different but interconnected directions, as each took advantage of the possibilities open to men and to women at this time.

Jordan was a model of the male scientist of his generation. Although his credentials were limited to an M.A. at a time when there were no clear requirements for hiring in the field, he chose to emphasize research over teaching as a means of getting ahead professionally. The controversy over the relative merits of teaching versus research in delineating the professional identity of scientists emerged slowly during this period.[80] Jordan, following the lead of Agassiz, chose to mark out a large field of endeavor as his own, to devote his summers to extensive field trips, and to publish his findings in impressive publications. Such efforts won him status and influence, and enabled him to move from teaching at the college to the university level as institutional opportunities became available, and thence into university administration where he could affect structural as well as intellectual change. While to some extent his career reflected personal proclivities, ambitions, and choices, he also pursued opportunities and used socially sanctioned means open to him as a man. He was not, however, unconcerned with teaching and gave some thought throughout his life to encouraging it as inseparable from professorial research activities.[81]

Clapp, by contrast, perceived her experience at Penikese in terms of enabling her to fulfill her commitment to teaching. In this she remained true to the role that Mary Lyon had defined for Mount Holyoke women. Moreover, she accepted the goals on which Agassiz had founded his school, rather than emulating his example. There is no evidence during these years that she had an interest in research or publishing.

The circumstances that allowed the seminary science faculty to specialize within their institution, also allow them to establish a new kind of relationship with men that traded on the men's status. Within the seminary they continued to regularly divide the labor of teaching the physical sciences with male visitors. While the teachers increasingly assumed responsibility for lecturing in biological science courses, which in any case favored the more desirable laboratory work and empirical study, male faculty from other institutions continued to come in to give courses of lectures, keeping their hold over the physical sciences. The trustees, who now included Young and Charles Hitchcock in their ranks, gave them higher professional titles and credentials than the women, who were still only designated as teachers. These men included Charles Thompson of Worcester Free Institute, who had replaced Shattuck in the 1870s and who lectured on chemistry. There were also the two trustees already mentioned: Charles Young, who lectured on astronomy and physics, and Charles Hitchcock, who lectured on geology. Both men would retain their posts until the end of the century.

In the biological sciences, it seems the teachers chose the men invited to lecture. In line with these teachers' more independent status, these men appeared infrequently and spoke as experts on specially designated topics of current interest. In 1884–1885, Clapp's friend and fellow Penikesian Edmund B. Wilson, now a professor at Bryn Mawr and a Ph.D., gave a special course of lectures on biology. Sedgwick from MIT, whom she preferred less, also lectured a few times during this period.

Young and Hitchcock's own professional advancement was intertwined with raising the status of the seminary as each gained additional credentials over the course of years. By 1887, the seminary catalogue lists them both as having Ph.D.'s. Moreover, Young had moved on from a series of college teaching posts at Williams and Bowdoin to Princeton College. The same was true of other lecturers. In the 1887 catalogue Professor Alonzo Kimball of the Worcester Technical Institute (which had been the Worcester Free Institute) was listed as lecturer in physics with an M.A., having over the years graduated from Amherst College and taught at a military academy, then at Worcester, receiving the title of Professor of Physics in 1872.

The slow rate at which the teachers took charge of lecturing was in part a matter of credentials, but also grew from their need to focus a great deal of time and attention on the design and furnishing of new laboratories, as well as on developing specialized curriculum for laboratory-based courses.[82] One positive result of the trend toward specialization was thus the introduction of laboratory teaching using a variety of the latest equipment. During these years, students began to do laboratory work in specialized subjects with their own hands under the direction of the teachers. There is no indication that they did research, however.

Teaching the new panoply of sciences based on laboratory work was aided by the construction and outfitting of new buildings on campus. Williston Hall, completed in 1876, housed lecture rooms and laboratories for work in chemistry as well as zoology and botany. In fact, Williston Hall contained the Natural History Cabinet, and a wealth of new apparatus for teaching physics, geology, and physiology. These included microscopes for the study of minerals—a method introduced at the seminary by Cowles, a set of plaster casts of dinosaur tracks, and a new mannequin and other models for the study of physiology. In addition, the new library's holdings for student and faculty use in the sciences were expanded during the 1870s to include the latest publications in science, including scientific journals. The construction of an astronomical observatory in 1880 made it possible for students to use a telescope with an eight-inch objective, a transit instrument, an astronomical clock, and other appliances.

Curricular reforms made during these years at Mount Holyoke introduced scientific approaches into nonscientific courses as well, most significantly in those concerned with religion. Anna Edwards, interested in the new Biblical scholarship, modified the reading list for her course in "Theism and Evidences of Christianity" to include both the traditional Butler's *Analogy* and the newer works that encouraged students to critically assess the Bible as a source of information about nature and history: Fisher's *Grounds of Theistic and Christian Belief* and Wright's *Logic of Christian Evidences*.[83] In her course on ancient history, she introduced pictures and artifacts collected on her travels to the Holy Land, as well as translated texts of ancient writings, including Greek myths, as primary data to be examined critically.[84]

As significant, the study of religion was no longer set as a cap on and a rationale for the study of science. In part this change was signified by the elimination of the course titled "Natural Theology" by 1887; and in part by the inclusion of a heavy load of science courses (nine) in the junior and senior years, with religiously centered courses reduced to one in the last half of the senior year. While Bible study was required throughout the four years and "Theism and Christian Evidences" was still offered in the senior year, these studies were complemented by a course in a more secularly oriented "Mental and Moral Science." By 1887, the study of science and religion seemed to have been set on more equal levels, increasingly separated from, if paralleling, one another in their emphasis on engaging students in independent critical thinking about empirical evidence. Character building in the old evangelical Christian sense of disciplining the body and mind was now at least divided and partly transferred to professional identity building of women scientists.[85]

Like the faculty, students were given some encouragement to specialize in science. Although a full-fledged elective system had to wait until the 1890s, by the fall of 1887 students could receive additional instruction in courses of their choosing on an individual basis if they had the interest and wished to devote additional time—although they had a broad range of subjects, of which the sciences were only a part. Postgraduate work in each special area was also available, although it is not clear in either case what sort of projects students took up.[86]

Life at the seminary outside the classroom changed much more slowly during the 1870s and 1880s. There was a marked division between the freedom and coeducational experience of Penikese for example and the still very religiously constrained existence of the family buttressed by the domestic system. Nevertheless, the changes that did occur were deeply intertwined with the teachers' commitment to science. The old lifestyle of the Mount Holyoke family based on self-denial and hard work to prepare students for religious communion with nature was gradually undermined by the introduction of material comforts associated with scientific progress and of reforms that gave students and faculty greater personal freedom. Both sources of change had a salutary effect as far as preparing the ground for a professional scientific culture to flourish at the institution.

The general enthusiasm for science and desire to be competitive led the senior teachers to introduce improvements in the physical plant to ease domestic work at the seminary during the 1870s and 1880s. An elevator, for which Shattuck collected subscriptions, reduced the need to carry loads up the stairs, while an artesian well fitted with a steam pump brought running water for cleaning and bathing to all floors of the seminary building. Steam heating introduced in 1870 made the building a comfortable space in which to study and work. Dubbing the elevator "the alleviator" and praising steam heat for creating "perpetual springtime," Mount Holyoke women found these technological changes wonderfully liberating. There is no hint of any concern that enjoying the material benefits of modern science in any way conflicted with the evangelical stand against industrial society's values.[87] Indeed, beginning in 1879, the seminary catalogues yearly promoted an image of Mount Holyoke as an appealing place where modern technological comforts abounded. Descriptions of the new conveniences now dramatically acknowledged acceptance of the industrial culture whose materialism science at the old seminary had fundamentally opposed.

Most remarkable, a new appreciation for the benefits of technological innovation penetrated into the very realm of science itself at the seminary. The catalogues devoted much space to descriptions and attractive engravings of airy and spacious science buildings, the cozy natural history cabinet, and lists of up-to-date equipment purchased for laboratories where students would obtain the best education that money could buy. The catalogue itself with its modern illustrations became a marketing tool for promoting the new scientific face of Mount Holyoke.

Such changes in the wider culture affecting science at Mount Holyoke were aided in part by support from several more recently appointed trustees. While the trustees had little hand in decisions about curriculum and life within the seminary, the appointment of male trustees who had close ties to business and were also strong supporters of benevolent causes aided the senior teachers in some of their reform efforts.[88] Perhaps the most important among them in advancing the special cause of science at the seminary was A. Lyman Williston, a wealthy manufacturer from Northampton whose mills shipped goods to a national market. As treasurer of the seminary he was not only familiar with the budget but also able to suggest ways to finance expansion. He proved to be an important benefactor of science at the seminary, contributing to the funds for the erection of the well-outfitted, spacious Lyman Williston Hall in 1876 and the Williston Observatory in 1880–1881, both of which were depicted in the catalogues in beautiful engravings that emphasized their size and elegant settings.[89]

There had also been an easing of regulations on dress and food consumption that bespeak a discerning if unofficial acceptance of middle-class materialism. Students and teachers often decorated their somber apparel with lace trimming and brooches for special occasions, for example, while sugared desserts were included on the menu. Photographs of Shattuck from this period reveal an elegant if reserved figure, offering an image of greater prosperity and worldliness than that projected in the portraits of Mary Lyon a generation earlier. Still, behavior was tightly monitored and community bonds privileged over private experience, even to the extent that teachers' mail continued to be set out on the mantel for all their colleagues to read.[90]

By the 1880s, faculty members at Mount Holyoke were faced with a paradox. They believed the changing content of science courses had remained consistent with the fundamentals of Protestant Christianity. At the same time, they had introduced methods of teaching that ran counter to the system of imposed controls over behavior the family community used to maintain conformity to orthodox belief. Now encouraging individual initiative and a desire for self-development through specialized knowledge was identified with careers. In addition, the general enthusiasm for new material comforts testifies to their growing acceptance of some of the values of capitalist industrial society that Lyon had vigorously opposed through the use of religiously sanctioned controls over consumption. By mid-decade, the contradictions implicit in this paradox began to cause problems. The unified character of family life that had allowed science to prosper and invade the academic fabric of the entire institution during the previous decade now began to seem at odds with faculty and students' experiences in the classroom and in the society beyond the seminary walls. A crisis arising from the struggle of Shattuck, Clapp, and their supporters to achieve collegiate status brought things to a head, resulting in this faction's affirmation of scientific culture as a unique foundation for the liberalization of the entire community of women into a modern college with a strongly professional bent. A new concept of science and collegiate status were as wedded in their minds as an older idea of science and seminary had been joined in Mary Lyon's imagination.

From Seminary Teachers to Collegiate Specialists (1887–1888)

From the early 1880s on to 1888, Mount Holyoke faculty members worked to gain the approval of the Massachusetts legislature for a college charter.[91] They found that a modern curriculum privileging science, improved faculty qualifications in specialized fields, and a well-equipped physical plant were not sufficient to draw potential students away from the new women's colleges in order to raise the enrollments necessary to preserve the institution. They had to choose between two, now seemingly conflicting, traditional purposes of their institution: "[converting] students to the great Christian work of saving a sinful world, . . . or remaining leaders in the cause of higher education of women."[92]

Choosing the latter course in which the former objectives became subsumed, Shattuck and her colleagues looked to certification as a college to make them competitive. Clapp recalled the fight this entailed, even with some of the trustees:

> In 1887 I began to kick the bedclothes about this college business. The trustees didn't work. Dr. Mary A. Holbrook was fired with indignation and the trustees thought that they would have to suppress her.[93]

It was not simply a matter of wishing to be able to grant degrees for their symbolic value alone. These women felt not only that collegiate status would give them stature within an increasingly credential-based system of higher education, but also that it would enable them to provide what American students and their parents now saw as an invaluable aid to social advancement through a career: a degree. As Miss Blanchard observed in her report of 1887, "[There are] several instances . . . showing that the lack of a degree renders it difficult for our graduates to obtain certain advantages that are open to those who have no greater attainment, but who have a degree."[94] Dr. Holbrook (MHS '78) (M.D., University of Michigan), a former student of the seminary, echoed this view in noting that those with college degrees could "step at once into positions as writers and speakers."[95] Thus, the teachers continued to adhere to the traditional belief that Mount Holyoke's claim to leadership in women's higher education was based on preparing students for useful work in society. But unlike Mary Lyon, who characterized teaching as a calling aimed at saving souls, they viewed the college degree as an aid in advancing a career, with all that implied about self-fulfillment and social leadership.

The faculty faced a dilemma, however: how to liberalize the family community and still maintain the religious character of Mount Holyoke. Seminary life had become a liability in the marketplace for students, and Mount Holyoke's reputation had suffered at the hands of the new women's colleges that were anxious to identify themselves with contemporary social mores, secular reform efforts, and liberal ideals of what a community of educated women should be. In the eyes of Wellesley faculty and students especially, Mount Holyoke Seminary epitomized all the rules and regulations, the religious exhortations and controls of an outmoded and oppressive system of women's education they had vehemently rejected for themselves. And they were only too happy to publicize this negative image.[96]

The answer to the dilemma was already there in the changes introduced through the aegis of science. In the midst of arguments over whether to keep the seminary or reform it into a college, a petition from 280 students to the trustees forced limited reforms that began the liberalization of family life at Mount Holyoke. Reluctantly, the senior teachers, including Shattuck and Anna Edwards, relinquished some control over the community's life by agreeing to abolish the "purgatory seat" and the accompanying custom of having students confess their transgressions of seminary rules in assembly.[97]

For Mount Holyoke, eliminating public confession was the first step in dismantling the old controlling culture of pious behavior that lay at the institution's heart. In bowing to the pressures of younger faculty and students in this case, the senior teachers began a process of liberalization that would allow students and faculty greater freedom and self-determination and opportunities for self-development in their daily lives. This new freedom complemented that already exercised in their experience with the modified elective system and in their scientific studies in preparation for work after graduation. Moreover, as discussed in the next chapter, the gradual elimination of the remaining rules and regulations would enable a younger generation of science faculty to reformulate rules and controls within their own disciplines along more restricted specialized professional lines, to create a scientific subculture at the college after 1890.

By 1888, when the Massachusetts Legislature granted Mount Holyoke a charter as a college with the right to offer a bachelor of science degree, significant steps had been made toward the creation of a professional culture of science within the former seminary's precincts. The accommodations that made the study of religion more scientific and separated science from religion provided a coherent, orderly, and secularly oriented intellectual basis for the institution's offerings; there was a division of labor within the institution among scientific specialties, and the teachers had begun to show that they cared about enhancing their own credentials as measures of expertise. Such impulses had led them to form a bridge between the confines of seminary life and the more worldly, affluent and fluid society of professionalizing science. The physical plant began to reflect this specialization of the seminary, with its elegant new structures devoted to the study of the sciences. Moreover, students could exercise independence in choosing to concentrate in science, where they could receive training certified with a degree. All this was done in an atmosphere filled with the spirit of academic competition and social advancement rationalized in Shattuck's explanation for gaining collegiate status:

> Since, therefore, the instruction of the seminary has had a scientific trend from the first without tendency to convert us into agnostics or infidels, since this is a scientific age and we are bound to keep abreast of the times, since every college has its own particular individuality, let us press onward in these lines till we obtain full recognition among the colleges of New England.[98]

The Foundations of Gender-Equal Scientific Work

The teachers' efforts to resolve the crises to save Mount Holyoke produced not only a college granting a bachelor of science degree, but also a redefinition of women's scientific work. Behind and supporting this redefinition were two factors: a concomitant rise in the status of science teachers within and outside the institution as they participated with the younger generation of men in the formation of new networks, and a loosening of evangelical customs and values over their daily lives accompanied by the transference of these values into a more disciplined practice in teaching science. The paradox was that institutional curricular equivalence with male colleges depended on women's circumscribing their career ambitions within the goals of Mount Holyoke.

Science teachers' reforms gave their teaching a social significance it had not previously had. They had not only made themselves saviors of the institution, but had given themselves the cachet of modernizers whose specialized knowledge and colleagueships enabled them to join Mount Holyoke with trends in the outside academic community and in American middle-class society. Of special importance, the nature of their work was now in line with trends in American science that emphasized laboratory-based study of nature. Even if they were not engaged in research and publishing, through the prevalence of laboratory teaching in the new curriculum, they had made their work compatible with and supportive of these activities. In this shift, the traditions of hands-on demonstrations, manipulations of equipment long identified in the minds of Mount Holyoke science faculty with raising their professional status, had served them well. In the atmosphere of academe, where empirical studies in the laboratory were fast becoming the basis of research, the teachers could coordinate what they taught about analysis and technical skills with the new information being produced by men doing research.

The weight given to the science faculty's work altered the position of religion at the seminary and the meanings it had once carried. First, the missionizing goals were subordinated to scholarly, scientific ones focused on secular ends, creating a fissure in the old family community. The preparation of missionaries became only one of several possible ways in which faculty prepared students, while a scientific course of studies became the foundation of all students' education, whatever line of work they intended to pursue after graduation. Second, religious values were transferred to scientific activity and used to justify it, without reference to the old biblical allusions and analogies. Instead, the belief that their science teaching and push to specialize were a means for Mount Holyoke to join the progressive march of American society took on the intonations of a crusade in which the science faculty were leaders. Third, this attitude about the importance of their scientific work shifted the Protestant work ethic and released them from the constraints that self-denial had exercised over their professional ambitions. Such a shift of values allowed the teachers to rationalize improvements that eased their domestic work and left them time to concentrate on educating themselves, improving their scientific work spaces and their teaching skills. In the new competitive era, teachers' consumption of space, equipment, and supplies the public considered the sine qua non of scientific work became a sign in the marketplace of their moral superiority and worth, as well as that of their institution.

If the character of their scientific work in their classrooms altered, the relationships with male scientists did as well, taking two different directions. Visiting male lecturers retained their hold over certain subjects, especially the physical sciences, where access to advanced education for women at the new technical schools and research universities was closed off. They even advanced that hold if we consider that by the 1880s there were several male science professors on the board of trustees, and the presence of clergy had diminished. In these areas, the women science teachers remained to do the recitations and laboratory classes, while gaining additional education in these subjects from these men or from study leaves to a limited number of institutions in the old manner. In these cases, they remained in the old position of tutelage sanctioned by evangelical Protestant custom, now more structured and intimately dependent on men for technical information. If Mount Holyoke boasted a chemistry curriculum equal to that of male colleges because of the connections Chadbourne, Thompson, and Kimball might have made, the status of the women teachers and their teaching responsibilities were lower than and different from those of faculty in these institutions where men took charge of all facets of instruction. It is unclear why the women teachers did not protest; however, they may very well have looked outside at the rebuffs suffered by women trying for advanced degrees in chemistry and physics, or they may have been cowed by the aggressively masculine workshop atmosphere of Worcester Institute of Technology and MIT experienced on their educational sojourns.

In the biological sciences, however, the women faculty had a new freedom in relationships with men on the move. This was especially true in the new field of zoology where methods, credentials, institutional bases, and even the body of basic knowledge were relatively undefined. Such circumstances allowed for a feeling of camaraderie and mutual support among men and women that loosened if not dissolved the old distinctions between men and women academics' scientific work. This gave Clapp in particular the opportunity to participate in the formation of an important new segment of the scientific community through teaching activities and further education that put her on a par with men at the colleges.

The change in the definition of their scientific work expressed and structured a highly gendered identity change going on beneath the surface of their personalities. Ironically, these identities drew sustenance from the very evangelical culture whose outward forms they sought to erase from their image. Shattuck's exchanges with Gray could not have proceeded on this high intellectual plane if evangelical Protestant culture had not already confirmed her in the exercise of her intellect and in the accessibility of nature to both sexes. For Clapp, neither intellect nor nature was gender neutral. She interpreted the salvation experience at Penikese, which committed her to teaching the "new" biology with feelings of enthusiasm, youth, and behavior unrestricted by convention, which she identified as masculine. These were to be the hallmarks of her persona as she fulfilled her newfound mission to save Mount Holyoke's position by improving herself.

In these decades, the science faculty laid the groundwork for their entry into the fields of modern chemistry, geology, and physics. But, they did so as second-class citizens serving to pass on information, albeit new information rooted in and disciplined by laboratory technical training, under the direct supervision of men with strong evangelical credentials who wrote the texts and presented the lectures. It would take a new set of trustees, a new generation of women who had access to higher degrees in these fields, and a generation of male scientists who turned away from stewardship over women's colleges to enable Mount Holyoke women to achieve control over the design, content, and objectives of courses in these fields.

The biological sciences stand in contrast. In botany, Henrietta Hooker, with the support of Shattuck, moved ahead easily to gain credentials and to build a department. This may have been because it was in a field that was becoming heavily feminized at this time. And no new economic avenues for people with such training had yet opened.[99] It was in zoology that Clapp moved the furthest, making herself and the zoology program participants in the formation of the developing scientific field through exchanges with male colleagues outside the seminary's walls whom she had known since the Anderson school. If she limited herself to teaching, rather than research and publishing at this time, she was not different from many men on college faculties. Moreover, her quest for advice and knowledge from men to improve her teaching won her respect almost unique among women in the field at this time. In the following decades, she would continue to lead Mount Holyoke in the direction of perfecting teaching at the college level. Embedded in a network of reciprocal relationships with men at higher ranks, Clapp would work with them to establish a structure and hierarchy within the field and within American science that would include Mount Holyoke faculty within a collegiate structure.

Mary Lyon, daguerreotype, 1845. The Mount Holyoke College Archives and Special Collections.

Portrait of the Reverend Edward Hitchcock, ca. 1845. Amherst College Archives and Special Collections.

Original seminary building c. 1845. The Mount Holyoke College Archives and Special Collections.

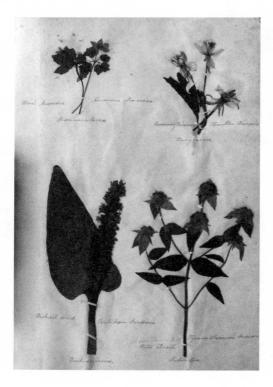

A page from the herbarium collected by Hannah Plimpton ('48) as part of her study of Wood's book on botany. The Mount Holyoke College Archives and Special Collections.

Lydia Shattuck, formal photographic portrait, 1860s. The Mount Holyoke College Archives and Special Collections.

"For the Elevation of Seminary students." Humorous student sketch commenting on Lydia Shattuck's effort at scientific improvements for the seminary, 1880. The Mount Holyoke College Archives and Special Collections.

Lyman Williston Hall with Shattuck Hall at left, before 1917 fire, postcard. The Mount Holyoke College Archives and Special Collections.

Ornithological alcove, Natural History Collection, Williston Hall, c. 1887. The Mount Holyoke College Archives and Special Collections.

Cornelia Clapp lecturing to zoology students in Williston Hall, c. 1892–1893. The Mount Holyoke College Archives and Special Collections.

Chemistry laboratory with students at work, Shattuck Hall, early 1900s. The Mount Holyoke College Archives and Special Collections.

Professor Anne Young, Chairman of the Astronomy department at the Mount Holyoke observatory, early 1900s. The Mount Holyoke College Archives and Special Collections.

Women and men at Mount Holyoke: Botany department, early 1900s. Dr. Henrietta Hooker is in the center; from left to right: E. Jackson, Miss Weston, Mary Kennedy, Sarah J. Agard, and Asa S. Kinney, who taught floriculture. The Mount Holyoke College Archives and Special Collections.

Tableau of Geology, Zoology, and Botany departments, Figures dressed as geneticist Gregor Mendel and fruit flies, 75th Anniversary celebration, 1912. The Mount Holyoke College Archives and Special Collections.

Zoology Professor Ann Haven Morgan showing student how to dissect using a microscope, 1930s. The Mount Holyoke College Archives and Special Collections.

Physiology instructor Hazeltene Stedman, F. G. Benedict, and Mount Holyoke students with apparatus Turner had developed for measuring women's metabolism, c. 1926. The Mount Holyoke College Archives and Special Collections.

Chemistry Professors Lucy Pickett and Emma Perry Carr, Department Chairman, in the laboratory with Halcyon Crawford ('58). The Mount Holyoke College Archives and Special Collections.

chapter 4

Redefining Scientific Labor in the Age of Specialization (1889–1900)

The MBL as the Source of a New Scientific Order

On a warm evening in the summer of 1890, Cornelia Clapp sat in the lecture room at the Marine Biological Laboratory (MBL) on the shores of Cape Cod. Clapp, her student Lucy Ella Keith, and her laboratory assistant Lucy Marsh listened attentively to Director Charles Otis Whitman present one of the decade's most important proposals for the restructuring of American science.[1] Significantly, Whitman titled his lecture "Specialization and Organization, Companion Principles of all Progress."[2] Arguing that specialization based on a division of labor characterized the social as well as the natural world, the new director of the first American marine laboratory proffered a compelling vision of a new order for American scientists, male and female, that established a gender-neutral ideal for reorganizing American society led by a scientific community devoted to research.[3] This vision was a secular reconfiguration of the old evangelical Protestant elite's goals of leading the nation toward spiritual salvation. In it, Whitman articulated a complex yet harmonious social web evolving out of the effort of scientists to structure their own research and teaching activities in accordance with an evolutionary hierarchy of mutually supportive and interdependent individuals and institutions in higher education, government, and industry. Intellectual competence, skills, and subject matter, not gender, would be the deciding factors scientists used to sort themselves and their institutions into a functioning system led by research discoveries to serve the new social ends. The lines of development Whitman laid out spoke to the entire situation in American science, wedding it to a larger social mission that opened the way for Mount Holyoke women to move into a position of equality with male college science faculty.

Whitman's words struck Clapp as particularly relevant to the situation at home, for the newly chartered college had already seen the beginnings of a trend toward specialization as it broke its last ties to the old seminary culture in the late 1880s. Important for Clapp were his words on the benefits to be realized from coordinating individual specialists' efforts to increase and disseminate knowledge within a social and intellectual hierarchy.[4] In 1890 Mount Holyoke's senior science teachers confronted a complex set of circumstances not unlike those that faced science faculty at men's colleges also in the throes of reform during the previous decade. The break with evangelical ministerial authority and mores in the 1880s had set them on new intellectual paths pursued in an ad hoc manner by faculty at each institution. But this break had also left them adrift in the fiercely competitive market of the late 1880s. The increasing numbers of doctoral degree granting universities and professional medical schools were a new factor in the demand for credentials, while participation in research increasingly became desirable as colleges sought to attract a growing middle class anxious for access to position and influence in industrializing America.[5]

In a period when "survival of the fittest" was a favored motto of powerful capitalists and Herbert Spencer's social Darwinism a favored rationale for stressful circumstances in industrial society, these Mount Holyoke women and their male and female peers sought an advantage in the emerging ecology of higher education and access to the wider society. The science faculty members' passionate desire to secure the new college's position among the best in New England engaged them in the same general enthusiasm for coordinating scientific activities along specialized lines felt by many academics, male and female, of the period. Like Veblen's industrialists who followed the scientists lead in these years, they vertically and horizontally integrated their smaller scientific enterprise into a rationally organized system. Whitman's plan (adapted from Spencer's ideas) offered a way to reconfigure the old evangelical culture into a modern professional one, still deeply Protestant in character. It gave them the right to leadership, a structure, lines of communication, and the security of a place within a hierarchy of the chosen devoted to a new national mission.

Within this hierarchy, Clapp held a special place—especially in the emerging field of zoology. Although she sat in the audience on this occasion, listening as Mary Lyon had done when Hitchcock discoursed on science teaching, she was a participant in Whitman's enterprise in ways that Lyon might have hoped for and understood, but not foreseen. Then a lecturer on the faculty of the MBL and the head of its library, and later to be the only woman trustee, Clapp could coordinate its program and that of Mount Holyoke more intimately than was possible for women from other campuses. She could establish working relationships with male faculty members that were to their mutual benefit. She could draw on the large view it gave her of developments in American science to design her departmental programs to accommodate graduate school requirements and new job opportunities for women. Reciprocally, she could help shape a coeducational national organization more directly than women and many men from other colleges.

Changes in her home institution that validated the rise in science faculty's stature allowed her and other science faculty to focus their time and energies on these intra- and intermural specialized activities. To some extent these changes at Mount Holyoke would parallel the new organization of the MBL, an example being when trustees decided to appoint a president rather than a principal to head the college—which was now a fully accredited liberal arts college divested of the old seminary program. Their choice, Mrs. Hiram Mead, from Oberlin College, established a modern departmental system based on the rational ideal of organizational ecology. But changes that eased their life outside the classrooms were equally important, as they raised teachers' standard of living to approximate that of the leisure classes and allowed them to earn higher degrees, engage in research to some extent, and focus on building their specialties into the curriculum.

The growing division of labor within the scientific community in the coming decade, accompanied by increasing job opportunities for women, validated the practical wisdom of pursuing this policy. As the following sections of this chapter show, the faculty members' reconfiguration and expansion of science courses within modern departments and their advanced degrees, accompanied by a new division of labor on campus and a reordering of campus life, encouraged them to develop a special identity and subculture that helped them integrate into the new national scientific community, while distinguishing them from women in other fields on campus. Only at the end of this period, just at the turn of the century, did they recognize that they faced a new set of paradoxes and challenges. Male scientists in the universities set the standards for collegiate access to degrees, research opportunities, and jobs.

Curriculum and Faculty Development

Whitman's genius was to articulate a way these women could give order and social significance to their efforts, as well as find membership in a cooperative community of like-minded people. Specialization of their science curriculum and their own knowledge base promised them and Mount Holyoke assimilation into an emerging national network on a relatively equal footing with men. At the same time, Whitman's suggestion that such activity would contribute to both moral and social progress appealed to the teachers' need for a higher justification.

Viewed within the context of American higher education in the 1890s, Whitman's MBL offered a practical framework and a rationale for scientists who would shape the programs at many of the new universities and reformed colleges during this decade. The idea of the division of labor gave them a useful way to conceive the organization, objectives, and thus the content of their curriculum along specialized lines. It also helped them clarify their own status and function and that of their institutions within a hierarchical universe where by 1900, as Roger Geiger has noted, "the province of a true university was then held to be higher learning, graduate education, and the advancement of knowledge through research."[6] Finally, the idea of a national laboratory provided this generation of science faculty and their students with an opportunity beyond their journals and associations to forge personal communication networks extending across the country. During the summer weeks spent away from their home campuses, they could meet one another to inaugurate the exchange of information about course content, teaching methods, employment, and graduate school opportunities, as well as research topics and publications, which would be exploited upon their return.

In fact, presidents of established male colleges found an accommodation with modern society along lines congenial to Whitman's vision in order to survive. They could not go back, although at Amherst and Oberlin, for example, short-lived efforts were made to scrutinize the morality and piety of the faculty during the 1890s.[7] Protestant America had changed too much for the old cultural forms and content to be functional or attractive to prospective students and faculty. If the colleges wanted to maintain their dual role of forming the moral character of male leaders of American society and preparing them for worthy careers, they would have to embrace some form of the new culture and professional science education in order to attract students. They thus had to decide how to proceed in developing the commitments already made to science on campus. On this count they faced another set of problems posed by the universities. By the second half of the 1880s, the research universities had grown in number and several more were on the drawing board. One difficulty presented by their growth stemmed from the demand these novel institutions created for qualified science faculty with doctorates to staff the graduate programs, thus making it difficult for the colleges to compete for personnel with the best credentials. For example, in the early 1890s, A. A. Mickelson turned down Oberlin's offer to hire him, informing the college that he preferred the new University of Chicago because of "the freedom of . . . the stimulating research atmosphere."[8] At Oberlin a student's article in the *Oberlin Review* criticized the college for not appointing men with advanced training and especially foreign training to the faculty.[9]

Another related and more fundamental problem arose from the increasing attraction that graduate degrees exercised over the aspirations of those students interested in science. In the late 1880s the universities did not yet require a bachelor's degree for entrance into their graduate programs and were beginning a heavily competitive effort to increase their size through enlarged enrollments that drew from the same pool as the colleges.[10] Moreover, students and qualified scholars found reinforcement and support for professional aspirations in new universities, particularly research universities. These combined the high status of the natural sciences with utilitarian objectives of education for careers and research-based graduate training into "the core value of the university": knowing through the exercise of reason, or cognitive rationality.[11]

How were the male colleges that had once stood at the height of higher education in America to redefine their curriculum, their educational goals, and the profession of college teacher to accommodate the preparation of students for careers in science at the highest level? Most of them had neither the financial resources nor the desire to become universities granting the doctorate, although as in the case of Williams they experimented with the possibility.[12] Williams for a time offered a Ph.D. in astronomy, hiring a very small number of graduates as assistants while they worked on their degrees. Professor Safford shepherded these students through their thesis research and saw that they published their results in respected journals. The college also attempted to turn the Berkshire Medical College into an affiliated medical school.[13]

The resolution of this problem was not an easy one and took over a decade to work out. Beginning in the late 1880s, scientists at the universities took the lead in establishing a hierarchy of requirements for admission and credentialling that privileged specialized fields of research. Certain strategies helped them strengthen and unify their efforts. Leaders among them like Ira Remsen at Johns Hopkins founded journals and professional organizations that allowed them to set the standards and define the important areas for research in their disciplinary fields, as well as to identify the leadership in their fields.[14] While Remsen, who by 1887 had become the secretary of Hopkins' academic council, was able to set priorities and establish a hierarchical division of labor for the chemistry profession, Charles Otis Whitman's efforts to do the same for biology need to be mentioned as well. During his tenure as chairman of the Biology Department at Clark University from 1889 to 1892, Whitman founded the American Morphological Society and its organ, the *Journal of Morphology*. More importantly, he played a leading role in founding the MBL at Woods Hole in 1888, a post that enabled him to advance his own interests and to exercise some influence over the organization and stratification of professional biology. As its first director, he used the summer school program and the MBL journal and annual reports to redefine the content and goals of academic biology in the 1890s.[15] Moreover, the MBL functioned as a powerful organizing force. By bringing together faculty from universities, colleges, high schools, and academies for research or instruction within a ranked system, it helped initiate a set of hierarchical working relationships based on distinctions between those who did research and those who taught, as well as between those engaged in teaching at universities, colleges, and high schools. He made these intentions quite clear in his first welcoming address, and elaborated on them two years later when he spoke on "Specialization and Organization, Companion Principles of All Progress— The Most Important Need of American Biology."[16]

The male colleges also found opportunities to define the terms of undergraduate and preprofessional education in science that allowed them and the university graduate system to mesh. In fact, science faculty members in the colleges by 1888 had already begun to establish some avenues for resolving this greater difficulty through their participation in the network of scientists whom they had met in college or abroad. By spending time at international meeting grounds such as Göttingen, Berlin, or Naples or bringing students to the U.S. Fish Commission laboratory, they made known the quality of their own work, their students and their institutions to colleagues from the universities. The colleges thus became natural recruiting grounds for research university graduate programs, especially since they shared the same religious biases. By 1888 Oberlin had sent seven graduates (all male) to Johns Hopkins, the largest contingent of any college, partly through the agency of Oberlin alumni already there and partly through the relationships established between Hopkins and Oberlin faculty.[17]

Male college science faculty also began to define their professional duties partly in terms of developing a curriculum that provided a certain amount of specialization with an introduction to research methods and theoretical developments for the most advanced students. In doing so, they in effect put brakes on directions they had already been pursuing, drawing back to complement the direction in which university graduate education was going while standing their ground on what they were already equipped to do. In this way, too, they began to establish preprofessional programs to meet entrance requirements established by Harvard and Johns Hopkins medical schools by 1901.

Instead of pushing forward to develop more increasingly specialized courses and expanding their research projects, college faculty burrowed downward and outward to detail the mechanics of what to teach, how to teach it, and how to keep abreast of new knowledge, techniques, and equipment in course sequences that were both self-contained and preparatory. At Williams, for example, the Physics Department offered three levels of courses, in which the first introduced students to basic theory, classic experiments related to these theories, and simple laboratory methods and equipment. In Third Level Advanced Physics, the second course required students to work on a research problem under the professor's direction. Interesting because of its unusual orientation toward applied science in the physics curriculum, the completion of the entire advanced sequence at Williams "enabled [students] to enter the final year of a technical school."[18]

In the Biology Department, Professor Clarke arranged his sequence in biology with prerequisites, so that introductory biology broadly explored the relationships between living things through a new combination of lectures, readings, and student laboratory work. Study of living things drew on a much more refined understanding and testing of hypothesis drawn from Darwin's ideas on variation, the struggle for existence and natural selection. Later courses included work with more complex equipment on specialized topics such as the study of bacteria and their relationship to health and disease. As for introducing students to research, no doubt because he was over-extended, Clarke indicated cautiously that "where it is practicable" students who planned to be teachers could work on a research problem under his direction.[19] Still, he made certain that the best students who might be promising biologists were able to do research during the summers at Woods Hole, Massachusetts. Oberlin and Western Reserve College took similar approaches.[20] Here the colleges took the first steps along vaguely perceived new avenues into scientific careers for college students. At the same time they initiated the basis for the division of labor within science, so that college faculty limited themselves to providing an introduction to major subdisciplines, techniques, and methods, important theories, and a taste of research—the last restricted to a special few.

The details of how this division was worked out within the colleges will require further study; however, it is clear from the records of the MBL that the science faculty from many elite colleges for men and women, with the notable absence of Amherst, kept their institutions active in the formation of professional science during the 1890s. Between 1888 and 1895, a total of twenty-seven universities and single-sex colleges from across the United States subscribed to rooms and tables there, and over 101 faculty members and their students from these two types of institutions attended. In 1886 the number had grown to thirty-nine and by 1899 it was up to fifty. In 1894 and 1895 the cooperative colleges and societies supporting the MBL, as opposed to simply renting space there, included Williams and Hamilton.[21]

Another measure of the MBL's role in steering both men and women college science faculty to participate in the professionalizing process comes from data published by the MBL on the research activity of its attendees. Gathered to counter efforts of a faction within its membership to make the MBL solely a research institution, these data actually try to privilege the research experience of those in the colleges and less elevated schools. While colleges and universities are lumped together and not identified by name in the data, the figures showed that between 1888 and 1895, 24 men who had worked under instruction there had published original work, as had an additional 25 men who had "work more or less advanced." The numbers for the women were 15 and 13, respectively.[22] Just as for their colleagues in the universities, research had become an important measure of professional status for the third generation of college professors and their students as well by this time.

Not surprisingly then, within ten months of Whitman's talk, his major ideas began to find expression in Mount Holyoke's science curriculum, in the activities of the faculty, and in the training students received, as well as in the entire college system that supported them. The 1890–1891 report of the new president, Elizabeth Storrs Mead, expressed the hope that new methods of work and administration inaugurated that year would be successful particularly because of their connections with science: The college was "bringing in of [sic] a larger life" that included a growing interest in "Biological research" and the formation of the "habit of scientific observation and classification . . . that must lead to valuable results."[23]

Through the influence of Cornelia Clapp, in parallel with the scheme outlined by Whitman, in the 1890s Mount Holyoke's science faculty saw to it that their program followed a pattern of growth that correlated progressively specialized course work with a emerging hierarchy of professional opportunities for women interested in science. Not only did the number of courses offered in science expand over the course of the 1890s, but they were organized within new disciplinary departments and stratified into majors that moved students from basic to more intensive studies with an opportunity to do research. Moreover, the curriculum increasingly focused on laboratory work, while a number of practical courses were introduced. Thus, the content of the curriculum reveals the science faculty's desire to take advantage of opportunities for select women to enter the new university graduate programs in science and medicine, as well as to prepare other students for lesser jobs emerging within these fields. Most departments thus partly geared their specialized course work toward the practical objective of preparing students to qualify for one new niche or another in the professional division of scientific labor. Faculty connections with scientists at other institutions undergoing similar changes also influenced the shape of the curriculum, helping to create an alignment between Mount Holyoke's program and the increasing stratification of American science.

In quantitative terms, the increased pace of specialization between 1888 and 1899 is apparent in the growing number of offerings in the sciences, exclusive of mathematics. These offerings expanded from seven to sixty-two. Although the Zoology Department had the greatest number of offerings in 1888 and remained strong with eight listings in 1899–1900, Chemistry with eight, Botany with ten, and Physics with eleven show the greatest growth as separate departments during the decade. By 1899, Geology boasted eight and Astronomy five courses each. Physiology, still taught by the campus physician, offered two courses and had separated from Zoology. At least one ancillary course testifies to faculty interest in creating functional links between departments that supported science. The new French Department offered a special course in "Scientific French" where students could learn the professional vocabulary by guided reading of semipopular French scientific periodicals, such as *La Nature* and *L'Année Scientifique.* "Theoretical Chemistry" required three previous courses in chemistry and at least one course in physics. Two courses were open only to chemistry majors: "History of Chemistry" and "Journal Club" (which had the former as a prerequisite). By expanding their departmental offerings, the faculty were able to channel students into more specialized paths and raise the level of their technical expertise in each of these. By 1899 they not only required students to select a major by the end of their sophomore year, but the young women had to choose one among a number of special sciences—each with its own departmental designation, such as biology or geology, not simply the general category of science.

The idea of a college education as a logically continuous process of narrowing and deepening one's expertise within a special field, which crystallized during this period, is clearly evident in the Chemistry Department's catalogue entries for 1899–1900. All courses in chemistry, save the "General Chemistry" that all students took, had a prerequisite. Moreover, there was a stair-step character to them, so that in order to take "Qualitative Analysis," a student had to have had the "General Chemistry" course, while "Qualitative Analysis" was necessary to qualify for entrance into "Organic Chemistry." Within the departments, which as Hugh Hawkins has noted co-opted an old name for a new entity, the science faculty coordinated and unified their specialties around the idea of intellectual advancement toward a high level of expertise in that specialty. They structured their course work in sequences with higher level courses having prerequisites. The result was that this progression became wedded to an exclusionary process, turning those who survived into an elite cadre.[24]

Despite faculty's focus on channeling students into one of a number of very different fields of knowledge, all the science departments they created shared certain characteristics. In particular, all featured courses heavily weighted toward laboratory work, with a strong focus on teaching students a variety of techniques, from preparation of slides to qualitative and quantitative analysis. The emphasis reflected the persistence at the seminary of older teaching customs that favored engaging in highly ritualized procedures involving interactions with material phenomena, manipulation of equipment, and teaching students to do the same whenever practicable. Mary Lyon's admonition that everything be done perfectly was translated into a stress on learning to perform these analytical techniques as precisely and efficiently as possible. At the same time, the faculty members now had enough funds to provide equipment and supplies for student use, and enough expertise themselves to teach these techniques to their students.

Continuing the tradition of educating women for useful work, faculty in the science departments designed their offerings with a view to preparing students for a variety of newly defined professional and technical paths. The curriculum showed a remarkable sensitivity to the hierarchy of positions within science outlined by Whitman, as well as to the specific types of jobs available. Both the Chemistry and Zoology departments offered special courses in laboratory techniques that gave young women the skills necessary for jobs as laboratory technicians. The "Practical Astronomy" course taught students how to compute their observations, a skill that was much in demand at the time as Edward Pickering at the Harvard College Observatory and others sought help with the tedious work needed to realize their vast projects of mapping the sky.[25] In botany, the "Floriculture" course taught students how to cultivate and propagate plants in a greenhouse environment, with an eye to their employment in commercial horticulture as much as in municipal botanical gardens and university plant houses constructed during the 1890s. Physiology, taught by the physician, contained a practical emphasis on sanitary science. Geology by 1899 included practical courses of "Economic Geology" and "Petrology."

Remaining true to their traditional commitment to educating women to earn their livings as teachers, faculty members in each science department attempted to meet rising standards for science teachers in primary and secondary schools. The Geology Department offered a "Structural Geology" course for those preparing to be teachers, and the Botany Department had a "Teacher's Training Course." A small number of women already primary and secondary school teachers returned to their alma mater to do advanced work, bringing their knowledge up to date and earning college degrees in order to maintain their certification.[26]

Mount Holyoke science faculty members during this period also prepared their most talented students to enter graduate school for advanced degrees by introducing them to research methods and the work of prominent researchers. At the undergraduate level, the Chemistry and Geology departments, along with that of Physics, offered special upper level courses that engaged students in contemporary issues and discoveries through reading and discussing the latest publications in their respective fields. As for Biology, the 1899–1900 catalogue described the activities of a Biology Club and a Journal Club. The Zoology Department also provided connections for students to do graduate study at the Zoological Station at Naples, Italy, and research in zoology and botany at the MBL, where the college maintained an investigator's room.

Hiring of their own graduates continued too, but also included those with advanced training educated at a variety of other institutions, with an eye to improving academic standards. A good example of this adaptation of an old tradition to take advantage of new circumstances came in chemistry. With the death of Alonzo Kimball, President Mead agreed to put women in charge of chemistry teaching—and the new Chemistry Department.[27] Finally the struggle for control over this subject was won. Almost immediately, the transformation of chemistry at Mount Holyoke began in 1893 with the hiring of Mary Frances Leach, who interestingly was also a staunch supporter of religious education.[28] Leach had more training than the fresh Mount Holyoke graduates typically hired in earlier years. After graduating from Mount Holyoke in 1880, she earned a B.S. from the University of Michigan in 1893. When Leach returned to Mount Holyoke that year as a faculty member, opportunities for women in chemistry were growing and the college needed to upgrade its program as it continued to move away from the seminary tradition.[29] Leach inaugurated the first step toward a serious chemistry program with the establishment of a more substantial curriculum of advanced undergraduate courses. Her successor Nellie E. Goldthwaite followed her example. In 1897 Leach wrote to Goldthwaite, that "As you see by the old curriculum we have heretofore only played at Chem. [sic] after the first year, taking it in 2 hr. courses."[30] Goldthwaite followed Leach's progressive reforms of the department offerings.[31]

Not unexpectedly, by the end of the century Mount Holyoke faculty entered modestly into the field of graduate education in science, offering advanced work and a master's degree requiring a thesis by 1899. This was not a casual step for any college to take at the time. "Such graduate work is exceedingly costly for both instruction and equipment," Professor Helen Searles warned in a 1902 Mount Holyoke magazine article on "Graduate Study for Women in American Universities," summarizing lessons learned over the previous few years.[32] Yet science teachers would develop this program even more fully in the decades after 1900.

While the rationale inaugurating this program is unclear, it seems to have filled a variety of needs that overrode or mitigated cost considerations. Information from alumnae files indicates that like their male colleagues who inaugurated graduate programs in the universities at this time, science faculty at Mount Holyoke found graduate students useful as an inexpensive source of labor, having them serve as assistants in their departments now heavily committed to labor-intensive and time-consuming laboratory instruction.[33] Certainly, master's students also gave the faculty a cachet of authority and some status in the hierarchy of academe. Those enlisting in the program saw it as a means of self-advancement towards better jobs and better preparation for university work. A list of students in the master's program shows that one of the four women admitted to the program that year had a B.A., while two students receiving degrees had a bachelor of science.[34] Three of these women who specialized in science had been Mount Holyoke graduates returning to their alma mater after teaching school for a time to gain advanced, specialized education: Grace Ella Berry ('92) and Susan Leiter ('99) in physics, and Olive Hoyt in chemistry ('97).[35]

One additional area for which the faculty prepared worthy students was medical school. The course Clapp offered in zoology reflects her perspicacity when it came to premedical education. Recognizing the growing number of openings in medical schools, demand for doctors, and the increasing influence of science on medicine within the university setting, she made Mount Holyoke a leader among liberal arts colleges in the field of premedical education. She gave her students the advantage of a broad and extensive preparation in the biological sciences, while avoiding vocational training tailored to specific medical practices. The program consisted of an impressive two-year elective course in 1892, arranged to meet the needs of two classes of students each with career goals that Clapp and her fellow teachers had matched to trends in the job market and university programs:

a) those desiring some knowledge of methods of teaching, and of practical work in the laboratory, and

b) those intending to study medicine[36]

Physiology and anatomy figured prominently among the ten courses listed for the premedical course. Also included were "Comparative Anatomy"; "Histology and Embryology of the Chick," already introduced in a general way in the 1870s; "The Essentials of Comparative Physiology"; lectures by a physician; laboratory work with special reference to human physiology; and a course in "Anatomy, Physiology, and Hygiene," required of all students. This latter course, an expansion of the old course taught by the college physician, included lectures on sanitary science as well. Instead of natural religion and natural history, the curriculum included a reading course in which the modern evolutionists Darwin, Weismann, and Wallace were discussed.[37]

These programs exemplify the way in which specialization and organization within the college served these women's ambitions to weave themselves into a web of mutually advantageous relationships with men in the world beyond Mount Holyoke's walls. For example, Clapp's inclusion of public health and sanitary science in the zoology program was probably not fortuitous. She had invited Professor William T. Sedgwick, who had inaugurated a public health program at MIT, to speak at the college during the 1883–1884 school year. Sedgwick, whom Clapp had known since Penikese, may have originated the idea to include sanitary science in the physiology program. Such a course would have served his desire to attract a clientele for his scientifically based program.[38] Sedgwick may also have made it possible for at least one student to enter the famous course VII in biology at MIT, in which he taught anthropology and general biology.[39] Mount Holyoke College graduate Clara Amity Bliss ('88) spent the year 1890–1891 at MIT in this program, where about one-quarter of the students were women destined for employment as teachers.[40] Developments occurring outside Mount Holyoke thus influenced the content of curricular reforms, as male scientists sought to win adherents to their specialties, and Mount Holyoke science faculty members did the same in an active spirit of enlightened self-interest.

Just as Edward Hitchcock had done before the Civil War, men still came to give courses of lectures on science at Mount Holyoke, and while there also gave their advice and counsel—but this tradition was on the wane and their paternalism not welcomed by everyone. Charles Hitchcock continued his annual visits from Hanover to lecture on geology, as did Charles Young from Princeton on astronomy. Young in fact provided much expert advice to Elisabeth Bardwell, in her dotage and increasingly ill, who depended on Young, himself getting on in years, to help her as she struggled valiantly to work the new astronomical equipment installed in the observatory.[41] Hitchcock was becoming dated.

There were divisions among the women on the issue of male scientists on campus. Encouraging continuation of long-standing male control over the hard sciences, President Mead made special mention in her report of 1892–1893 that physics, astronomy, and geology had benefited from the expertise of male specialists who presented courses of lectures that year. In the same report, Mead singled out Professor S. F. Wright from Oberlin College, her former home and employer, for bringing the study of geology up to date that year. She diplomatically commented that "New methods, differing standpoints, and wider experience have a broadening effect."[42] These measures may have been Mead's way of compensating for the fact that the departments she mentioned all lacked strong female leadership. However, it also seems possible that Mead, coming from coeducational Oberlin where women were being integrated into the full college curriculum, which had been limited to men, was guiding Mount Holyoke College toward a future in which men might be hired as regular faculty members.

Even if there may have been some resentment from younger, more independently minded and more qualified faculty toward the paternalism of these men who came on extended visits, the men came to South Hadley under circumstances different from earlier decades. Unlike lecturers in the antebellum years who seem to have initiated their own visits or been invited by the trustees, the women had taken partial charge in deciding whom to invite.

Yet control of invitations also provided Mead with the opportunity to be selective in the ties she forged. One of the new relationships she tried to establish with some results was that between Oberlin science faculty and Mount Holyoke. President Mead probably served as a conduit for changes in the Chemistry Department, for example, which closely resembled reforms made within Oberlin College during the previous decade when she was there. Her husband had left his post as minister of the South Hadley Congregational Church to head Oberlin's Department of Theology in 1869. In this coeducational college Mrs. Mead had served on the Women's Board of Managers (1869–1881), and after her husband's death in 1881 taught English there for two years. She not only had a strong interest in science, of which those who recruited her for Mount Holyoke were aware, but her knowledge of happenings within the coeducational institution remained strong throughout the rest of her life, for her son-in-law was a professor of church history at Oberlin and she retired there in 1901.[43]

As discussed in Chapter 3, at Oberlin, in parallel with Mount Holyoke during the late 1870s and 1880s, faculty had pressed to expand the scientific course, but Oberlin was much more advanced than Mount Holyoke in chemistry in the 1880s because its president had made it possible for three faculty members in succession to devote a major amount of their energies to it, while at the seminary the figure with the strongest interest in chemistry, Lydia Shattuck, was physically declining. In particular, Frank F. Jewett, A.M., professor of chemistry and mineralogy, worked from 1880 on into the 1890s to develop a chemistry curriculum very similar to the one that would be found at Mount Holyoke in the 1890s.[44] Unlike Mount Holyoke, however, Oberlin students had a choice between pursuing a general course in chemistry, or electing the experimental course in lab practice. Moreover, they had more elective courses. Yet Mount Holyoke followed Oberlin's lead in accepting a number of special students and postgraduates who wanted to pursue advanced work in chemistry, particularly chemical research.[45]

In addition to President Mead, the teachers themselves served as agents of cultural transfer, bringing back ideas for curriculum development and teaching methods gleaned during summers spent at research institutes and years away in graduate study. They also invited the men they met to lecture on their specialties in South Hadley. The influence of the MBL on the zoology curriculum at Mount Holyoke stands as a good example of how this worked. From the very beginning of Clapp's association with the MBL, she drew on its program for the design of the zoology courses at Mount Holyoke. There is a strong correlation between the courses offered at the MBL from 1888 through the 1890s and those listed in the Mount Holyoke catalogues for the same period, for example. Instruction at Woods Hole included vertebrate and invertebrate zoology, embryology, histology, physiology and comparative anatomy—all subjects that Clapp incorporated into the Zoology Department program or that were found in the courses offered by Dr. Lowell, the resident physician. The Mount Holyoke "Cell Biology" course no doubt arose out of Clapp's own work begun at the MBL under Whitman and continued with him at the University of Chicago. Her decision to include behavioral biology and to use birds to study evolution in the zoology curriculum also suggests a similar origin.[46]

Clapp was certainly attuned to Whitman's emphasis on organizing knowledge into packages of courses designed in accordance with what they both considered a progression leading from basic knowledge to independent research. Like those programs Whitman designed at the MBL and later at the Biology Department at the University of Chicago where she studied with him, her program combined teaching and research functions, considering that all class work was a form of preparation for investigation as well as "a number of other purposes of a practical nature for teachers."[47] Moreover, Clapp's curriculum shows how thoroughly impressed she was with Whitman's views on the centrality of laboratory work in science, as all the zoology offerings attest. Many years later she recalled what Whitman had taught her first summer at Woods Hole: "The thoroughly scientific spirit which was evident and the complete absence of sensationalism was shown when he honestly told us that we should not waste our time with *lectures* [sic]."[48] It is easy to understand how graduates in zoology from Mount Holyoke could move on without much culture shock to do advanced work at the MBL or with any of the men at other laboratories and universities who had studied with Whitman. The same would be true for students in other science departments whose course designs were based on outside models.

Other examples of such cultural transfer by the female faculty need to be documented; however, Clapp's case serves to indicate fairly vividly how she and her fellow science teachers helped align the intellectual focus and function of their departments with the larger male-dominated institutional forces shaping American scientific education and employment.

Intellectual Growth, Credentials, and a Scientific Subculture

The faculty could not have accomplished this alignment without becoming specialists themselves, heading programs in ways that resembled the hierarchy outlined by Whitman for the MBL. During the 1890s they underwent a process of professionalization that allowed them to take increasing responsibility for all aspects of science education at Mount Holyoke. President Mead diplomatically noted in 1893 that "It would be difficult for me to measure the importance to the girls of contact with gentlemen as well as lady teachers." But she also suggested there was new opportunity for women teachers to replace the men invited to give courses of lectures by affirming that "The time will come, I trust, when we can add other specialists to our corps of instructors."[49] Such encouragement brought results. Not only did the number of women teachers specializing in science increase dramatically during the 1890s, but the level of faculty expertise rose as those of Clapp's generation earned advanced degrees and the college hired younger women already possessing master's degrees and the new Ph.D.

The 1888–1889 catalogue provides one benchmark for measuring the progress of specialization. It lists nine faculty members teaching science: two each in botany and chemistry, and one each in astronomy, zoology, physics, geology, and physiology. This number is somewhat deceptive, since Shattuck, who is identified as responsible for botany, was ill and did not live to see the end of the semester. The fact that several of these teachers taught more than one subject also suggests that faculty were less expert than the catalogue suggests: Marcia Keith taught mathematics and physics, while Clapp was in charge of gymnastics, as was Alice Carter, who also taught botany—most probably in her case growing out of the tradition at the old seminary of seeing the activity of collecting as a morally beneficial way to combine exercise with learning. By 1899 there were fifteen science faculty divided among six different departments, plus the elderly Elisabeth Bardwell, whose duties were reduced to directing the observatory; the female physician who taught physiology courses; and one man, Mr. Kinny, the gardener at the botanical garden, who taught floriculture. Faculty members now taught only in one department and the size of those departments had grown. Chemistry took the lead with four faculty, while Physics and Zoology had three each, and Botany two. Taken together, however, the biological sciences were the most prominently represented. By the turn of the century, Mount Holyoke could boast a more impressive array of science faculty than Smith, Amherst, Williams, or even Wellesley.

Although during this decade there were no official degree requirements for hiring college faculty, Mount Holyoke pushed its faculty to become specialists by returning to school for degrees. And, like other competitive colleges and universities of the period, senior faculty and administrators showed a growing preference for applicants whose academic credentials at least equaled the ones being awarded to their students. For these women whose careers spanned the shift from seminary to college, returning to school could mean simply additional study during the summer, as Elisabeth Bardwell did at Dartmouth College in the 1870s, or a combination of such study with a master's degree, as was the case with Louise Cowles. She earned an M.A. from Smith College in 1892. This had been preceded by a year divided between the Worcester Institute of Technology and MIT from 1880–1881, and followed by summer school courses at Cornell University (1894) and Amherst College (1895). Another variant was gaining a college degree to replace their seminary certificates, as Clapp and another Shattuck protégée, Henrietta Hooker, did, and then going on to get doctorates. Both also did postdoctoral study in Europe—but they were unusual in this partly because of finances and partly because opportunities for women to do advanced research were difficult to obtain and their benefits to college faculty unclear. In 1898 Clapp took advantage of fellowships for women from the newly formed Naples Table Association for Promoting Laboratory Research by Women to support a summer's study at the famed biological station in Italy, following in the footsteps of Samuel Clarke at Williams and of Whitman himself but also competing with women from the colleges for a place.[50] Only after 1900, under Mary Woolley's presidency, were doctorates required for faculty.

New and younger faculty hired in the 1890s came with at least a college degree, however. Thus, in 1899 Mount Holyoke's science roster listed two members with Ph.D.'s (Cornelia Clapp and Henrietta Hooker), one with a master of science degree (Anne Young), three with B.S. degrees (Nellie Goldthwaite, Mary Frances Leach, Marcia Anna Keith), and five with A.B.'s (Louise Wallace, Mary E. Holmes, Seraph Bliss, Vernette Gibbons, Susan Leiter). Only two listed in the 1899–1900 catalogue, Effie Read, an assistant in zoology, and Grace Baker, a teacher of botany, had no degrees listed after their names, but they were not full-fledged teachers. Thus, faculty claims to be specialists were not in actuality wholly dependent on the level of the degree one held, and the college recognized this situation by retaining the title of "teacher" rather than designating them as "professors." President Mead made it clear in the 1895–1896 Report of the President, however, that the college's reputation depended on making higher degrees a requirement:

> Our success as a college seems now to be absolutely dependent upon our ability to call teachers properly qualified for the position of heads of departments. The inability to do this makes the situation embarrassing.[51]

She was clearly anxious that the college's need for qualified faculty made it vulnerable in an academic market place where salary was now an incentive.

Mead's remarks point to the fact that real salaries at Mount Holyoke did not rise much in this decade. In ridding the institution of evangelical culture, they did away with outmoded fiscal arrangements but not with ideals of economizing. As the trustees eliminated the practice of faculty tithing that had helped maintain the old seminary by returning a certain percentage of teachers' salaries to the treasury in the manner of church members, teachers had to assume some of the costs of room and board.[52] Low salaries, coupled with heavy teaching duties, may have discouraged non–Mount Holyoke graduates from accepting jobs there, and if they did come, they were not inclined to stay. Thus, Nellie Goldthwaite, for example, had only a B.S. from the University of Michigan in 1894 when she was hired to head the Chemistry Department during the later 1890s. When she had the opportunity to pursue a doctorate in 1905, she left Mount Holyoke and did not return, preferring a career in research elsewhere. In contrast, Abby Turner, who graduated from Mount Holyoke in 1896, was hired as an assistant in zoology just after graduation. She later took a leave to earn a doctorate when this became a requirement for faculty, but returned to eventually head the Physiology Department formed especially for her.[53]

Faculty members also appreciated the benefits of membership in professional societies and organizations. They joined the American Association for the Advancement of Science (AAAS), as well as more specialized societies in their own fields such as the American Chemical Society, where they could hear and present papers on the latest research, meet colleagues, and find new ideas to take back to their students. Among them, Cornelia Clapp undoubtedly held the most influential professional position outside the college. Clapp became a member of the teaching faculty when the MBL opened, even before she had received either her bachelor of philosophy or her doctorate, and was elected the only woman trustee of the new MBL. However, she did not become a member of the American Society of Naturalists, which Samuel Clarke founded in 1883, even after she had earned the doctorate they seemed to require of their women members. Her preference was for male-dominated organizations that allowed her to take an active role that would benefit Mount Holyoke. For this reason, coupled with the unpleasant attacks on Mount Holyoke from women in the new women's colleges in the 1880s, she did not work to form organizations solely with women from other colleges, although she shrewdly recognized that the Naples Table Association was useful to her and participated in its meetings.[54]

The impulses that led the faculty members to specialize were complex, but clearly money was not much of an incentive, although there were salary differentials based on seniority. Moreover, if they gained credentials and new knowledge, it was not out of a wholehearted subscription to the cult of research either. None of the women in the science departments during this period did much research, even those who attained their doctorates, nor did they publish a great deal. In this behavior they were not unlike their male colleagues at other institutions. Outside of Johns Hopkins University, American universities and colleges tended to emphasize research only in relationship to teaching. Moreover, teaching, setting up new laboratories, and creating specialized courses—all required for the inauguration of this new professional science culture—took up large amounts of time and energy. In this context, the rewards for their efforts were in the new kinds of symbiotic relationships they began to establish with men outside the colleges and the new forms of status they won for themselves: Specialization and organization of their departments had helped make them members of a professional group, and it enhanced the stature of their own college in the eyes of potential students as well as of the employers, graduate and professional schools, and laboratories these students would later approach.

Faculty efforts to promote specialization raised their stature as teachers in other ways as well. It justified their placing all their energies into teaching-related activities. The administration and trustees supported them in this by making a number of changes in the wider culture of Mount Holyoke during the 1890s that dismantled the remaining structures of the old family life. The result was that faculty were relieved of other duties and left free to create a distinctive female scientific subculture within the college. This subculture distinguished science faculty and students from other women on campus, even as it forged a cultural bridge between them and male scientists in the professionalizing world of scientific specialists organizing beyond Mount Holyoke's walls.

The final breakup of family life and the unified, religiously based community it promoted can be charted in the enactment of four reforms that freed up life on campus. First, the domestic system was entirely abandoned so that students and faculty no longer had to spend part of their time doing chores related to the maintenance of the campus. Reducing the claims of the domestic system on student and faculty energies signified that physical labor was no longer esteemed as a virtuous way to bring the body into a state of physiological equilibrium with nature. Second, after 1896 students and faculty no longer lived together under one roof.

Third, the administration eliminated the self-reporting system that had placed students under the close moral observation of the teachers. Other rules that constrained the women's behavior were also abandoned. These included bans on material display, secular music, and even eating processed food—all outlawed in the old seminary to ensure adherence to a religiously defined code of nature. Finally, the study of religion was separated from other courses in the curriculum, so that it became an intellectual subject taken for credit, just like any other course. Moreover, the practice of religion had shrunk to the communal rituals of morning prayer in the college chapel and Sunday services in the town church. Religion remained a required subject for all students, but in the secularized form of "Biblical History," separated from nature study and from courses in other departments, including the sciences.[55]

If these reforms freed up life on campus, the administration introduced others that reconfigured it into a system of subcommunities offering individuals a variety of structured choices. Such choices gave them the opportunity to reorganize themselves along the more modern lines of their common specialized interests. First, the administration inaugurated a new system of separate dormitories housing students and faculty in smaller groups. Although President Mead proposed the plan for this new living arrangement when she came into office, the opportunity to implement it came when the old seminary building burned to the ground in 1896. As Helen Horowitz has described the rationale behind this more intimate living arrangement, the women's colleges favored this smaller scale as psychologically and physically healthier. President Seelye of Smith College, for example, argued against housing women students under one roof in order to "prevent the great harm of the seminary—the creation of a separate women's culture with its dangerous emotional attachments, its visionary schemes, and its strong-minded stance to the world."[56] Ever sensitive in these years to the image Mount Holyoke presented to the world, President Mead avoided being defensive about her college's seminary roots and chose to emphasize that smaller housing units were a practical measure against the spread of disease on campus.[57] Even if the students were not housed according to their academic specialties, these new dormitories did introduce the experience of living in smaller, independent groupings.

Other reforms encouraged faculty and students to focus their attention on their particular specialties. One extremely important reform in this respect was the new division of labor on campus that replaced the old domestic system. Organized on a hierarchical principle with teaching at the top, it was specifically intended to privilege the teachers' efforts to specialize, and it freed students as well to do the same. In a spirit completely at odds with Lyon's ethos, President Mead argued in 1893 that assigning the faculty domestic duties would be an unconscionable drag on a professional lifestyle: "We cannot ask Teachers who must have time for study and recreation to give an hour a day to domestic cares."[58] Instead of students and faculty, matrons were hired to supervise the upkeep of each dormitory and women from the town did the cooking and the dishes. Henceforward, science faculty would have a moral claim to be judged on the basis of their specialized work and a moral right to expect a living environment that made work comfortable.

When the requirement that all students select a major is also considered in light of this division of labor, then students and faculty were, as Mead's words indicate, morally constrained at this time to pursue their education, teaching, and organized leisure within the confines of a specialty. As a result, the science teachers as well as others were set in a professionally defined system of stratified, value-laden work that defined their personal development in terms of the degree of intellectual specialization they had attained.[59]

Science constituted the most specialized professional option on campus, and it is not surprising that it drew the greatest number of faculty and students. Other, nonscience, departments also developed structured courses of study; however, their stated career goals were limited to providing prospective teachers with knowledge about special fields of study such as history, but not with research skills or preprofessional or graduate preparation per se. Contrary to the sciences, these departments pursued the ideal of liberal education, which Laurence Veysey has shown became a popular solution to the identity crises faced by men's colleges of the period.[60] In fact, controversial Darwinian ideas were isolated in the curriculum of the biology departments, whose students were a self-selected minority. Instead, all students were required to take the less theologically problematic science courses in "Introductory Chemistry" and "Physics" as part of the freshman foundation courses that Mead felt were designed to develop character.[61]

Even leisure time on campus, something that had not even been thinkable in the old seminary, offered science faculty an additional opportunity to encourage specialization as a form of self-improving leisure. The appearance of an extracurriculum on college campuses in the 1890s allowed students to chose how to spend their free time in activities established through student initiative. At Mount Holyoke these activities had their utilitarian possibilities. While choices included secret societies, Greek letter sororities, and Glee Club and Banjo Club (formed in 1894), students could also build a social life with like-minded people in more professionally oriented groups. In marked contrast to the Banjo Club, whose members dressed in fancy white gowns to sing and play popular songs for the annual campus show, the Biology Club (founded in 1892) served as a place where students could report on their independent research, hear faculty and visitors lecture, and generally meet on a more informal basis.[62]

The addition of new or expanded scientific facilities for teaching and laboratory work offered faculty and students who chose to specialize in this area
their own distinctive physical spaces in which to congregate. Of the five
buildings used for teaching, three were partially or entirely devoted to science, including the new Lydia Shattuck Hall (1896) housing the Physics and
Chemistry departments. Shattuck Hall boasted a private study and laboratory for the professor. Botany faculty members and students now had new
plant houses, an arboretum, and a botanical garden for their use.

These spaces thus had distinctive features that made specializing in science different from doing so in any other field. Sociologists of science Bruno
Latour and Steve Woolgar have coined an apt phrase to describe the culture
that characterizes scientific activity: laboratory life.[63] Their point is that science not only means research, but an entire set of personal interactions, hierarchical arrangements, values, methods, and materials that constitute a particular culture and produce certain personality types. We do not have written
descriptions about what work in the laboratories was like at Mount Holyoke
during this decade; however, a number of photographs and course descriptions provide a clue. Not only did laboratory work differ from work in other
special departments such as history because students worked with physical
matter—plants, animals, minerals, and fossils—but it required them to ma-
nipulate a whole range of equipment, and to use precise technical methods
for producing standardized results. Students in the science labs used their
hands as they weighed and measured, analyzed and dissected. They recorded
their observations in the language of formulas and drawings, as much as in
words.

These ways of thinking and doing were carried out in social spaces quite
different from those of the history or English classrooms. The laboratories
were large rooms fitted with tables and sinks, but they were not neutral
spaces. Just the nature of the work required that faculty and students move
about and consult one another. Cornelia Clapp sacralized the space of her
lab by posting a plaque with Louis Agassiz's famous dictum on the wall, recalling Penikese and imitating the MBL where Agassiz's original plaque now
hung. Students, teachers, and laboratory assistants interacted with one another in less formally structured ways than their counterparts in the humanities who relied on the lecture–recitation format. As the photograph of
Cornelia Clapp in her lab with several students suggests, their messy work
required them to dress differently from their fellows for class. Aprons and
simple clothing were a practical necessity that became a sign of their particular specialty. We cannot glean anything about the division of labor within

the laboratories from these photos, although the catalogues make it clear that the laboratory classes were staffed by both assistants and teachers. Moreover, students and faculty spent a great deal more time in these spaces than did other faculty in their classrooms, simply because the equipment they both needed for their work was in these rooms. For zoology at least, the cultural life of the lab extended into and was reinforced by the exchange of information on the latest research that went on in the Biology Club.

The scientific subculture associated with laboratory life in many ways suggests an extension and revision of the old seminary family. It was after all marked by a cooperative spirit, shared values, and idealistic goals; however, its goals were no longer personal salvation by achieving a spiritual union with God through subordination to nature. Instead, it was personal development through the pursuit of specialized knowledge about the natural world. In place of the Mount Holyoke ideal of the self-denying woman who tried to subordinate herself to a design laid out by others, and accepted her own biology as the basis for defining her social work, there developed another for whom nature was something to be dominated: the woman of science.

The changed institution in fact opened possibilities for women beyond its walls as higher education, industry, and government expanded demand for trained personnel that extended into the next century—sometimes in spite of the school's own interests. Leach's efforts to upgrade her own training eventually led her away from Mount Holyoke: She left for further study in Europe at the University of Göttingen in 1897–1898, and at the Polytechnic of Zurich in 1898–1900. She then gave up her appointment at Mount Holyoke, earned a Ph.D. at the University of Michigan in 1903, worked as a research assistant there for a year after taking her degree, and published at least one scholarly paper.[64] From 1907 to 1923 she returned to the circle of Mount Holyoke, but not the mother institution, spending the rest of her career as a professor of chemistry and hygiene at Western College for Women. The college's policy of hiring faculty members with B.S. degrees and expecting them to work on doctorates during summers and leaves of absence, intended to raise the quality of its own faculty, thus could work to individual rather than institutional advantage in an expanding market. As already mentioned, Leach's successor at Mount Holyoke, Nellie Goldthwaite, also a protégée of Lydia Shattuck, took a job at Mount Holyoke in 1897 with a B.S. from Michigan in 1894. By continuing her own studies during summers she earned a Ph.D. from the University of Chicago in 1904 and continued to teach at Mount Holyoke until 1905. She resigned when she decided she wanted to conduct research in home economics, which was apparently not acceptable at Mount Holyoke.[65]

In addition to Leach and Goldthwaite, the college hired five women as assistants in chemistry, mostly fresh college graduates. Of the total of seven women who started work at Mount Holyoke in the 1890s, five earned doctorates later in their career, one earned a master's degree, and one went on to a career as a missionary. Three of these women made careers teaching at other colleges and three others spent significant parts of their careers in industry or at agricultural experiment stations.

Toward a New Configuration of Gendered Science

If one were to put it in biological terms, by 1900 the new generation of Mount Holyoke science faculty belonged to a distinct subspecies of educated women by virtue of their specialized focus and the advantages it gave them in a scientific enterprise that transcended institutional walls. No wonder Whitman's version of Darwinian evolutionary theory had such broad appeal to them. It offered more than a metaphorical image of the process of development through which they and the organisms some of them studied had passed—it validated the differentiation this process had produced between them and other faculty in the college as the working world of male and female science faculty began to take on a more bureaucratic shape that cut across institution-based communities. They had achieved an advantageous position in the new institutional ecology whose structures and functional relationships they helped lay down by 1900.

Margaret Rossiter has described the years from 1888 to 1900 as full of openings and blockages for American women wishing to engage in science—whether in research, employment, or educational opportunities in university graduate schools and medical schools.[66] Rightly so, Rossiter's position is that women should have been able to do what they wanted to do without restrictions placed on them by men because of their sex. The example of Mount Holyoke science faculty in these years suggests that women in science cannot be conceived as a unified social group, however. These women did not think of themselves in terms of such solidarity because institutional loyalties and personal ambitions came into play. In fact, Mount Holyoke women's aspirations as scientists separated them from women at the other colleges—and in great part intentionally. Despite the fact that religious belief, credentials, and evangelical lifestyle lost their intensity in these years at Mount Holyoke, the religious culture of the old seminary remained a factor in shaping the way Mount Holyoke faculty members perceived their situation, gained an advantage for Mount Holyoke through participation in the process of

specialization and organization, and integrated themselves into the more bureaucratized community of academic science with the assistance of men.

There is no evidence that faculty members such as Clapp felt blocked in
attaining their goal of establishing Mount Holyoke's leadership among the
colleges on a scientific basis. Quite the contrary, the virtue of identifying
one's own stature with that of collegiate status in these years meant that the
teachers avoided the frustrations faced by women who aspired to be university professors. They, like Lyon, accepted the circumstances of this world as
less than perfect and sought to reform them through institutional means.
Their vision, like hers, focused on the general situation and on how Mount
Holyoke teachers might improve their position by joining with men at other
institutions in rectifying the disorder and stress that interfered with the work
at hand. This was quite a different strategy from that of women who formed
separate organizations and raised scholarship and endowment funds to buy
individual women places in graduate programs and research laboratories—
although as in the case of Clapp and the Naples Table Association, they
could use the organizations' support for their own purposes.

There is no sign that Mount Holyoke science faculty members showed
much interest in the growing feminist movement, and for obvious reasons.[67]
They saw their advantage lay in making common cause with men for a goal
that seemed above politics, rather than in calling attention to themselves and
their special circumstances. It was also a strategy that gave them an advantage over faculty members at other women's colleges, especially when the
consequences of Clapp's friendships with men she had known since Penikese
are taken into consideration. Her willingness not only to accept Whitman's
grand scheme, but also to work to implement it, gave her authority and influence in the scientific establishment that other women lacked. His wish to
award her these advantages ultimately came from his conviction that she
could help him achieve his goal because they shared a common vision of a
world led by a certified scientific moral elite and because they both had institutions they could use for this cause. And Clapp made clear her commitment to this ungendered professional ideal rather than to the interests of all
women—or even all women in science—when she sanctioned the move at
the MBL to eliminate amateurs (most of whom were women) from its ranks.
This was a move that benefited her and Mount Holyoke in a variety of ways.
It is difficult to see how men blocked Clapp and the other senior teachers in
any way from attaining the credentials, the positions, and the authority they
desired in these years.

We can see traces of the old helpmate tradition in Clapp's relationships
with Whitman and other men at the MBL during these years. However, the

coeducational character of the setting and the advent of research institutes and universities awarding doctorates had broken down the old divisions of labor between men and women teachers and made women and men on college faculties more equivalent by putting them under a new institutional umbrella. In these circumstances, Mount Holyoke faculty members found themselves competing with male college faculty members to appear equally competent and with women college faculty members to appear more competent. As they earned advanced degrees to divest themselves of their dependency on college men to give courses of lectures, they also worked to identify themselves and their curriculum with male scientists at universities in order to best their rivals in the women's colleges. One of their tactics in this struggle on two fronts was to try to gain control over conduits to certain types of jobs and advanced training opportunities for their students. The consequences of their efforts allow us to understand how Mount Holyoke teachers contributed to the making of the professional scientific world in this decade, rather than sitting at its fringes trying to get in.

One consequence of this effort was to contribute to the creation of women's work in science. Rossiter and others have noted with well-founded dismay that in the post-Civil War period certain trends began to mark the role women played within American science.[68] Such work was heavily weighted towards the empirical and the technical. The explanation for this situation has been that it was imposed on women by men who took research and theory for themselves and allocated the supportive, less intellectually challenging roles to women, as in the computing positions at the Harvard Observatory that the astronomer Edward Pickering filled with women.[69] The example of Mount Holyoke faculty indicates that at least in their case women faculty members took some responsibility for this situation by designating the jobs their graduates would perform in science and defining the job requirements, including the more technical ones. As in the case of Lyon, who saw the opportunities that feminizing teaching offered her in a country in need of teachers, Clapp's descriptions of her program in the catalogue reveal a similar perspicacity.

To some extent, the question of whether these jobs were intended by men for women or women claimed them is a problem of the chicken and the egg. However, there is no doubt that the strong emphasis on laboratory work combined with the custom of paying attention to detail and perfecting the execution of tasks would have fitted Mount Holyoke students very well for jobs that required such skills. On the other hand, when these positions first came open, the duties were not well defined and men often performed them. A better explanation, given Clapp's position at the MBL and her own pointed

references to employment in the catalogues, is that she helped professionalize these jobs in terms she made certain prospective employers knew her
graduates in particular could meet. Rather than suggest there was a sense of
irony at work when she transformed skills faculty had once deemed suitable
for men—that is, the manipulation of equipment—into women's skills, her
actions reveal her shrewdness in making a synthesis of skills and standards
already part of the Mount Holyoke tradition.

The other significant consequence of science faculty members' actions
was that they set the precedent for an identity filled with ambiguity about
what it meant to be a woman scientist in a college. Just as Lyon had used
evangelical assumptions of intellectual equality to claim the male college
model for her seminary teachers to emulate in educating women, the science
faculty at the college adopted the standards, organizational structures, and
status symbols of men in the universities for their own, based on the same
assumption. However, as has been discussed, unlike their predecessors, they
possessed the same credentials in many cases as their male counterparts.
Clapp in particular may not have engaged in much research during these
years, but she and President Mead recognized its importance and made it a
cornerstone in establishing their status and the status of Mount Holyoke in
the eyes of men who mattered. If they made a clear division between themselves and university graduate and professional school faculty on the basis of
differences in their curricula, degrees awarded, and to some extent in the career paths men and women students were being prepared to follow, they
blurred the distinctions between their own status and that of university men
in an important way. They established the custom of mimicking the university men who had willingly trained them in terms of respect for credentials,
research, laboratory work, and empire building as means to their own advancement. In the expansive decades after the turn of the century, a new generation of science faculty with the support of President Mary Woolley
would fully exploit the possibilities this identity offered in the way of professional advancement for women in male-dominated fields both within and
outside the college. But as the old egalitarian strains of evangelical culture
faded with the advent of competition and coeducation, the character of that
identity became increasingly associated in the public's mind with a peculiar
twisting of female traits into masculine behavior. This perception would
cause them difficulties and eventually bring their vision to a crises. The history of this period and the denouement of their tradition are the subject of
the next chapter.

chapter 5

Apogee and Defeat of the Female Science Mission (1901–1937)

Mary Woolley: More than Complementary Equals

Mary Woolley's inaugural address as president of Mount Holyoke College in 1901 was both audacious and conservative. Seated on the dias with the male presidents of Amherst and Brown, and the female presidents of Bryn Mawr and Wellesley, she affirmed the tradition of complementarity at the college, but gave it a new, more aggressively detailed feminist twist. At a time when coeducation was on the rise, she claimed new ground for the school in educating women intellectually, professionally, and socially. Her words regarding science reiterated the long-standing belief in women's intellectual and educational equality with men, but added that women's natures encompassed the qualities possessed by men and then some. In a period of American higher education that saw the rise of the research university with its commitment to graduate education and the culture of rationalism, Woolley advocated that the women's colleges emphasize research to produce women who "think," "who create as well as absorb." In an era that saw the beginnings of the scientific study of sexuality, she proposed that women were not only as capable of rational thought and invention as men, but they made better scientists. Woman's gift of "intuition," the new President elaborated, and "the genius for detail, accuracy, and perseverance wrought into her nature by generations of training in her home province, especially fit her for scientific and historical research. . . ." All this was sketched out, along with a continuing emphasis on college education as "preparation for service in the broadest interpretation of that term."[1]

Taking Woolley's words as their cue, for the next thirty years, science faculty made their departments sites for the successful education of more women who went on to get advanced university degrees in science and mathematics than any other undergraduate institution, single-sex or coeducational.[2] They would also educate a large number of women who worked at jobs which drew on their science training. They themselves almost uniformly held doctorates. Yet, the value system established by the department heads under Woolley's aegis gave a certain feminist direction—closely associated with professional goals—to the tradition Lyon had established. Still committed to the ideal of the unmarried woman professional, the culture that evolved, while successful by many measures, was neither unflawed nor impregnable. By the 1930s the stratification of scientific work, the poor economy with pressures to hire men over women, and strengthened social pressures on women to marry made that value system obsolete.

It is worth taking a closer look at Mary Woolley's inaugural address, for she not only engaged the subject of defining women's intellectual abilities, but defined the areas on which she felt the college should focus its educational energies. In both cases, she seemed to extend the scope for women in science, but also opened the door to new problems they would face. Intellectually, she assumed that the world of nature that scientists endeavored to know was in some sense neutral or at least as accessible to women as to men. In fact, she argued that women had at their disposal ways of doing science that might reap more and better knowledge than men. In so doing she went to the heart of the scientific endeavor—what can we know and how can we know it? To this she added an implied challenge: Who can know it best? Intuition and attention to detail were talents women possessed that could be used to increase scientific knowledge. In part Woolley considered these talents inherited traits specific to the female sex; in part they were fostered by the domestic environment that had been women's traditional place. Woolley, like Lyon well over a half-century earlier, leveraged women's authority with the weight of their skills at detail. But she surpassed Lyon with a brilliant tour de force. Taking what in her time were commonly considered female traits that weakened women's claim to intellectual equality with men, Woolley turned the tables, making them into virtues that would allow women to surpass men in scientific endeavors. What she did not foresee was that these characteristics would eventually prove problematic.

Her interest and that of her listeners in the subject of women's mental traits (as they were termed at the turn of the century) was no doubt stoked by current discussions in scientific and educational circles about women's abilities. Not only were psychologists such as G. Stanley Hall writing on the subject to the detriment of women, but earlier the work of Charles Darwin and the writings of the American physician Edward Clark had helped fuel arguments against women's mental equality with men.[3] Refuting these claims was a young woman psychologist Helen Thompson Woolley (then Thompson) who had done work establishing the intellectual equality of the sexes. Thompson, soon to join the Mount Holyoke faculty, in fact provided a study based on testing of male and female students at the University of Chicago that showed there was little if no difference in general ability between the sexes.[4]

Mary Woolley's social vision for the school took for granted that Mount Holyoke was equal to men's colleges in its faculty, its intellectual caliber, and its ability to educate students for service. She did, however, put science toward the end of her talk, after teaching, social work and motherhood. Perhaps simply reiterating the founding tradition of accommodating a range of ranked possibilities for contemporary women, she introduced the idea that Mount Holyoke College now was interested in providing an education that would also prepare women for this highest professional role, as well as for the others. Not only did she continue the tradition of educating women to go on to work in the world at careers open to them—which now added scientific positions to teaching—but she opened the doors of the school to women whose main objective would be marriage and motherhood rather than missionary teaching as their major form of service to society. It was a vision that would appeal to a broader range of young women wishing to go to college. It was certainly true that under her aegis the school became more religiously diverse, drawing Episcopalians, Catholics, and making efforts to include Jews, as well as foreign students into the ranks of the student body. Racial diversity was another matter. The college only grudgingly tolerated African Americans—in some cases admitted before their race was known to officials.[5] Moreover, the numbers of students who married increased and the time span in which they did so after graduation decreased during the later years of her tenure.[6]

The science professors generally shared Woolley's views on science, but their understanding of it was of course much more detailed, drawn as it was from the point of view of scientific practitioners. They saw the world of nature as a harmonious whole that the scientist aspired to understand through the use of reason. Professor Abby Turner, who headed the Physiology Department, put both an evolutionary and an evangelical moral spin on the value of her science. Physiology filled two needs, she wrote in her 1940 article summarizing current trends in this scientific field: Its study enabled people to achieve an "agreeable adaptation of the conditions of life" and it helped them in their "search after a harmonious idea of life and the world."[7] Identifying its study with the early efforts of Edward Hitchcock to teach hygiene at the school through the use of a mannequin, she fleshed out Woolley's suppositions by presenting a picture of nature that was as gendered as his.

The biological sciences are of course the place where one will find the most elaborated vision of nature infused with gendered images. Professor Ann Haven Morgan felt nature was filled with "vitality," a force that connected all living things. James Needham affirmed Morgan's views in his forward to her book *Field Book of Ponds and Streams*, published in 1930: "All are born to feed and grow and reproduce, to hunt and be hunted, to strive for a livelihood; and in so doing to fill a place in the household of nature." While he was speaking here of aquatic life, his words were equally applicable to her general views on the study of ecology, the science of living systems.[8] There was competition in the world, but it was mitigated in a vision in which most survived in a system she characterized as vastly varied, yet interconnected through an arrangement of supportive economic and social domestic relationships.

There was no doubt in the minds of science professors that women had the mental ability to study this vast structure, or that women were intellectual equals of men in this endeavor. Where they stood on those special characteristics that Woolley had identified is discussed in this chapter. As they grappled with the realities of the job market for women in science, it became clear that what their president claimed were virtues that would add to scientific knowledge could also be taken as limitations on women's abilities to do science and to teach it at the highest levels. It is in fact in the teachers' social vision of science and of the role of the college in educating women in science that we may begin to sense some of the contradictions that the professors of science met as they sought to prepare women for service in the broader world.

What was their social vision? They saw the school as preparing three categories of women: those who would not be scientists and who needed a general education in science; those who would work in science at lower levels such as technicians and primary and secondary school teachers; and those who would do research and teach at the college or university level like themselves. This last group comprised an intellectual elite who would grapple with the study of nature alongside men. Implicit in their categorization, however, was the idea that women were not only segregated in the scientific work force, they were ranked. Hence, also implicit was the idea that students who married would fall into the first of these three categories. Even if they prepared for the other two, as soon as they married it was expected that they would probably not work. The school's policy of taking alumnae off the roles of the placement office when they married in fact reinforced this attitude.

Socially, for all three groups some general knowledge of the sciences was deemed necessary by the professors. In addition, they felt that the study of science was beneficial to the family and participated in activities directed at the social applications of science. Ann Morgan, for example, participated in a conference organized by the American Social Hygiene Association focusing on education for marriage and social relations. There she was asked to share her outline of "class and laboratory studies of sex, of animal and human social relationships, as given in our course in General Zoology."[9]

In sum, the vision of Woolley and the professors in science entertained an expanding society of opportunities where women in science would take their place and make their contributions alongside men. The departments were the training grounds in which these ambiguities and contradictions were played out by 1937. The family was the psychological and cultural context for the dissemination of these values.

The Departmental Structures

The new primacy of the departments during Mary Woolley's administration is apparent in the celebration of the seventy-fifth anniversary, just twelve years after she took office. In the pageantry that year, faculty and students dramatized the distinctiveness of the individual discipline. Not only did they present themselves by department, but Cornelia Clapp had the Zoology Department students present a tableau of costumed fruit flies under the tutelage of the great geneticist Gregor Mendel, while the Geology Department students were also appropriately dressed. The humorous nature of this conception suggests a certain comfort and pride in belonging to a group with a special identity. The photograph that documents the celebration suggests faculty and students consciously wished to define themselves by associating with a broader, male-dominated scientific tradition, and even with contemporary scientific discoveries, rather than with the history of the school.[10] Within the context of departmental structures the sciences grew rapidly during the Woolley years. The number of departments increased. In 1900 there were seven and in 1930 there were eight. In 1900 there were eleven faculty members with rank of instructor or above. In 1930 there were thirty-six.

The largest departments were Chemistry, Zoology, and Botany, with three faculty each. In 1930 of the thirty-six faculty members, there were six each in Zoology, Chemistry, and Physics, five in Physiology, and four in Psychology (taught as a laboratory science). Several men were permanent members of the science faculties—one teaching psychology, another in the Physics Department, and later in the 1930s one in the Geology Department.

Course offerings increased along with departmental size. In addition, the college kept pace with other colleges such as Amherst and Smith. In some cases, as in the premedical offerings and in the emphasis on organic chemistry, Mount Holyoke distinguished itself.[11] The practical bent of the school was apparent, as well as its continuing interest in health care, in the premedical course maintained in the curriculum. Smith College had no course of study nor courses listed as premedical until 1925, and only offered introductory-level zoology. Amherst College listed a "Hygiene and Physical Education" course with emphasis on human anatomy and physiology. It included the study of data gathered on male college students. The catalogue declared that the special aim of the Biology Department is to "furnish the student of medicine and biology with a broad foundation for his future studies." Williams College also did not declare a premedical course of studies until 1925.[12]

The faculty grew in numbers so that Mount Holyoke became the third largest employer of women faculty members in science in the country, with twenty-five in 1938 at the professor or assistant professor level.[13] Interestingly, the courses offered in psychology (taught as a laboratory science) put Mount Holyoke, with fifteen, above Vassar, Wellesley, Bryn Mawr, and Amherst, with only Smith offering more.[14] Department budgets grew so that by 1935–1936 the Chemistry Department and Zoology Department respectively had the third and fourth largest budgets in the school with about $3,000 each, coming just after the Speech Department and English Literature and Drama Department. If allotments for the biological sciences departments are added together, then biology comes at the head of the list.[15] The doctorate degree became common and then mandatory for those holding professional ranks.[16] The professors were very proud of theses newly won signs of institutional as well as professional status. However, Ann Morgan wrote to Mary Woolley with a touch of cynicism about women's real professional stature, "More titles should be used. I believe it for our own professional good. I don't expect to turn the tide!"[17]

During the Woolley years independent women anxious to build their separate departments emerged to head the sciences. To some extent they were part of a trend that had begun under Elizabeth Mead and benefited from the efforts of Cornelia Clapp. Some years after Cornelia Clapp's retirement, her Department of Zoology was divided into two parts in 1922, each headed by one of her protégées. Ann Haven Morgan, who received her Ph.D. from Cornell and came to Mount Holyoke in 1906, headed the Zoology Department. Abby Turner, a Mount Holyoke graduate who received her doctorate from Harvard in 1926, chaired the new Department of Physiology. In addition to them, Emma Perry Carr, Mount Holyoke 1901, who did her graduate work at the University of Chicago, took charge of the Chemistry Department, while Mignon Talbot did the same for the Geology Department until 1935. Helen Thompson did groundbreaking doctoral research at the University of Chicago, already mentioned at the beginning of this chapter, and during her short tenure at Mount Holyoke established the research laboratory in psychology in the early years of the century. Ellen Talbot, who received her Ph.D. from Yale, headed the Philosophy and Psychology Department during the teens and twenties, when it grew to have a large mental testing research program. Botany had Alma Stokey. Less prominent in terms of funding and numbers of students were the departments of Physics (offering a major as of 1905), Mathematics, and Astronomy.[18]

In two cases, men figured importantly in the development of the departments. One was Samuel Hayes in the Philosophy and Psychology Department, who took charge of the psychology offerings, laboratory work, and research after Thompson left. The other was Robert Balk, who came to Mount Holyoke from Hunter College in 1935, replacing Mignon Talbot as chairman of the Geology Department that year. Rogers Rusk in Physics was less dynamic.

Aided by their departments with leaves and funding, faculty also maintained and expanded their networks with the educational world. On an institutional level, links were made to increasing numbers of universities as these became the centers for graduate education in the United States. Mount Holyoke faculty received advanced degrees from all of the seventeen institutions listed by Margaret Rossiter as granting the doctorate to twenty or more female students during 1938.[19] These included the University of Chicago, the University of Michigan, Ohio State University, the University of Missouri, Johns Hopkins, Harvard, Cornell, and Yale Universities. There were connections with recently formed foundations supporting scientific work, among then the Rockefeller and Carnegie Institutes.

Such networks growing out of the departments were not only institutionally based, but often strongly personal. The science professors continued to do cooperative research with men, but now at places throughout the United States and in Europe. For example, chemistry professor Dorothy Hahn spent the year 1907–1908 at Bryn Mawr working with several men in the Chemistry Department there. Chair of the Physics Department Elizabeth Rebecca Laird had pursued further research at J. J. Thompson's laboratory at Cambridge University in the summer of 1905 and settled on a research topic on x-rays produced by cathode ray tubes. In the 1920s Emma Perry Carr, who established a broadly collaborative research program as chair of the Chemistry Department, carried on extensive correspondence with men in her field and made it her business to spend time in several laboratories abroad to assure she remained engaged in the most advanced work in her field. Cornelia Clapp during her summers at Woods Hole gleaned the latest developments in biology from social interactions and course work offered there. In the summer of 1912 she wrote Jordan that the "investigators are putting up houses, and making plans for summering here: Among them E. B. Wilson, Calkins and Morgan of Columbia; Loeb, of Rockefeller Institute, and Lillie and Conklin of Chicago." She might have added that students and faculty from Smith, Williams, Johns Hopkins, and Amherst were also there.[20]

Cornelia Clapp until her retirement in 1915 and even afterward continued to ask advice and favors from David Starr Jordan on a variety of matters. In 1903 she wrote him for assistance in finding women candidates for the scholarship offered by the Association for Maintaining the American Women's Table at the Zoological Stations at Naples and for Promoting Scientific Research by Women. Jordan spoke at the college in 1907 about Louis Agassiz and also gave a moving address in chapel the next day.[21] In 1912 as preparations for the seventy-fifth anniversary celebration drew near, Clapp wrote to Jordan, perhaps at the request of Mary Woolley, who shared Jordan's enthusiasm for the world peace movement, asking for his help in publicizing the celebration in West Coast newspapers. Her concern, as she wrote, was to disabuse people of "Various false or inadequate notions . . . more or less prevalent in regard to the college. In some quarters even our right to be called a college is questioned, although for more than twenty years we have had a college charter."[22] She also arranged for him to speak at Woods Hole on the occasion of the fiftieth anniversary celebration of the Penikese Island school.[23] Emma Perry Carr corresponded with Professor Victor Henri of the University of Zurich, in whose laboratory she had worked during the spring of 1925 and again during 1929–1930. Less prominent faculty were also engaged in these readjusted relationships with male scientists, now at universities and research institutes rather than long-term visitors to Mount Holyoke. Hazeltine Stedman, a lecturer in physiology in the early decades of the twentieth century, worked with Francis G. Benedict, pursuing research and teaching on women's metabolism, which complemented his own research on men. In some cases she used apparatus perhaps designed by Professor Abby Turner, head of her department, and also actively collected information on women's physiology based on studies of Mount Holyoke students.

While Hahn and Clapp went to learn from these men, it could work the other way. In the case of Abby Turner, who worked with Cecil Drinker of the School of Public Health at Harvard, Drinker was anxious to have information about her work in physiology.[24] In addition, the faculty presented lectures at meetings and on other campuses. Ann Morgan gave three lectures at the Massachusetts Agricultural College during one year.[25]

Students also reinforced and even helped expand these networks. In 1933–1934 the fifth annual Student Science Conference was held at Smith College. Six hundred people registered at this event, at which Janet Wilder from Mount Holyoke presented a paper on the anatomy of water beetles.[26] Students also helped the school reach into the emerging areas of government and industrial employment. It is important to point out several trends here. In counting there were at least 233 different institutions with which graduates were associated through advanced work or through employment between 1901 and 1940. Those in zoology continued to spend summers at the MBL, taking courses and meeting students from other schools as well as the major figures of the period in United States biology. Graduates went on for advanced degrees at the same schools their professors had attended and added others to the list. Many of these were employed at universities, colleges, medical schools, and hospitals. They also held jobs at research laboratories such as Cold Spring Harbor where they worked doing field surveys for the eugenics studies of Charles Davenport.[27] One graduate worked at the Tennessee Experiment Station, and others at the Mellon Institute and at the National Bureau of Standards. Graduates in chemistry often secured jobs in industry. Such was the case of Elizabeth Stokes Matlock ('35) who worked as a research assistant testing white pigments for the DuPont Company.[28] A large number of graduates still went into teaching in public and private school, primarily in the Northeast. While many of them taught general subjects, a number taught in their specialties of math, biology, and chemistry as American secondary education was increasingly divided into specialized subjects. A few even kept ties with foreign missionary-based schools strong. For example, Edith Marion Coon ('13) went to teach at Madras College in India, while Ida B. Scudder ('25) worked for thirty-six years at the Women's Union Medical Missionary College, Vellore, India, founded by her aunt, where she developed the Radiology Department.[29]

Thus, this web of relationships between the college and the outside world became more complex, extensive, and varied during the years of Mary Woolley's tenure. To some extent these new and expanded networks represent the integration of Mount Holyoke into the expanding and diversifying system of scientific elites characterized by an interrelationship of colleges, universities, research centers, governments, and industry—it would seem Mount Holyoke fit right in at the highest levels of collegiate-based science. The question is whether this new situation structured a more egalitarian intellectual relationship between men and women.

It is true that this web of relationships was of a different character than what had gone before. On the surface it was more professionalized. The alumnae and faculty files in the Mount Holyoke archives from these years are filled with the apparatus of professionalism. There are placement bureau forms, evaluations, and letters of support, as well as correspondence between former students and Helen Voorhees, the indefatigable and ever vigilant head of the placement office. Evaluations of students and letters of recommendation from faculty members and employers chart virtues and flaws in personality and abilities in and outside of jobs, promotion, and further education sought, won, and sometimes lost or curtailed.

In terms of departmental organization and structure, we have on the surface a picture of greater equality with men. Relationships with men had changed somewhat. Within the departments, female professors were no longer dependent on men. They now had full charge of lecturing as well as recitations. Each department had fully equipped laboratories. Teachers used texts, a few of which they had written themselves. Among these were the laboratory manual written by Ann Haven Morgan.[30] In addition, they ran research laboratories and engaged students in their research. Moreover, it was now the rule that those with professorial appointments had credentials equivalent to those of men. A pecking order existed, however, even at this college dominated by women. The departments boasted additional members who held the title of assistant. These were women with no advanced degrees, some of whom were married.

This meant that the hierarchical organization of the departments at Mount Holyoke was somewhat analogous to that at male colleges, but it also mimicked in truncated form that of universities and private industry. Departments had strong chairwomen who set examples as fine teachers and researchers for their faculty and students. There was even a graduate program in zoology and chemistry that granted master's degrees.

New Family Values

The old values transformed and adapted to more professional circumstances created a productive atmosphere in which departments grew and expanded. At the same time, these values tended to constrict possibilities. What were these values? Were they the old ones writ large, or altogether new ones? The ways in which faculty and employers assessed students tells us much about the values faculty shared with the broader world of science to which Mary Woolley had pointed with assurance. Their best students, those whom they hoped would go into college teaching and graduate research, were characterized in terms such as brightness, inquisitiveness, independence in thinking and carrying out research. Of Christianna Smith ('15), a protégée student who became a leading light in the biology department, her teacher Cornelia Clapp wrote, "We expect that she will prove the good teacher that we want, and certainly she has the right qualities for success." Alma Stokey was more specific: "Her work, while not brilliant, was of unusually interesting quality because of her ability and willingness to think for herself. We found her a student of a most desirable type, not only pleasant in manner in class and laboratory but interested and independent in her work. She has a good mind."[31] Of Gladys McCosh ('20), who became a professor of zoology at Wellesley, Ann Morgan wrote: "Miss McCosh is one of our most able students. She is independent, original, full of energy and enthusiasm, and she has an ardent desire to learn to teach. . . . She took the Invertebrate course at Woods Hole in 1919 and was there regarded as one of the most promising members of the class."[32]

Among the important qualities valued for the best students were several having to do with emotional responses to doing science. Enthusiasm, energy, ardent desire, all the old responses associated with religious experience seem to have become identified with commitment of the highest order to science. In view of common distinctions between irrational religion and rational science, it is important to ask whether, in the minds of faculty, these sentiments were associated with the exercise of intuition, that quality that Woolley had enthusiastically endorsed as a gift to be cultivated: the insight into human nature, the sensitiveness to conditions, the ability to "feel" "what one cannot explain by logical processes".[33] Was there, in other words, an approving recognition of the ways in which scientists can use imagination to approach the study of natural phenomena?

There was, interestingly, no specific use of the term "intuition," a mental ability that Woolley had cited as characteristic of women's ways of thinking. Occasionally, however, a professor would laud a student who had a biological way of thinking, perhaps referring to something like the intuitive identification with organisms that Evelyn Fox Keller described in her book *A Feeling for the Organism*, a biography of biologist Barbara McClintock.[34] Certainly, Ann Haven Morgan found a spiritual side to the study of ecology, while Abby Turner's reflections on physiology resonated with the feeling that she experienced a sense of wonder at the existence of a higher moral order when she studied the workings of the human body. Yet the professors rigorously distinguished between the emotional feeling one could have about doing science and the rational nature of the enterprise itself. In so doing they avoided identifying the abilities of the best women students with specifically feminine characteristics as Woolley had done.[35]

The exclusiveness of the school continued, although in the 1920s and 1930s it was slowly being modified to include Jews and Catholics, although not as faculty.[36] As was the case with most private colleges of that period that were not specifically designated as Negro or American Indian, not only were all the best students White and Protestant, but faculty letters reveal a conscientiousness about promoting a Christian ethos. Letters from employers often remarked that the former Mount Holyoke students had good Christian character. The atmosphere at Woods Hole—which was not unique in its socioreligious makeup—was strongly racist in character, as Kenneth Manning has shown in his study of the black biologist E. E. Just.[37] Mount Holyoke, as we have seen, was actively involved in that enterprise. While there are no overtly discriminatory comments from faculty, such as those found earlier concerning Catholic students, the women continued to accept if not openly espouse, along with men in science, an enterprise that was White and Christian. As Cornelia Clapp had written Jordan, Mount Holyoke College was still the seminary writ large. To some extent this approach was evident in the interest they had in course work on heredity. It was also apparent in the biases toward White, Christian, college-educated women used by Abby Turner to set standards for women's metabolic rates.[38]

This attitude of being special and superior was also evident in the course work on heredity. A. Elizabeth Adams not only covered the theories of Darwin and the work of Gregor Mendel in her heredity course, but student notes from the 1923 course listed the possibilities for racial betterment. They noted that "the effect of inbreeding, then, depends entirely on the stock used." Citing Guyer's book *Being Well Born*, the student iterated that the question comes down to "segregation vs. sterilization." She wrote:

> An educated public sentiment [is] [sic] the most valuable eugenic agent.... Education of women in eugenics is especially needed—woman is the deciding factor.... If we are of good stock ourselves we should recognize that it is highly desirable that we give to the race at least four children.... Good traits inherited as well as bad, also a certain capacity for alternative action.[39]

Such biases echoed in the work of Charles Davenport, the influential head of the eugenics movement in the United States, who employed several Mount Holyoke graduates anxious to put their scientific training to "socially useful" work.[40]

Despite these signs of full equality with men in science, the old ideals of an extended family of Christian women assisted by men were alive and well within the departments of science. Although, as we have already seen, relationships with men were now on a more professional basis and men were no longer depended on within the school to provide the broad intellectual framework, the relationships were not necessarily ones based on equality. Cornelia Clapp's correspondence with David Starr Jordan continuously asked for his advice and assistance. While she invited him to speak on various occasions, her invitations were not reciprocated. Dependency on men persisted, although in a new, more professional context. Mignon Talbot noted in her Annual Report of 1922–1923 that Miss Cooley, a junior member of the department, was "in contact with many of the younger men in geology."[41]

As for Abby Turner, her relationship with her adviser Cecil Drinker at Harvard School of Public Health and with F. G. Benedict, director of the Carnegie Institution's Nutritional Laboratory, offer good examples of the way in which complementarity was not always a relationship of equality. This was so even when the work they did fit together to serve the larger social goals of public health research in the 1920s. There is a letter to Turner from Benedict asking her to consider working with him on a project that would be based on Mount Holyoke and derive from her own work begun at Harvard. Benedict admits that although "most of these reasons are those of expediency ... scientifically if one has the combination of two people who understand each other and who are scientifically sympathetic," it can be done. His appeal is also couched in terms of the moral necessity of group solidarity in difficult times. "There is trouble enough ahead for all workers in physiology," he wrote.[42] Yet the tone of his letter is paternalistic and full of self-serving flattery offered in return for information from her. From Drinker's point of view, the relationship was one of unequals, in which Turner would be assisting him.

Inequality was also accepted in the realm of employment. Positions that these Mount Holyoke women held in women's colleges obviously constituted a form of sex segregation, albeit, self-selected. A few graduates such as Virginia Apgar and Helen Vincent McLean, both of whom were medical doctors, worked at high levels and in influential posts in coeducational settings. Other graduates fell in the realm of what Margaret Rossiter has called "women's work in science." Most of the science graduates who went on to employment in science did so as schoolteachers, research technicians, and secretaries working under male supervision. These positions, often seen as being without influence or import, did make some small differences according to the letters we have about those who held them. Taken as a group, women in these positions tended to help shape and reinforce the emerging division of labor within the world of the sciences in the twentieth century—whether or not they approved.

There was also some emphasis on scientific women's subjects with an eye toward employment opportunities. During the years of World War I, when there was an immediate need for increased numbers of medically trained personnel and for greater food supplies, the school offered courses and preparation for nursing and home economics.[43] Strong interest in women's physiology and health continued to be set within a broad context that included both sexes, but took on increasing importance with the growing feminism of the 1920s. By this time the course offerings might be characterized as providing a solid balance that connected the subjects with teaching students about the female role in reproduction. For example, mammalian embryology focused on the development of sexual characteristics and reproductive organs. As noted earlier, Professor A. Elizabeth Adams's ('14) heredity courses set human inheritance and the study of racial betterment through proper breeding within the study of evolution and genetic theories of inheritance.[44] By 1930, the general zoology and physiology courses, offered through the Zoology and Physiology departments, included a large amount of time in the study of sex and reproduction, suggesting a long period of development and enrichment on this topic.[45]

Not all attention was focused on human reproduction. In 1932 Ann Morgan was asked to summarize what had been and was continuing to be taught on the subject of "sex, development, and adjustment." Her report, included in the department's annual report of 1932–1933, is a six-page outline and four-page bibliography that she handed out in the introductory zoology courses that all students took. Topics included the biological definitions of sex, procreation, pregnancy, and birth process; genetics; heterosexuality and homosexuality as having their fundamental basis in plant and animal life; the commercialization of sex, as well as anthropological dimensions of cleanliness, fresh air, good water, exercise, and diet; and informed understanding of human physiology, including reproduction and development.[46]

Faculty members and some students were well aware of the separation between women and men and of the trend toward inequality. Carr fought it by emphasizing equal professional objectives over gender divisions when it came to doing science. Thus, she responded negatively to the proposal for a separate formal organization for women within the American Chemical Society, saying efforts should be to produce "original work of sufficient value to present at the meetings." Clapp exercised some humor in regard to the situation. Calling her summer cottage at Woods Hole where students roomed with her an "Aladdin House," she referred to the "harem" she had there. One student, writing in an essay on the standard of oral recitations at Mount Holyoke College, admitted a sense of inferiority: "True enough, M.H. is labeled the technology of woman's colleges, but the students haven't the strength of men to stand hard work."[47]

Yet the faculty's efforts to adapt the tradition of the family to the new circumstances of a departmentally organized campus tended to strengthen the bonds among women pursuing useful work in the outside world. The old concern for turning student attention to such employment took the form of directing their professional goals toward science. Commitment to cooperative work continued in the form of collectively organized research projects. These were especially strong in the Chemistry Department under Emma Perry Carr, but were also a way of organizing research in the Zoology Department and Physiology Department.[48] It also continued in the system of domestic work, now transposed to the labs where students shared the chores of cleaning up.[49]

These values helped maintain a continuing responsiveness to the positions that were open to them as women. The faculty continued to try to "fit in." Here those values Mary Woolley claimed as the special talents of women were identified with special types of jobs in science. For the most part these jobs were "women's work in science"—that is, low-level positions as laboratory technicians and research assistants working for men. The adjectives used to describe the students emphasize their appropriateness for such positions: "conscientious," "painstaking," has "tactfulness and sociability," "wholesome," "good-tempered," "accurate, scientific," has "common sense," "loyal, hardworking." There are also numerous comments on students' physical appearance, noting when they were attractive.

Faculty disliked complaining or insubordination, noting critically those who were "conceited," showed too much egotism, or were erratic in their work. The professors fretted over the students who lacked the preferred virtues, and they encouraged improvement. Abby Turner wrote of one student that:

> If it were not for this manner of seeing all the difficulties as she works, I could recommend her much more highly. . . . If she goes at something whole-heartedly and forgets that she is working, she has qualities which may make her come out well. If this temper is an expression of exaggerated self-esteem which it sometimes suggests, it may interfere with the end result. I should be inclined to risk her in a piece of moderate difficulty to hope for the best.[50]

Letters from employers in schools and laboratories both guided and reinforced the professors' standards. B. F. Kingsbury, professor of histology and embryology at Cornell, wrote of one former Mount Holyoke student then doing graduate work with him: "We found her most conscientious in her teaching, in the preparation for her teaching and in her research work. In the latter she fully made up for what she may have lacked in 'brilliancy' by hard work and dogged persistence."[51] Typical was the letter one school principal wrote about another former student:

> She has established a reputation for *unusual ability* as a *teacher,* for having a character that is *strong* and *pure,* for possessing an unusual amount of *common sense* and *every* sense of the word *successful.* Her pupils are fond of her, her discipline is *good,* and not *fussy.* Her presence is an inspiration to her pupils. She is a *woman.*[52]

A woman director of the Bureau of Social Education for the National Board of the YWCA wrote with surprising approval that the Mount Holyoke science graduate they had hired was "without much initiative. In her work she is accurate, painstaking, and faithful . . . constant attention to detail gives her unusual degree of dependability which I prize in a co-worker."[53] If the professors seem complicit in affirming the system of scientific employment by emphasizing those virtues and tasks identified with women's very nature, they seem to have done so because of their commitment to finding employment for their former students. In this way they remained faithful to the original objectives to train women for useful work and matched their traditional values to those of the market.

They also persisted in giving precedence to the single woman graduate as the ideal worker. Mary Woolley may have marked out a domestic role for educated women, but the science professors encouraged them to remain single in order to pursue their profession. While professors may have helped married students informally, it was the policy of the college to remove the names of students from the placement bureau roster when they married. It was possible through special request to remain inscribed and to receive assistance, however. A few biology students who married during these years are on record as receiving help from their professors. Lois Smedley ('35) was one such student. She remembered with great affection that Christianna Smith had helped her work through the potential conflicts between having a boyfriend and doing her research. When Smedley married after earning an M.D. degree, they continued to be in contact. Helen Voorhees, while not a faculty member, assisted other married students in finding employment that would enable them to continue their household duties.[54]

In all these endeavors the science faculty members showed great awareness and sensitivity to some of the changes occurring in American society. They were attuned to a job market that was itself undergoing change as the sciences became an increasingly important part of the American economy and culture. They were also responsive to a new tolerance on campus and in American society in regard to educated women's lives. Faculty members are pictured in college photographs in their own laboratories, worlds they had created for themselves and their students. They published papers and books, belonged to professional organizations, and won prizes. Their accomplishments as scientists were recognized alongside those of men in the prestigious directory of *American Men of Science*. With the award of the Garvan prize to Emma Perry Carr in 1937, special recognition was given to them as individual women successfully working in science.

There were also changes in their lives mirrored in the new freedom on the campus itself. The move in the 1920s to democratize the college encouraged students and faculty to express a sense of individuality there. Thus, campus life eased for everyone. Not only were dancing and smoking now allowed, but there were coeducational dances and parties in which men were invited for informal social occasions on a regular basis. Already enjoying more social intercourse with their male colleagues in the outside world of science, the science faculty, along with colleagues and administrators, now lived singly and in pairs in their own homes, where they entertained students and male and female visitors.[55] They adopted independent lifestyles and manners of dress. Ann Haven Morgan in the 1920s began to wear slacks and blue ties in a masculine dress style that marked radical change from the restrained black, often dowdy dresses formerly worn by faculty.

Whatever the private relationships between these women, their success as unmarried women scientists was reinforced and rewarded by the college during the Woolley administration. There is both elation and regret we can feel at the picture we have of women who had built their own world, partly on their own terms at the college, one that mirrored in slightly distorted ways the world of male science outside.

The Decline of the Professional Family in Hard Times

Circumstances in the 1930s put this set of values and the science departments themselves under duress. Pressure for change came from two sources. First, students began expressing a wish that the school help prepare them for marriage and family, teaching them the graces that President Harris of Amherst College had advocated for the school at the turn of the century. Like their peers in other women's colleges, more Mount Holyoke students were marrying and doing so earlier than had their predecessors. The *Mount Holyoke News* ran an article in February 1931 by a student predicting that "most of us expect to get married at least ten years after we graduate." She went on to suggest that what was needed was the application of science to courses that prepared students for domestic life, such as "plain everyday cooking." At the same time, a campus committee proposed lectures on community, family life, marriage, and friendship.[56] It may have been because of these changing interests on the part of students that Morgan was asked for a summary of what was taught in her courses on sex and procreation. At a time when women were faced with the conflict engendered by hard economic times and social pressures to accede to men in the working world, Abby Turner in her departmental report wrote in some dismay that many recent biology graduates were married already.[57]

These new trends were accompanied by implied criticisms of the unmarried women faculty, especially those in the science departments. The request for information on instruction about sex in 1932 suggests uneasiness on the part of trustees and some administrators about how these single women were influencing the values of their young students. There was certainly a sense that faculty and students in science were different from other women in the college that rose alongside growing uneasiness in American middle-class society regarding women's friendships.

As early as 1902 a new stereotype of the odd woman scientist had crystallized to the extent that a student in the Library Department poeticized the Mount Holyoke science major:

My Zoölogical Flame

Dear Girl, I wish I knew her well,
And yet I dare not call,
For spiders' webs and mud wasps' nests,
And ugly things that crawl,
Cocoons and bugs and toads adorn
Her desk and stand wall.

Sweet girl, I'd love with her to walk,
If only I could stop her,
When she picks up, upon the spot,
An innocent grasshopper,
And tells his whole anatomy.
I do not think it's proper!

Bright girl, I'd like to chat with her,
But she speaks of Hymenoptera,
Of the stages of the Blastula,
And the various Orthoptera,
Of segments, somites, symmetry,
And of the Coleoptera.

Fair girl, I'd like to be her friend,
But may the gods protect me!
Perhaps she'd give me some such name,
Or else perchance dissect me,
Examine, analyze, and draw,
And n'er again collect me.[58]

Here was, albeit in caricatured form, the offspring of Cornelia Clapp, Lydia Shattuck, and ultimately Mary Lyon, descended from a line of women who three generations back claimed a resemblance to the entire seminary population. She possessed the passionate love of nature and the intellectual power to objectify, analyze, and organize it that made her a scientist—and a strange and threatening personality, unwomanly in the eyes of others.

These trends at the school had their culmination in the hiring of Roswell G. Ham as the first male president of Mount Holyoke in 1937. Married with a child, trustees justified Ham's appointment partly on the grounds that he would help to build a healthy family atmosphere on campus.[59] The reference was not to the extended family of women that Mary Lyon had had in mind for Mount Holyoke, but to the nuclear family with a father at its head and a mother as helpmate. This more conventional middle-class model of the family was in direct conflict with both the old helpmate arrangement between males and unmarried female teachers and the more recent one of complementary equals. Ham also advocated a stronger emphasis on literature and the arts in women's preparation for married life, and thus put himself at odds with the traditions of the school on the issue of where science stood in the curriculum and even with the very purpose of the curriculum. His appointment came as a shock to many on campus, including the science professors, many of whom vehemently protested it.

The second change during the Depression years, one that the science professors did attend to from the beginning, was a change and a drop in the market for women trained in science. The recognition of the change in work opportunities and the departments' commitment to adapt to them can be found in the comments of Ann Haven Morgan in her 1933–1934 annual report:

> Technical positions, especially in hospitals, have been often available during the past two years when nothing else cold be secured. This situation accounts for the rather unfortunate eagerness for "practical" and "medical" courses.[60]

Pressures to hire males over females for faculty positions were based on the argument that men were family heads and needed the jobs more. Openings for women graduates with bachelor's degrees were increasingly limited to technical positions, as women's work in science increasingly demanded less responsibility and initiative. Teaching positions became scarce.[61]

Changes in the presidency of the school and in the market were interconnected. The Depression drove women to marry as opportunities for jobs declined or became less appealing.[62] It also encouraged general pressures on the middle classes from whom Mount Holyoke students were drawn to emphasize the hiring of men and the education of women to be helpmates to educated men.[63] Faculty were extremely sensitive and alert to this trend in the job market, which threatened the opportunities for their unmarried students.

It was otherwise with Ham's appointment. His nomination seems to have come as a surprise to the women science faculty, perhaps because in many ways they had distanced themselves from the general life of the school. Ensconced in their departments, attending to their own faculty, their careers, and their students, they were out of touch with the concerns of trustees and families of the young women at the college. Their responses centered on the new presidential appointment. To the immediate threat of a male president, they responded by making public statements that called attention to the traditions of the school as a place where women had always been educated in the sciences.

In 1935 Zoology Professor A. Elizabeth Adams sent out a circular to trustees, alumnae, and the press opposing Ham and asking for support for a woman candidate, while Ann Haven Morgan published a letter arguing for a woman on the grounds she would be much better qualified than any male interested in the post. Emmy Perry Carr spoke on Springfield radio station WIXAL in 1936. In her talk she discussed the chain of protégées who "built wisely and well upon the foundation laid by Miss Lyon" to establish a great "scientific heritage." Coming as it did at the climax of the struggle between a number of faculty and trustees over the appointment of a married male English professor as president, the themes of her talk affirm the traditions of Mount Holyoke as strongly scientific and strongly woman-led, while acknowledging the support men have lent to women scientists' efforts there. As in the past, she argued, the secret of Mount Holyoke's future success as a college—not a women's college—would lie in continuing support for science.[64]

What they could not respond to, however, was the issue raised for them by Ham's appointment: that of how to combine marriage and career for their women graduates. The obvious way to synthesize the traditions of the school with the new trend of college women to marry was to forge a value system that allowed for this combination and to create a support system that made it possible. This the Mount Holyoke science professors were helpless to enact.

That the appointment of Ham constituted a watershed for the women science faculty at the college is born out by Ham himself. Looking back on the 1930s in his Presidential Reports of the 1950s, he declared the feminism at the school "false," saying he was glad it was gone. The idolization of women that he felt had marked the centennial celebrations of 1937 was in his view counter to Mary Lyon's ideals.[65] Even more germane in understanding his position on the sciences is the way in which he rationalized placing the Natural Sciences and Mathematics after the Liberal Arts in the 1956–1957 report. He explained:

> It is not that these departments are less active than those in the languages and arts; on the contrary, they have at times been falsely placed by outsiders as the principal claim to excellence of Mount Holyoke! (The field of science, however, is no more nor less than part of a well-rounded and integrated college, contributing ably its share to the common heritage.) . . . [66]

Thus the period of Mary Woolley's presidency saw shifts in the school. Proceeding along lines already laid down by Elizabeth Mead, the science departments became more autonomous within a school that was increasingly less centrally organized and more individualistic in its stance. The science teachers were hence less influential in its overall direction. At the same time, they became a powerful subculture in the school, forming strong scientific departments with active heads, faculty members engaged in teaching and research, funded often by grants, and in structure modeled on scientific departments at graduate schools and in the emerging scientific world of industrial and governmental work. They focused their attention more narrowly on an increasingly more organized and professionalized scientific community, maintaining and expanding their networks with men at universities, at research centers, and in industry, where they sent students for advanced work and for employment.

For the science departments the ethos of complimentarity was maintained as a value system in which ideals of a family of select women working together in concert with men of Christian character remained strong, and commitment to the ideal of the single working woman prevailed. The success of this stance can be measured in terms of the number of women from Mount Holyoke who went on to get advanced degrees in the sciences during this period. At the same time the 1930s economy, which favored hiring men, and middle-class values, which favored educating women for marriage, destabilized the science professors' policies. They faced what seemed a fundamental rejection of Mary Lyon's original mission when the trustees appointed a male president. This decision opened the way for first men and eventually also married women to enter the science faculty in significant numbers, as Mount Holyoke kept abreast of social forces and market pressures to retain its position in science.

President Ham took over a campus with a divided mission, each faction laying claim to the founder's tradition. On the one hand, there was a group whose leaders included science faculty who drew strength from Lyon's commitment to single women teachers, to women who worked for a living, and to the importance of science. On the other, there was the new president, and important trustees, alumnae, and some faculty who looked back to Lyon's ideal of Mount Holyoke as a family community, educating women to enter a broad continuum of roles wherein education as a vocation united single women teachers with those who married, had children, and contributed to building a national leadership in noneconomic ways. During the 1920s, encouraged by Woolley's ambitious policies and growing demand for access to scientific training, the science faculty's engagement in the professional marketplace had produced a divide between women committed to self-development within a specialized career track and those who chose to remain single, and those who wanted to marry and to have children. Their efforts to follow Woolley's assertion of women's intellectual equality with men, to meet the challenge to be better than their colleagues in the male colleges, had had both positive and negative consequences for them in the increasing press of professionalization that established individual contributions to research as an end whose rewards were status, status for their college, and membership for themselves and their students in a community of academic specialists.

To tell the truth, they were only following the customs and negotiating the realities of life in American society as academic science and middle-class life became structured around economic and professional measures of success. What had been a powerful synthesis in Lyon's time, made viable by the missionary movement and the demand for teachers with scientific knowledge, had become a clash of contradictions for women faculty members faced with hostility to working women and promarriage values in the 1930s. By 1937 women science faculty members confronted the necessity of trying to hold on to their own positions, their authority, and that part of Lyon's legacy on which these claims rested in order to preserve what they could of the college as they had known it. The Second World War, coming just four years after Ham took office, ushered in an era of national growth and social change that turned college and faculty's attention away from these conservative prospects to the revitalization of science accompanied by the creation of a liberalized, multicultural, and mixed-gender faculty culture.

{ chapter 6 }

Conclusion

There are certain images that exemplify the history of women science faculty at Mount Holyoke: Mary Lyon in her white cap striving to be perfect in her understanding, explication, and administration of natural laws.[1] Cornelia Clapp in an apron working with students in her research room at the Woods Hole Marine Biological Laboratory. Emma Perry Carr in a tailored suit and pearls seated before a spectrographic microscope. Ann Haven Morgan in rubber boots and fisherman's hat seining for mayfly larvae with her students in the campus pond.

Or this: Mary Lyon surveying the geology of western Massachusetts with Edward and Ora White Hitchcock. Lydia Shattuck correcting Asa Gray's botany text. Cornelia Clapp lecturing on developmental biology to men and women scientists at the MBL. Emma Perry Carr declining to participate in a special women's section of the American Chemical Society.

And finally, snapshots offering a glimpse of what has become of the traditions in the decades following Ham's appointment: Curtis Smith arrives with his wife and children to be the first male faculty member in the biological sciences at Mount Holyoke. Anna Jane Harrison, Chemistry Department chair, graduate of the University of Missouri, becomes the first woman president of the AAAS. Married women faculty work with students in their laboratories while their husbands, on leave from the college, care for the babies.

Continuities and Paradoxes of Science (1837–1937)

This book on the history of science faculty at Mount Holyoke began with a thesis and two questions whose answers might revise understanding of women's participation in the formation of American science. Looking across a century that stretches from the founding of Mount Holyoke to Roswell Ham's inauguration, several striking features on the historical landscape

meet the eye. Some affirm the wisdom of Lyon's plans and strategies for getting ahead through science teaching by establishing quid pro quo relationships with men from the Protestant colleges. Others reveal, not so much weaknesses in her approach to the expanding market place—which were few—but
paradoxes arising from the faculty's decision to use religious beliefs regarding the equality of men and women to define and enlarge the scope of women's
work in science whenever the opportunity arose.

Paramount throughout this period is the fact that the science faculty continuously played a significant role in the life of the institution. Science remained prominent as a subject in the curriculum, as a focus of teaching activity, and as a site for the faculty's introduction of gendered Protestant
beliefs and values. These women helped maintain Mount Holyoke's competitive position in higher education by always keeping their eye on the job
market and on shifting public demands for science education. They helped
equilibrate these economic forces by earning advanced degrees and reforming their departments and programs in accordance with the changing character and organization of scientific knowledge and standards of performance and certification. Their working alliances with male scientists enabled
these efforts.

Mount Holyoke remained committed to teaching as its central focus and
source of strength. Emphasis on laboratory work, empirical analysis, specimen collecting, and hands-on teaching aimed at technical proficiency continued. Moreover, faculty members had creatively integrated, built outward
from teaching recitations, collecting and offering demonstrations to embrace
lecturing and laboratory research activities tailored to the undergraduate setting and to those jobs in which they determined women might contribute.
And by the 1930s they also engaged in the public activities of writing, publishing, and even the popularization of science.

They also remained committed to their Protestant roots and the Protestant ideals of male and female equality—within a comity of the elect. However, they had transferred and transformed Protestant ideals and missionary
goals into professional scientific values regarding measures of worthiness,
definitions of work, and the sexual division of labor. From initially pushing
the envelope of possibilities to raise the status of teachers to that of ministers, they ended by becoming college scientists, engaging in research, publishing, and teaching in specialized fields, thereby helping to define professional scientific life along with men. They continued to respect and even
protect the Protestant community's distinctions between the roles of single

and married women to their own advantage. Their primary mission went from using science to form leaders with certified Christian character to producing women with the highest qualifications to work within the circuit of professional scientific specialties.

Throughout this period, they had used their New England location to build extended, reciprocal networks among a variety of individuals, institutions, and organizations. Members of their network changed over time in tune with the weakening of clerical influence in academe and the emergence of a secularly oriented demand for scientific personnel in colleges, universities, private research laboratories, government, and industrial research. The faculty's mission was framed in terms of forming and maintaining such alliances, although some students continued to find ways to use their science education in missionary work.

Thus, the history of Mount Holyoke provides some answers to the questions of why women entered science and how they came to be concentrated in certain fields and types of work. The history of science faculty at Mount Holyoke is partly a microcosmic view of the history of women's engagement in a complex process of cultural change whose code word is "professionalization." This process was not a phenomenon that occurred in a separate male sphere that women sought to invade or even perfectly mimic, nor was it a modernist case of outsiders as insiders. Rather it can be considered a phenomenon of social ecology driven by highly ambitious and visionary science faculty members using institutions of higher education to advance their common purposes. Mount Holyoke science faculty were members of that developing social ecology. The history of four generations of science faculty at Mount Holyoke allows us to understand just how women could use an interdependent relationship with male scientists to raise their status in tandem with science faculty at the men's colleges.

Evangelical culture and a growing demand for better-credentialled faculty ensured that this group of women had much in common with their male counterparts in the colleges. These two factors also ensured that they would maintain a distinctly gendered identity within which there was room for diversity. Their own identities and culture contributed to the character and dynamic of professionalizing science and were shaped by it at the same time. Mount Holyoke faculty members are exemplary in this case because their history is also a part of the history of science in the American college, an institution that historians interested in tracing the rise of the research university have seen as inconsequential after about 1870.[2] Although they were relatively small in number, as a group their connections within the evangelical community and later within Protestant academic circles gave them an advantage over women faculty in other colleges in establishing working relationships with influential male science faculty at the most highly regarded colleges and universities. As for the eastern women's colleges founded after the Civil War, although Mount Holyoke's ties to religion and its antebellum roots give its history a different character from all of them save perhaps Wellesley, it is also part of the common experience of higher education for women.

The previous chapters have recounted a story that helps explain the seeming contradiction between Mount Holyoke faculty's commitment to single-sex education and to intellectual equality within the framework of professionalization. The answer lies in the ideology of American Protestantism; its adherents spawned a cultural system and set of educational institutions that valued the study of science by both men and women to prepare them for complementary careers through which they could exercise moral leadership. In the period before the Civil War (1860–1864), evangelical Protestants responding to the disrupting forces of industrial capitalism gave enormous encouragement to the study of science in sex-segregated colleges and seminaries preparing their graduates for new job opportunities.[3] Although the American population's enthusiasm for evangelicalism subsided in the 1850s and 1860s, this movement left its mark on the social relations between men and the women science faculty at Mount Holyoke and on the aspirations and goals of these women faculty members. As importantly, it set in motion a dynamic relationship between specializing trends in college science offerings, faculty professional qualifications, and the changing market for women with higher education in science. This market which correlated job opportunities in science with the demands of women clientele forced Mount Holyoke faculty and administrators to periodically alter the science curriculum and the religious character of the culture of the institution to conform to a more secular-focused, university-dominated, and masculinized science community in the late-nineteenth and twentieth centuries.

If religion as an all-encompassing value system and set of goals serves to distinguish the experience of Mount Holyoke's science faculty from that of its colleagues at other women's colleges, the institution's religious heritage makes comprehensible the large numbers of Mount Holyoke women in the scientific teaching community. The persistence of values and customs derived from that religious culture also helps to explain the gendered division of scientific labor that occurred within American higher education during that period, as well as the framing of current issues that confront women science faculty and their students in terms of aspirations for a reworked version of full professional status. As will be discussed in the next section of the conclusion, of particular importance in revising Daniel Kevles's model and refining Margaret Rossiter and Evelyn Fox Keller's interpretations of women's situation in the professionalization of science are the results of recent studies on the advisability of single-sex education for women.

Ideological support for science education at Mount Holyoke came from religious values and goals that endowed those women who taught science with special authority, although initially their professional status also depended on their ability to manage a broad range of responsibilities in a scientific manner. Evangelical Protestants in American towns and villages provided a social framework that justified the scientific study of nature by both men and women. Science offered a means of systematically understanding the divine order of nature as well as disciplining the mind and body in accordance with this order. It was a step all Christian souls could take towards salvation from the materialism of American society. Thus, men and women faculty members and their students were encouraged to share the same knowledge base, and their intellectual capacities were deemed equal. In the 1820s and 1830s these same evangelicals also supported the founding of sex-segregated colleges and seminaries to provide institutional mechanisms for forming minds along these lines, an effort which encouraged both men and women faculty members interested in science to professionalize their activities. While the goal of these institutions was to produce men and women who would cooperate in the realization of a common moral objective, the culture within these single-sex institutions, heavily influenced by arrangements within the churches, encouraged women and men to teach science differently while sharing a common knowledge base. Moreover, the preparation they offered students distinguished between men and women on the basis of the differences between the careers and social roles open to each. The fact that by definition the colleges and seminaries operated in a market where demands for higher education in science were constantly growing, however, encouraged science faculty to liberalize its religious commitments, to bring its science programs into conjunction with university offerings, and to attune its curricula to changing job opportunities for men and women in order to remain competitive.

By and large the faculty members' efforts were a success. On their own terms, they had succeeded in building active, all-female departments with strong heads—especially in Zoology, Physiology, and Chemistry. Carr's accomplishments alone represented the realization of Lyon's efforts to take charge of chemistry teaching and was thus an enormously important affirmation of Lyon's legacy, a fact which Carr herself fully appreciated. However, as was also seen in the previous chapters, the faculty continually faced resistance from men with whom they cooperated over the issue of who would control knowledge and create new knowledge and who would be the supporting agents, handling the technical and repetitious work.

The continuities and alterations were means of survival in a competitive world. Like all adaptive strategies, those who adopted them were changed along with their environment. The science faculty members as a group increasingly evolved their own subculture and a professional persona analogous to that which male science professors were developing in the universities. Using the ideal of genderless scientific knowledge as the basis of their claim to professional equality with men, they increasingly adapted the working relationships and lifestyles of their married male peers to their own existence in a world of single women. In the 1920s and 1930s, they broke Lyon's culture of evangelical conformity that enforced group solidarity and hence the solidarity of single women faculty with other women in the old, extended Mount Holyoke community—single, married, mothers, non-specialists, non-scientists, engaged in domestic and volunteer activities. If they adapted successfully to an increasingly specialized niche in an increasingly specialized academic market during the long period of national growth, when that vast national environment constricted in the 1930s, they and their hybrid culture were in trouble.

The Depression forced an economic crisis in the scientific community, which was experienced at Mount Holyoke as crises in the entire culture of science and in the integrity of the college, which was so closely tied in the minds of science faculty to the fortunes of science. The trustees' decision to hire a man—a family man and English professor—to be president promised a way to prosperity that rejected the entire set of mutually reinforcing relationships that had given the science faculty such authority over Mount Holyoke for so many years. What would have happened had war not broken out is hard to say. It is clear that the Second World War brought science back to the center of American life, the national economy and Mount Holyoke; however, the six decades after Pearl Harbor would see the old traditions reformed into very different and much more liberalized configurations.

Continuing Traditions in the Scientific Enterprise (1940–2000)

The Second World War opened possibilities to escape from the dilemma President Ham's policies had posed for women science faculty. In the decades after 1940, circumstances encouraged the rejuvenation of traditions that stressed science, women science faculty participation in defining women's scientific work within a wider enterprise, and the importance of a collegiate community for women in supporting these efforts. Their way led forward into a new economy for universities and colleges and more socially liberal society, rather than back to a pre-Depression era, however. It brought the faculty and administration to reform and update these traditions to build a culture that included both married women and men. To use a watery metaphor, the Cold War, Sputnik, and the Civil Rights and women's rights movements were on the other side of a historical watershed that cut off some old streams of habit and tradition, redirected others into new channels, and opened new sources that transformed the culture of science at Mount Holyoke.

In the long view of the years from Ham's inauguration to the present, we can chart a recommitment to science at the collegiate level; to traditions of teaching science combined with research; to laboratory-based science; and to educating women for useful work with emphasis on paid employment. Faculty members continued to maintain high technical standards for performance, with stress on laboratory teaching and on remaining viable in the academic marketplace. Added to these continuities has been the liberalization of faculty hiring to include married women and women with children, as well as to increase the number of men and to embrace religious and racial diversity. A final change of great significance is the culture that supports working parents, and thus seeks to resolve one of the most vexing difficulties middle-class women face in contemporary economies where the supportive, extended communities offered by the missionary movement in Lyon's day no longer exist.

The Mount Holyoke faculty and college remain integrated in the now vast field of scientific enterprises where independent, single-sex colleges have found themselves increasingly challenged to survive. This field is characterized by big science: the appearance of large, complex and interlocked institutions, government agencies, and corporations that are part of a billion-dollar economy employing hundreds of thousands.[4] Research universities became a major feature and force in this new, very competitive environment. The post-Sputnik era, with its enormous increase in demand and funding for scientific training and personnel, required that small colleges in New England—and nationally—rethink their role in science education. One of the most dramatic efforts came in the 1980s when independent colleges joined together to aggressively promote their collective value as a resource for science in this country. Out of this effort that had its antecedents in the strategies of nineteenth-century evangelical Protestant science faculty came new and renewed networks, cooperative resource sharing, integrated programs, and a fresh focus on contemporary developments in science.[5] In 2001, the National Science Foundation has launched initiatives to attract and retain women and minorities in faculty positions and science and technology degree programs to replace traditional sources of scientific workers (White, native-born men).[6] Most importantly, despite the rapid decline in the number of women's colleges since World War II, from over 130 to less than fifty, Mount Holyoke remains as steadfastly committed to promoting women's science education as to serving the interests of professional science in the name of a higher purpose. The notes of religious enthusiasm found in Mary Lyon's 1837 seminary announcement can still be heard in the moral tones with which recent college catalogues describe the institution's goals.[7]

Countering the trend toward decreasing numbers of independent colleges, of single-sex colleges, and of scientists with baccalaureates from these institutions, Mount Holyoke has continued to be a leader in producing graduates who went on to receive doctorates in science and mathematics from American universities.[8] In 2000 the National Science Foundation reported that Mount Holyoke ranks number 33 in a field of 641 institutions of higher education in terms of total research and development (R&D) expenditures in science.[9] While below Bryn Mawr, Smith, Amherst, and Williams, it is close in ranking, and the difference may be attributable to differences in the size of the student bodies.

At Mount Holyoke, women faculty members benefited from the war as it stimulated demand for women college graduates, offering them jobs that carried patriotic as well as scientific significance. There were also relatively substantial research grants awarded by the federal government to some of the science departments, particularly Chemistry and Physiology. The impetus for integration into the emerging world of big science brought further changes after the war. In the 1940s and 1950s, the retirements of science department chairs Ann Haven Morgan (Zoology), Abigail Howe Turner (Physiology), and Alma Grace Stokey (Botany), made it possible for the administration to reform these strongholds of single, Mount Holyoke graduates. In the 1950s, Zoology, Botany, and Physiology were reorganized into a single Department of Biology, in part to consolidate shrinking enrollments in some of them and in part to open the way for incorporating changes in contemporary research that cut across these old disciplinary categories. As the costs of scientific equipment and facilities increased, Mount Holyoke joined in cooperative degree-granting ventures and sharing of facilities with other nearby institutions, contributing to the creation of a four-college genetics program in the 1950s and five-college coeducational programs in physics and astronomy in the 1970s.[10]

In the 1950s the college continued the prewar trend to diversify the faculty and have it mirror contemporary society more accurately. Thus, in this decade men, most with families, were hired for the first time in the formerly all-female Chemistry and Zoology departments, and a bit later in the consolidated biological sciences department. In the 1970s, married women began to be hired and retained on the faculty even when they became pregnant and had small children. There was also a liberalization of religious strictures. Not only was attendance at chapel no longer required, but the faculty began to include Jews, African Americans, and women from Third World countries, moving Mount Holyoke radically away from the religious and racial parochialism of its prewar history. Moreover, increasing numbers of newly hired women faculty had received their undergraduate education at colleges other than Mount Holyoke. Among them, Anna Jane Harrison, a graduate of the University of Missouri, eventually took over the chairmanship of the Chemistry Department, so long dominated by Mount Holyoke graduates stretching back to Mary Lyon. Thus, the protégée chain that had been such a powerful mechanism for transmitting and reshaping the values of the founder was broken. At the same time, removing the stricture against married women having careers in science broke the social framework that had encompassed dedicated single women but marginalized or excluded their married counterparts.

Many of these changes came about as a result of Mount Holyoke's responsiveness to the new opportunities opening up for graduate work and jobs in science and a greater willingness on the part of social institutions, including Mount Holyoke, to fill those needs with a more diverse range of women. There were also pressures from the federal government as laws against sexual and racial discrimination were passed and enforced. Such changes have made it possible during recent decades for the college to maintain the high rate of science majors and of graduates pursuing further degrees in science. Perhaps the greatest symbol of this change and of the stature of Mount Holyoke science faculty was the election of Anna Jane Harrison to the presidency of the AAAS—the first woman to hold this office in the nation's major scientific society.

Nevertheless, these changes do not constitute a complete sweeping away of the old values and traditions in science. These were reconsidered and reformulated in the late 1960s when Mount Holyoke, along with numerous other single sex colleges in the United States, had to come to terms with radically different mores, aspirations, and ideals of the baby-boomer generation that constituted its new clientele. Many of these colleges broke with their original mandates and became coeducational as part of an effort to accommodate. Mount Holyoke found another way. In 1970 Mount Holyoke, under the aegis of a committee that included strong representation from the science departments, opted to recommit itself to the higher education of women. As a result of this decision, the sciences were reinforced as one of the long-standing strengths of the institution.[11]

Within the science departments themselves certain traditions were revitalized beginning in the 1970s and the following decade, primary among them the commitment to educating women for useful work in fields within the collegiate purview. Articles in the alumnae magazine and conferences held on campus have made science one of the foci and major selling points of the college. Integrating research and laboratory teaching has become part of the well-articulated professional reasons for deciding to seek posts in a liberal arts college. Professor of Biology Rachel Fink, who received her doctorate from Cornell University, chose college teaching because "the time spent with our students in laboratories teaching them how to answer scientific questions . . . is the core of what we do."[12] In the Department of Earth and Environment (formerly Geology, Geography, and Astronomy departments), Professor M. Darby Dyer, whose doctorate is from MIT, offers a detailed picture of just what this coproduction of science entails in her laboratory: "These students have run my laboratory operation, conceived and performed their own research projects (including publishing and presenting the results), and assisted with nearly every piece of research done in my lab."[13]

The continuing focus on professionalization has in fact been reinforced with the introduction of more structured majors, the holding of job fairs, and strong measures for counseling students about preparation for employment and graduate school applications. Increased attention is being paid to making students aware of the opportunities available to them in science and to pointing out that these are the same as those available to men. Moreover, problems of how to take advantage of these opportunities, of how to confront discrimination and the "glass ceiling," as well as how to deal with marriage and career, are openly discussed informally as well as in organized forums, something that was only done on an ad hoc basis and not well articulated before 1940.

The emphasis on professional goals at Mount Holyoke has tended to deemphasize the old concerns with setting scientific work within the context of a Christian calling—a trend that had already begun before 1940. This does not mean that faculty's moral commitment to teaching as a vocation identified with earning a living has disappeared. Quite the contrary. Personal sense of calling has taken other forms as these women strive to keep teaching at the center of their work, while participating in the research and publishing necessary to making them effective contributors to the scientific workforce. And this objective remains closely associated in their minds with the contributions scientists make to American society. Where Mary Lyon used the evangelical mission to morally leverage employment for single women teachers in higher education, postwar generations of women science faculty members at Mount Holyoke (whether single, married, divorced, or mothers) have looked to the democratic mission of the United States to ensure their right to equality with male colleagues in a joint endeavor. Their efforts reflect the democratizing trends of the Cold War, when the practice of science became broadly identified with serving the causes of democracy, truth, and national defense. The call to save humanity from tyranny tended to replace Christian salvation as justification for the high value placed on scientific work, and the moral onus was on institutions of higher education to create democratic environments where standards of fairness and equality were put into practice.

Their efforts also reflect the press of economic necessity on middle-class women over the past five and a half decades that has made equality of opportunity a central issue for women beyond those who are single. Two-income families, high divorce rates, and single-parent families have encouraged college education for women to become more than ever preparation for paid employment that will be personally satisfying and socially meaningful. The struggle to realize the promise of the Equal Rights Amendment has intensified on campus and in American society at large, while women's employment and promotion in science have become the focus of attention and personal advancement a major incentive and measure of satisfaction.

As for the domestic system and the concept of the family, they too have changed. The former no longer exists; work-study funding has come to replace group participation in laboratory maintenance with hired student help. While the term "family" is no longer one used to describe the social arrangements in the laboratory, following the relinquishing of the role of *in loco parentis* by the college, it is in the nature of scientific activity to be social and hierarchical. At Mount Holyoke, as elsewhere, science continues to be learned and practiced within a group setting structured by the professor or teaching assistant. What has changed is often the degree of formality and deference that prevails within the laboratories, as well as the fact that faculty are much more varied in their own lifestyles and experiences. As such, they provide a panoply of role models and mentors for young women with differing degrees of ambition who do not necessarily want to choose between marriage and career. Networks with other colleges and universities that formed the basis of an extended family crucial to Mount Holyoke's success continue to be built and encouraged, but they too are more extensive and varied than formerly, reflecting the changes that have occurred in the scientific world as well as Mount Holyoke. They now include as a matter of course women who hold professorships and head departments and laboratories at coeducational colleges, universities, and research institutions.

What then of the overarching ethos of complementarity? Earlier in this chapter reference was made to breaking the old vision in which men and single women were encapsulated in a system in which women filled the interstices while sharing a common set of knowledge. The only equality and identity they could share with men was that of intellectual ability, while they separated themselves from their married sisters and from non-Christians. In the postwar years at Mount Holyoke, after the retirement of President Ham and especially under the renewed female leadership of Elizabeth Keenan, it appears that a new vision of complementarity has arisen, one that both integrates men and women in the colleges into the scientific professions on an equal basis and refuses to accept the notion of "women's work in science." At the same time, it embraces all professionally qualified women, whatever their religion, race, and marital and family status. If this is the realm of the possible that now has legal recognition in the form of federal legislation, at Mount Holyoke it is being played against frustrating realities of glass ceilings, boring low-level technical jobs designated for women, competitive job markets, and poor child care and pregnancy leave options for graduates. Current graduates, however, feel a greater flexibility exists in the job market, allowing some of them to see advantages that well-paid part-time employment can offer those raising families.[14]

Broadly speaking, Mount Holyoke and its faculty hold an important place in the history of science at liberal arts colleges, in the history of the relationship between religion and science in this country, and in the history of women in American science. It is possible to see that the overarching culture of Mount Holyoke invests its history with broad implications for the study of women in science in the past, but also for the design of strategies for integrating and advancing women into the scientific enterprise in the present and future.

The current generation of Mount Holyoke science majors and their professors struggles with the mechanics needed to realize a new dynamic arrangement. At the same time, their efforts are part of that restless dynamic that is the essence of the American scientific enterprise. Although many of the characteristics of their current vision are radically different from the original that informed the teaching of science at Mount Holyoke and suited different circumstances and opportunities, this current vision has much in common with old structures and goals, and hence with that earlier formulation.

The ethos of complementarity, in the ways it integrated considerations of sexual identity and gendered roles with a particular understanding of the scientific community and its multiple objectives, bridged a psychological and social gap that has been a source of frustration, ambivalence, and confusion to many women and minorities. That separation is, and has been, experienced as what Elizabeth Fox-Genovese has termed a painful state of "twoness."[15] By espousing the individualism of Western capitalist society, members of marginal groups such as women and African Americans have become caught up in a dialectical tension between a feeling that part of their individuality lies in their difference, and their membership in a larger society that includes them on some generic level but denies them full membership as individuals. Not unrelated to Fox-Genovese's analysis, but more directly addressing the issue of women in science, philosopher Sandra Harding asks if there is a way that feminism can integrate science and transform it into something new so that there is no contradiction between women's sense of their individual identity and the values of the scientific community—that is, no tensions or divisions between women scientists and the profession of science.[16]

For Mount Holyoke scientists, individualism and radical feminism were not compatible with institutional goals and values that stressed community and integration into the economy on the basis of moral, economic, and intellectual equality—not identity—with men. A major objective has been to help women to deal with the hard realities of the American market place. For well over a century, save for the crises in the late 1930s, their culture has allowed faculty members and students to avoid the dialectical abyss of "twoness" with its encouragement of social alienation and introspection, creating as it did a way for women to intellectually and socially integrate themselves into the scientific community while mitigating any problematical contradictions in their position as unmarried women. Their culture in essence was able to establish for them and for many of their graduates a functional, enclosed intellectual and social space comprised of male scientists (married and unmarried) and unmarried women scientists in which certain essential forms of equality and capability were believed in, and others aspired to. In addition, their cosmologies, natural as well as social, took into account male and female differences and similarities, while accepting female sexual differences as part of a natural plan, but not a weakness to be overcome, nor a cause for alienation. Institutionally, the seminary and college were and still are seen as places where women develop their strengths and abilities as a means of working themselves into the system and thereby altering it. Mount Holyoke was a place where women learned to coordinate their relationships with men—not where they learned to separate and oppose themselves into an isolated female culture.

Even with the shrinking of this culture from a campus-wide to a departmentally centered value system, the type of feminist individualism that Fox-Genovese criticizes was not the dominant characteristic of Mount Holyoke scientists in any of the three periods studied here. And when it threatened to become so, the entire community was impelled to look back to Lyon's corporate vision. Where it did figure was at the institutional level, for as a seminary and college for women that emphasized science, Mount Holyoke was caught in periodic assessments of its identity, strengths, and weaknesses vis-à-vis the wider world of male dominated science. There was a kind of institutional individualism, yet even here the commitment of Mount Holyoke to what its faculty and administration considered a nongendered, socially beneficial goal shared with male scientists undercut any tendencies toward alienation from the mainstream of science. This proved to be a great strength. It was, in particular, a means of survival and participation in the professionalization of science.

Given these continuities and differences, there are two ways that might end this study. One ending is with an anecdote exemplifying both the great strides that have been made and very familiar dilemmas that face women scientists in a profession where they are attempting to realize sexual equality. Today some women faculty at Mount Holyoke worry that the new egalitarianism on campus may favor married men, as the college grants postpartum leaves of absence to new fathers as well as mothers. The fear here is that men will parent differently than women, enabling them to use this time freed from teaching duties to increase their publication output, while their wives tend to the baby and temporarily reduce their intellectual productivity. Old stereotypes and sex roles, even with the best institutional support, will be long in disappearing in the competitive world of science.

The other ending is more optimistic, a biological metaphor derived from a science to which Mount Holyoke's founder was particularly attached. It can be said that the cultural seeds that Mary Lyon planted so long ago have produced sturdy stock. Through institutional hybridization and intellectual grafting performed by science faculty, this stock has proven capable of continuous adaptation, diversification, and social contribution—all signs of persistent and continuing vigor.

Notes

N.B. Where possible, I have referred the reader to printed texts of archival documents and printed references to them in notes, for greater ease of access. Some archival documents can be accessed via the Mount Holyoke College Archives and Special Collections web site. Throughout the notes, I have used the following abbreviations: AC (Amherst College), MHCA (Mount Holyoke College Archives), and MIT (Massachusetts Institute of Technology).

Preface (pp. ix–xiii)

1. *College: The Undergraduate Experience in America* (New York: Harper and Row, 1987), p. xii.

1. Introduction (pp. 1–18)

1. Histories of Mount Holyoke include: Arthur C. Cole, *A Hundred Years of Mount Holyoke College: The Evolution of an Educational Idea* (New Haven, Conn.: Yale University Press, 1940); Frances Lester Warner, *On a New England Campus* (Boston and New York: Houghton Mifflin Co., 1937); Elizabeth Alden Green, *Mary Lyon and Mount Holyoke: Opening the Gates* (Hanover, N.H.: University Press of New England, 1979); Lisa Natale Drakeman, "Seminary Sisters: Mount Holyoke's First Students, 1837–1849" (Ph.D. diss., Princeton University, 1988); Beth Bradford Gilchrist, *The Life of Mary Lyon* (Boston: Houghton Mifflin, 1910); Sarah D. (Locke) Stow, *History of Mount Holyoke Seminary, South Hadley, Mass., During Its First Half Century* (South Hadley, Mass.: Mount Holyoke, 1887); Charlotte King Shea, "Mount Holyoke College, 1875–1910: The Passing of the Old Order" (Ph.D. Diss., Cornell University, 1983); Elizabeth M. Tidball and Vera Kistiakowsky, "Baccalaureate Origins of American Scientists and Scholars," *Science* 193 (20 Aug. 1976): 646–52. Kenneth Hardy places Mount Holyoke second in the period 1920 to 1939; see "Social Origins of American Scientists and Scholars," *Science* 185 (9 Aug. 1974): 501. On sources of doctorates for Mount Holyoke faculty, see Margaret Rossiter, *Women Scientists in America: Struggles and Strategies to 1940* (Baltimore: Johns Hopkins University Press, 1982), pp. 35, 144–158.

2. I wish to thank Professor Rosalind Williams for her suggestions for summarizing this material. Professor Rosalind Williams personal communication to author, 1 December 2003.

3. Charles Rosenberg, "Science in American Society: A Generation of Historical Debate," in *The Scientific Enterprise in America: Readings from* Isis, eds. Ronald Numbers and Charles Rosenberg (Chicago: University of Chicago Press, 1996), 3–14; and his "Afterword," ibid., pp.15–20, present a summary and analysis of these trends in research on the history of science. Also see: David Hounshell, "Rethinking the Cold War; Rethinking Science and Technology in the Cold War; Rethinking the Social Study of Science and Technology," *Social Studies of Science* 31 (April 2001): 289–297; Michael Aaron Dennis, "Historiography of Science: An American Perspective," in *Science in the Twentieth Century*, eds. John Krige and Dominique Pestre (Amsterdam: Harwood Academic Press, 1997), 1–26; George Sarton, "Remarks Concerning the History of Twentieth Century Science," *Isis* 26 (Dec. 1936): 53–62; Miriam R. Levin, "Center and Periphery in the History of Science," in *Reconstructing History: The Emergence of a New Historical Society*, eds. Elisabeth Lasch-Quinn and Elizabeth Fox-Genovese (New York: Routledge, 1999), 322–346.

4. See Robert K. Merton's preface to his *Science, Technology and Society in Seventeenth Century England* (New York: Harper & Row, 1970).

5. Thomas Kuhn, *The Structure of Scientific Revolutions* (Chicago: University of Chicago Press, 1962). See also comments by Rosenberg, "Science in American Society," p. 7 and n. 7.

6. Bruno Latour and Steve Woolgar's contributions come from the field of science studies, and historians of science have transposed this ethnographical approach into historical settings. See Bruno Latour and Steve Woolgar, *Laboratory Life: The Construction of Scientific Facts* (Beverly Hills: Sage, 1979); and Latour, "On Recalling ANT," *Keynote Speech: 'Actor Network and After' Workshop*, Keele University, July 1997. http://www.comp.lancs.ac.uk/sociology/stslatour1.html. On the relationship between the design of these spaces and the character of scientific activity within them, see Stuart Leslie and Scott Knowles, "'Industrial Versailles': Eero Saarinen's Corporate Campuses for GM, IBM, and AT&T," *Isis* 92 (March 2001): 1–33. On the design of science buildings as helping inaugurate modern trends in women's colleges see: Helen Lefkowitz Horowitz, *Alma Mater: Design and Experience in the Women's Colleges from Their Nineteenth-Century Beginnings to the 1930s* (New York: Houghton Mifflin, 1986).

7. David Kaiser, "Making Tools Travel: Pedagogy and the Transfer of Skills in Postwar Theoretical Physics," in *Pedagogy and the Practice of Science*, ed. David Kaiser (Cambridge, Mass.: MIT Press, Fall 2004). In 2002, MIT hosted a series of workshops on the subject of pedagogy in the sciences: "Training Scientists, Crafting Science: Educational Formation in the Physical Sciences, 1800–2000," held 25–26 January 2002 and 20–21 September 2002.

8. Daniel Kevles, *The Physicists: The History of a Scientific Community in Modern America* (New York: Vintage Books, 1978), a study in the rise to power of a particular group of men and how they came to epitomize their profession. George H. Daniels was also a

major figure in introducing the study of the scientific profession. See George H. Daniels, "The Process of Professionalization in American Science: The Emergent Period, 1820—1860," *Isis* 58 (Summer 1967): 150—166; and *idem, American Science in the Age of Jackson* (New York: Columbia University Press, 1968).

9. Margaret Rossiter, *Women Scientists,* chap. 3; and *idem,* "Women's Work in Science, 1880—1910," in *The Scientific Enterprise in America,* pp. 123—141.

10. In *Women Scientists,* pp. 22—28, Rossiter frames the history of women scientists within this professional model, where research activity and university positions are the sine qua non and teaching an impediment to individual success. Searching out the strategies women used to cope with discrimination and to contribute to research, she characterizes the women's colleges as offering less desirable, problematic alternatives to university posts. Evelyn Fox Keller, *A Feeling for the Organism: The Life and Work of Barbara McClintock* (New York: W. H. Freeman, 1983), refers to women's colleges as places for women who lacked the drive necessary for high-level research. Historically women's colleges sought their highest measure in men's colleges, not universities, at the same time remaining conscious that women's education was distinctive. Roger L. Geiger points out that between 1887 and 1910 the U.S. Bureau of Education made this measure official when it began publishing reports ranking women's colleges into two categories, depending on how well they measured up to men's colleges in the Northeast and on their ability to satisfy the "demand with respect to women's education." See his "The 'Superior Instruction of Women,' 1836—1890," in *The American College in the Nineteenth Century,* ed. Roger Geiger (Nashville, Tenn.: Vanderbilt University Press, 2000), pp. 192—193.

11. Roger L. Geiger, "The Era of Multipurpose Colleges in American Higher Education, 1850—1890," *American College,* pp.127—152 passim.

12. Robert Merton, preface to *Science Tecnology and Society in Seventeenth Century England,* p. ix; Max Weber, *The Protestant Ethic and the Spirit of Capitalism,* Second Roxbury Edition (Los Angeles, Calif.: Roxbury Publishing Company, 1998).

13. See Thomas Nipperdy, "Max Weber, Protestantism, and the Debate around 1900," pp. 73—82, and Hans Rottmann, "Meet Me in St. Louis," pp. 357—384, in Hartman Lehman and Gunther Roth, eds., *Weber's Protestant Ethic* (Cambridge: Cambridge University Press, 1993). Also see Magali S. Larson, *The Rise of Professionalism: A Sociological Analysis* (Berkeley: University of California Press, 1977); Magali S. Larson, "In the Matter of Experts and Professionals, or How Impossible It Is to Leave Nothing Unsaid," in Rolf Torstendahl and Michael Burrage, eds., *The Formation of the Professions: Knowledge, State and Strategy* (London: Sage Publishers, 1990), pp. 24—50; Burton J. Bledstein, *The Culture of Professionalism: The Middle Class and the Development of Higher Education in America* (New York: W. W. Norton and Co., Inc., 1976), who overemphasizes the break between the pre— and post—Civil War secular attitudes as throwing off religious values altogether in favor of objective rationalism.

14. Max Weber, *Protestant Ethic,* pp. 13, 21—23, 168, 249.

15. Weber, *Protestant Ethic,* p. 62—63.

16. Weber, *Protestant Ethic,* p. 62—63.

2. Sanctified Scientific Teachers—Teachers of Science
(1837–1859) (pp. 19–50)

1. For accounts of Lyon's intentions in opening Mount Holyoke, see: Cole, *A Hundred Years*; Elizabeth Alden Green, *Opening the Gates*; Amanda Porterfield, *Mount Holyoke Missionaries*. In an 1836 letter promoting Mount Holyoke Female Seminary, Mary Lyon presented the rationale for her radical vocational goals in terms that mixed ambition, subservience, moral superiority, and marketability, pointing out how her agenda for her faculty would help fill a vacuum in the leadership of the evangelical mission to change the nation. See Kathryn Kish Sklar, "The Founding of Mount Holyoke," p. 200. On Lyon's own scientific education, see: Porterfield, *Mount Holyoke Missionaries*, pp. 41–43; Gilchrist, *Life of Mary Lyon*, pp. 39–83; Stow, *History of Mount Holyoke*, pp. 17–18.

2. Richard W. Wilkie and Jack Tager, *Historical Atlas of Massachusetts* (Amherst: University of Massachusetts Press, 1991), pp. 28–36; Winifred Barr Rothenberg, *From Marketplaces to a Market Economy: The Transformation of Rural Massachusetts, 1750–1850* (Chicago: University of Chicago Press, 1992); Jonathan Prude, *The Coming of Industrial Order: Town and Factory Life in Rural Massachusetts, 1810–1860* (New York: Cambridge University Press, 1983); Charles Sellers, *The Market Revolution: Jacksonian America, 1815–1846* (New York: Oxford University Press, 1991). Daniel J. Boorstin's account of this period captures the multifaceted enthusiasm contemporaries had for higher education, specifically for college teaching. See Boorstin, *The Americans: The National Experience* (New York: Random House, 1965), pp. 152–161.

3. For background, see Donald G. Mathews, "The Second Great Awakening as an Organizing Process, 1780–1830: An Hypothesis," *American Quarterly* 21 (Spring 1969): 23–43. And more recently *The American College in the Nineteenth Century*, ed. Roger Geiger, provides a collection of articles treating both the historiography and history of these institutions. On the social composition and origins of the student body, see: Colin B. Burke, *American Collegiate Populations: A Test of the Traditional View* (New York: New York University Press, 1982), esp. chapter 3 and p. 275, n. 3; David Allmendinger, Jr., "Mount Holyoke Students Encounter the Need for Life-Planning, 1837–1850," *History of Education Quarterly* 19 (Spring 1979): 27–46; *idem, Paupers and Scholars: The Transformation of Student Life in Nineteenth-Century New England* (New York: St. Martin's Press, 1975); Charles Roy Keller, *The Second Great Awakening in Connecticut* (New Haven, Conn.: Yale University Press, 1942); Leonard I. Sweet, *Health and Medicine in the Evangelical Tradition: "Not by Might nor Power"* (Valley Forge, Penn.: Trinity Press International, 1994); Robert A. Wauzzinski, *Between God and Gold: Protestant Evangelicalism and the Industrial Revolution, 1820–1914* (Rutherford, N.J.: Fairleigh Dickinson University Press, 1993); Stanley M. Guralnick, *Science and the Antebellum American College* (Philadelphia: American Philosophical Society, 1975); Frederick Rudolph, *Curriculum: A History of the American Undergraduate Course of Study since 1636* (San Francisco: Jossey-Bass, 1977); Daniels, *American Science*, esp. chap. 2; Sally G. Kohlstedt, "Reassessing Science in Antebellum America," *American Quarterly* 29 (Fall 1977): 444–

453; Robert V. Bruce, *The Launching of Modern American Science, 1846–1876* (New York: Alfred A. Knopf, 1987), pp. 75–93.

4. On the formation of the American scientific community and Hitchcock, see: Sally G. Kohlstedt, *The Formation of the American Scientific Community: The American Association for the Advancement of Science, 1848–60* (Urbana: University of Illinois Press, 1976); Daniels, *American Science*, esp. chapter 2; Stanley M. Guralnick, "Geology and Religion before Darwin: The Case of Edward Hitchcock, Theologian and Geologist (1793–1864)," *Isis* 63 (Dec. 1972): 529–543; Philip J. Lawrence, "Edward Hitchcock: The Christian Geologist," *Proceedings of the American Philosophical Society* 116 (Feb. 1972): 21–34; Bruce, *Modern American Science*, pp. 122–126, 167, 251–252.

5. Lyon kept books of subscribers and subscription amounts. A list from some of them is published in Stow, *History of Mount Holyoke*, pp. 40–41, 59–60. Stow makes special mention of the importance Lyon placed on the first donation of $1,000 that came from Ipswich Female Seminary teachers; ibid., p. 60.

6. Mary Lyon to Zilpah P. Grant, February 4, 1833. Quoted in Edward Hitchcock, *The Power of Christian Benevolence Illustrated in the Life and Labors of Mary Lyon* (Northampton, Mass.: Hopkins, Bridgman, and Company, 1851), p. 172. Lyon wrote: "It is desirable that the plans relating to the subject [improving the middling classes] should not seem to originate with *us*, but with benevolent *gentlemen*. If the object should excite attention, there is danger that many good men will fear the effect on society of so much female influence, and what they will call female greatness" (his italics). For an example of this strategy used with Edward Hitchcock, see Stow, *History of Mount Holyoke*, p. 41.

7. See quote in Sklar, "The Founding of Mount Holyoke," p. 200.

8. "A General View of the Design and Principles of Mount Holyoke Female Seminary," February 1837, quoted in Stow, *History of Mount Holyoke*, p. 72.

9. On the composition of the board of trustees, see listings in the yearly catalogues for Mount Holyoke Seminary for this period; catalogues from 1837 to 1900 are accessible online through the Five College Archives Digital Access Project, http://clio.fivecolleges.edu/mhc/catalogs/. Also see Cole, *A Hundred Years*, pp. 24, 46, 51–52; and Stow, *History of Mount Holyoke*, chap. 4.

10. Mary Lyon, "Mount Holyoke Female Seminary" (also known as "The Character of Young Ladies"), pamphlet from 1835 (Boston: Directors of the Old South Work, 1903 [reprint]), MHCA. Quoted in Shmurak and Handler, "'Castle of Science,'" p. 316.

11. Cole, *A Hundred Years*, pp. 22–23.

12. "First Annual Catalogue of the Officers and Members of the Mount Holyoke Female Seminary, South Hadley, Mass., 1837–8," p. 9.

13. These practices may have been adopted by Lyon from personal observations of Amos Eaton's teaching methods and participation in the popular activity of botanizing, as well as her acquaintance with the Troy Female Seminary Program. She, like Almira H. Lincoln Phelps, had studied with Eaton. See: Amos Eaton to Mary Lyon, ca. 4 January 1825, MS 0500.1, Series A, Mary Lyon Collection, MHCA. She also may have

adapted the methods Hitchcock used to teach geology and to build Amherst College's natural history teaching collections. On avid student botanizing see: Susan Tolman, Journal Letters, 24 May and 7 June 1847, MHCA; Cole, *A Hundred Years*, p. 62; Rossiter, *Women Scientists*, pp. 2–3 and nn. 6, 7. On natural history museums at colleges, see Sally G. Kohlstedt, "Curiosities and Cabinets: Natural History Museums and Education on the Antebellum Campus," *Isis* 298 (Sept. 1988): pp. 406–429.

14. Almira H. Lincoln Phelps, *Familiar Lectures on Botany, Practical, Elementary, and Physiological; With an Appendix, Containing Descriptions of the Plants of the United States and Exotics, &c., for the Use of Seminaries and Private Students*, 4th ed. (Hartford, Conn.: F. J. Huntington, 1835), pp. 13–14. Phelps played a major role in promoting botany as a subject of study for women and wrote textbooks widely used in the 1830s and 1840s in seminaries that are particularly interesting for their emphasis on learning from nature at a time when this pedagogical approach was controversial in higher education. On Phelps, see Rossiter, *Women Scientists*, pp. 6–7, 76, 95, 103; Emma Lydia Bolzau, *Almira Hart Lincoln Phelps: Her Life and Work* (Lancaster, Penn.: The Science Press, 1936).

15. Lyon to Zilpah Grant, 17 March 1837, Mary Lyon Papers, Series A, Subseries 1, MHCA. On the history of laboratory teaching in this period, see Deborah Jean Warner, "Commodities for the Classroom: Apparatus for Science and Education in Antebellum America," *Annals of Science* 45 (July 1988): 387–397.

16. Rossiter, *Women Scientists*, p. 9, gives ratios for the number of women to men on the faculties of women's seminaries and academies, but does not elaborate on the different types of appointments that existed. For Hitchcock's courses of lectures, see annual catalogues for Mount Holyoke Female Seminary, 1837–1860.

17. Paul H. Mattingly, *The Classless Profession: American Schoolmen in the Nineteenth Century* (New York: New York University Press, 1975), pp. 37–43. He argues that the history of professionalization in the colleges is best understood in terms of the professionalization of teaching in which faculty at different types of institutions defined their functions in light of the emerging bureaucratic structure of American education. See *ibid.*, including the section "Bibliographical Notes."

18. The identification of women with botany, and its concomitant fall from a high ranking in the panoply of scientific courses, rested on the popularity of collecting and the growing number of amateur women botanists. See Rossiter, *Women Scientists*, pp. 83–86 and nn. 25 and 26.

19. Rebecca Fiske, Journal Letter, 3 June 1848, MHCA. Also see n. 13 above.

20. Trustees. See minutes (1836–1890), MHCA. Also see discussion of selflessness and Lyon's views on pride in Porterfield, *Mount Holyoke Missionaries*, pp. 14–15.

21. Porterfield, *Mount Holyoke Missionaries*, pp. 14–15, speaks generally about Lyon's decision to restrain herself from breaking into public life directly.

22. David F. Noble, *A World Without Women: The Christian Clerical Culture of Western Science* (New York: Alfred A. Knopf, 1992), pp. 250–256. Leonard Sweet, *The Minister's Wife: Her Role in Nineteenth-Century American Evangelicalism* (Philadelphia: Temple University Press,

1983), pp. 5–11, 76–106. Sweet paints a less radically segregated picture, yet makes clear that women might pray in public in some congregations, but faced censure in many eastern Baptist, Congregationalist, and Presbyterian circles for speaking to a mixed audience. In any case, they could not preach—a way to keep the minister's professional authority inviolate. See *ibid.*, pp. 78–79, 121–122. On conversion, see Virginia Lieson Brereton, *From Sin to Salvation: Stories of Women's Conversions, 1800 to the Present* (Bloomington: Indiana University Press, 1991), pp. xi, 3–28.

23. See Lyon's comments on natural foods and on exercise in Cole, *A Hundred Years*, pp. 82–84.

24. *Ibid.*, 55.

25. It was an experience that her devoted student, the missionary Fidelia Fiske, offered as a model for others. See principal's reports for these years, MHCA. Fiske's description of Mary Lyon's salvation experience is included in Stow, *History of Mount Holyoke*, p. 21. See also Fidelia Fiske, *Recollections of Mary Lyon, with Selections from Her Instructions to the Pupils of Mount Holyoke Female Seminary* (Boston: American Tract Society, 1866). Porterfield, *Mount Holyoke Missionaries*, pp. 50–67, discusses the experience of salvation and its role, practice, and origins at the seminary at some length. She also points out that for Lyon it originally provided an encouragement and means of canalizing her energies, while subordinating her self-doubts. This experience was especially important for women preparing to enter work that required calling attention to themselves in a society that discouraged them from speaking in public, even within the confines of evangelical churches with their more egalitarian attitudes toward women's right to salvation. See Noble, *A World Without Women*, pp. 250–256, and Susan Juster, *Disorderly Women: Sexual Politics and Evangelicalism in Revolutionary New England* (Ithaca: Cornell University Press, 1994), esp. chaps. 2, 5, and 6. Juster's discussion of women's conversion narratives identifies the feelings of commitment they had to a group of the chosen. For background see Mathews, "The Second Great Awakening," pp. 23–44.

26. Quoted in Carl Degler, *At Odds: Women and the Family in America from the Revolution to the Present* (New York: Oxford University Press, 1980), p. 299.

27. Mattingly, *Classless Profession*, pp. 41–43.

28. *Memorial. Twenty-fifth Anniversary of the Mt. Holyoke Female Seminary* (Published for the Seminary, South Hadley, Mass. [Springfield, Mass.: S. Bowles & Co., Printers, 1862]), p. 51.

29. *Ibid.*, p. 17.

30. Cole, *A Hundred Years*, p. 99; Stow, *History of Mount Holyoke*, pp. 159, 178–179; and Porterfield, *Mount Holyoke Missionaries*, pp. 37–38, all note this emphasis. Porterfield elaborates on Lyon's obsessive-compulsive behavior in this regard, especially at the end of her life (pp. 53–54).

31. Cole, *A Hundred Years*, p. 98.

32. *Ibid.*, p. 70.

33. *Ibid.*, p. 99.

34. See Daniels, *American Science*, p. 52 and n. 38.

35. Cole, *A Hundred Years*, p. 55.

36. Letter from Sarah A. Stearns (former Ipswich pupil) to Lyon, 26 December 1838. Mary Lyon Papers, Series A, Sub-series 2, MHCA.

37. Cole, *A Hundred Years*, pp. 54–55, 132–133.

38. *Ibid.*, p. 62.

39. Susan Tolman, Journal Letter, 7 June 1846, typed manuscript, p. 85, MHCA.

40. Lyon wrote of the student: "She is a member of our present Senior Class. She is very much interested in the natural sciences & by giving her direct & almost exclusive attention to them, I think she might excel. But she has not acquaintance in giving chemical experiments. This would scarcely be expected of any lady unless she should attend to it with the definite expectation of occupying such a place." Mary Lyon to Rev. Charles C. Beatty, 15 July 1845, Mary Lyon Papers, Series A, MHCA. In an earlier letter to Beatty dated June 30, 1840, Lyon wrote: "Some of my best scholars attend to chemistry before they come, so I have no knowledge of them in that branch, except by their examination. I might not however fear to give them such a department in our seminary. I should expect that they could learn. . . . By the way, will you please write & state whether you consider it important that the candidate should have had any experience in giving experiments." Mary Lyon to Charles C. Beatty, Mary Lyon Papers, Series A, Sub-series 1, MHCA.

41. Susan Tolman, Journal Letter, 27 January 1847, MHCA.

42. See MHS principal's reports, 1854 to 1865. Chadbourne also later published a book of lectures on natural theology: Paul Ansel Chadbourne, *Lectures on Natural Theology, or, Nature and the Bible from the Same Author* (New York: G. P. Putnam and Son, 1867). A number of science lecturers also led the school in morning devotions during their visits.

43. Unsigned Journal Letter, 26 May 1852. MHCA.

44. Journal Letter, 23 July 1856, MHCA.

45. Rev. Edward Hitchcock, *The Coronation of Winter: A Discourse Delivered at Amherst College and Mount Holyoke Seminary, Soon After a Remarkable Glacial Phenomenon, In the Winter of 1845* (Amherst, Mass.: J. S. & C. Adams, 1845). On Hitchcock see also: Kohlstedt, *American Scientific Community*; Daniels, *American Science*, esp. chap. 2; Guralnick, "Geology and Religion before Darwin"; Lawrence, "Edward Hitchcock: The Christian Geologist."

46. Hitchcock, *Coronation of Winter*, p. 20.

47. Quoted in Cole, *A Hundred Years*, p. 84 and n. 69.

48. *Ibid.*, pp. 57–58 and n. 46.

49. These lectures were published in the book he coauthored with his son, Edward, Jr.: *Elementary Anatomy and Physiology: For Colleges, Academies, and other Schools* (New York: Ivison, Phinney & Co., 1860).

50. Cole, *A Hundred Years*, pp. 82–84.

51. Hitchcock, *Elementary Anatomy*, paragraph 814 and p. 430.

52. Cole, *A Hundred Years*, p. 110; Porterfield, *Mount Holyoke Missionaries*, pp. 48–50.

53. Stow, *History of Mount Holyoke*, p. 111.

54. Shmurak and Handler, "'Castle of Science.'"

55. Cole, *A Hundred Years*, p. 124. Little has been written on these institutions. For an

overview, see Margaret A. Nash, "A Salutary Rivalry," in *American College*, pp. 170–173. Nash offers a sketch of the Western Female Seminary in Oxford, Ohio, a "daughter school" very closely modeled on Mount Holyoke. Presbyterian minister Daniel Tenney, its founder, visited South Hadley in 1854 to enlist Mount Holyoke teachers for his new seminary. See p. 170, n. 5 (*ibid.*) for sources on the other sister and daughter institutions.

56. Cole, *A Hundred Years*, pp. 124–125.

57. *Ibid.*, pp. 116–118.

58. Ibid, p. 68, n. 65.

59. See Guralnick, *Science and the Ante-bellum American College*; Richard Hofstadter, *Academic Freedom in the Age of the College* (New York: Columbia University Press, 1962); Rudolph, *Curriculum*. The information available on men's colleges of the period suggests that the seeds of systematic professional culture were more heavily sown at Mount Holyoke. Guralnick does not indicate that men's colleges were concerned with identifying scientific study and character building with particular occupations, as at Mount Holyoke. The male colleges don't seem to have been either as programmatic or as disciplined as Mount Holyoke in their methods of teaching science or in the institutional arrangements that supported and justified its teachings.

Nor were men's colleges such as Amherst and Williams particularly committed to associating the study of male physiology with preparation for specific occupations. Indeed, physiology had a smaller place in their curriculum than at Mount Holyoke: see the catalogues of Williams College and Amherst College for 1837–1860. Male faculty members were, however, as much interested in rebuilding their identities as specialists as were the women faculty members at Mount Holyoke—but along lines that did not conflict, but did imply power relationships.

60. See catalogues for Amherst, Williams, and Bowdoin colleges for these years.

61. Wilmott B. Mitchell, "A Remarkable Bowdoin Decade: 1820–1830," Paper read at Town and College Club, Brunswick, Maine, December 1950 (Brunswick, Maine.: Bowdoin College, 1952), pp. 22–23; Laurence R. Veysey, *The Emergence of the American University* (Chicago: University of Chicago Press, 1965), pp. 34–35. Also see Allmendinger, *Paupers and Scholars*.

62. Mattingly, *Classless Profession*, pp. 61–83, 139–142, 152.

63. See Allmendinger, *Paupers and Scholars*.

64. Mattingly, *Classless Profession*, pp. 104–112.

65. Quoted in Daniels, *American Science*, p. 52 and n. 38. See also Sally G. Kohlstedt, "The Geologists' Model for National Science, 1840–1847," *Proceedings of the American Philosophical Society* 118 (April 1974): pp. 179–195.

66. Cole, *A Hundred Years*, 130–131. Albert Hopkins's brother Mark was more famous than he; however, Albert made his own mark on American science as a professor of astronomy and natural history at Williams where his brother served as president. According to Cole, p. 130, Albert was responsible for organizing the construction of the first observatory in North America erected exclusively for astronomical observations.

67. His book on this topic was quite successful. By 1857 it had gone into its second

edition, having sold 12,000 copies. Edward Hitchcock, *The Religion of Geology and Its Connected Sciences* (Boston: Phillips, Samson, and Co., 1857).

68. Helen Peabody, Journal Letter, 24 March 1851, MHCA.

69. Edward Hitchcock, *The Power of Christian Benevolence.*

70. Cole, *A Hundred Years,* pp. 96–97.

71. Lucy T. Lyon, Journal Letter, 18 August 1845, MHCA.

72. Cole, *A Hundred Years,* pp. 116–123.

3. Taking the Academic Science Path in an Era of Collegiate
Innovation (1860–1888) (pp. 51–92)

1. Rosalind Rosenberg, *Beyond Separate Spheres: Intellectual Roots of Modern Feminism* (New Haven, Conn.: Yale University Press, 1982); Geiger, preface to *American College,* pp. vii–viii; *idem,* "The Crisis of the Old Order: The Colleges in the 1890s," in *American College,* pp. 264–276; Peter Dobkin Hall, "Noah Porter Writ Large? Reflections on the Modernization of American Higher Education and Its Critics, 1866–1916," *American College,* pp. 196–220.

2. Ronald L. Numbers, *Darwinism Comes to America* (Cambridge, Mass.: Harvard University Press, 1998), pp. 24–57; A. Hunter Dupree, *Asa Gray, American Botanist, Friend of Darwin* (Baltimore: Johns Hopkins University Press, 1959), p. 275; Margaret Lynch, "Darwinism at Mount Holyoke Seminary: An Educational Response" (Thesis for degree of bachelor of arts with honor in history, Mount Holyoke College, 1981). For contemporary responses to lectures presented by the Rev. Joseph Cook in 1876 and 1877, see Stow, *History of Mount Holyoke,* p. 249, and Journal Letter, 5 June 1867, MHCA. Jane Maienschein, ed., *Defining Biology: Lectures from the 1890s* (Cambridge, Mass.: Harvard University Press, 1986), pp. 4–5; Edward Lurie, *Louis Agassiz: A Life in Science* (Chicago: University of Chicago Press, 1960), pp. 379–381, and *idem, Nature and the American Mind: Louis Agassiz and the Culture of Science* (New York: Science History Publications, 1974), pp. 25–45.

3. See Miriam R. Levin and Pamela E. Mack, "The Transformation of Science Education in the Gilded Era," Proceedings of the American Historical Association, 1986; Margaret Rossiter, *Women Scientists in America,* pp. 19–89; and n. 2 above.

4. Physicians Report, 1862, MHCA. Health Service Records, Series B, Folder 1, and Cole, *A Hundred Years,* pp. 137–138.

5. See discussion in Regina Markell Morantz-Sanchez, *Sympathy and Science: Women Physicians in American Medicine* (New York: Oxford University Press, 1985), p. 25. One of the best known proponents for the separation and subordination of women on the basis of their biological and psychological frailty was President Eliot of Harvard. Eliot's views are discussed by Barbara Miller Solomon, *In the Company of Educated Women: A History of Women and Higher Education in America* (New Haven, Conn.: Yale University Press, 1985), pp. 25–26 and n. 1.

6. For biographical information on Lydia Shattuck, see *Notable American Women, 1607–1950: A Biographical Dictionary,* ed. Edward T. James (Cambridge, Mass.: Belknap Press of

Harvard University Press, 1975, c. 1971); "Death of a Veteran Teacher," *Springfield Republican,* 4 November 1889; Henrietta Hooker, "Miss Shattuck as a Student and Teacher of Science," in *Memorial of Lydia W. Shattuck: Born, June 10, 1822, Died November 2, 1889* (Boston: Beacon Press, 1890), p. 38. MHCA.

7. Cornelia Clapp to Ann Haven Morgan, "Notes Taken During Talks with Dr. Clapp," typescript, 6 June 1921, Cornelia M. Clapp Papers, Box 2, Series C, Folder 4, MHCA, p. 2.

8. Mrs. H. M. Paine, "Sketch of Miss Shattuck's Early Life," Lydia W. Shattuck Papers, Box 2, Series C, Folder 1, MHCA. This quotation is from Chemistry Notebook, Series B, Folder 2, Shattuck Papers, MHCA, c. 1860–66, p. 114.

9. Cole, *A Hundred Years,* p. 157. Also see Margaret Lynch, "Darwinism at Mount Holyoke." For contemporary responses, see Stow, *History of Mount Holyoke,* p. 249.

10. Dupree, *Asa Gray,* pp. 28–34.

11. Maria L. Owen, "The Connecticut Valley Botanical Society," *Rhodora, Journal of the New England Botanical Club,* 1:6 (June 1899), p. 96.

12. Shattuck to Asa Gray, 30 June 1864, Lydia W. Shattuck Papers, Box 1, Series A, Folder 2, MHCA. Gray does not date his reponse.

13. 24 December 1873, Lydia W. Shattuck Papers, Box 1, Series A, Folder 2, MHCA.

14. *Ibid.*

15. Alan Rocke, *The Quiet Revolution: Hermann Kolbe and the Science of Organic Chemistry* (Berkeley: University of California Press, 1993).

16. Asa Gray, *Gray's Lessons in Botany and Vegetable Physiology* (New York: Ivison, Blakeman, Taylor, 1868), p. 173.

17. Dupree, *Asa Gray,* p. 275.

18. On the disagreement between Gray and Agassiz over Darwin's theory of evolution, see Dupree, *ibid.,* pp. 247–248, 257–265, 321–324. David Starr Jordan's memoir *The Days of a Man: Being Memories of a Naturalist, Teacher, and Minor Prophet of Democracy* (Yonkers-on-Hudson, N.Y.: World Book Co., 1922), pp. 106–114, describes both his debt to Agassiz and the Swiss scientist's liberal attitude that encouraged students to think for themselves based on the evidence they found about this issue. Very suggestive as a way of thinking about the change in mentality that accompanied the change in science teachers' personal interaction with the material world is the chapter by William Coleman, "From the Lecture to the Laboratory," in *The Investigative Enterprise: Experimental Physiology in Nineteenth-Century Medicine,* eds. William Coleman and Frederic L. Holmes (Berkeley: University of California Press, 1988). Also see Cynthia E. Russett, *Darwin in America: The Intellectual Response, 1865–1912* (San Francisco: Freeman, 1976); Theodore Dwight Bozeman, *Protestants in an Age of Science: The Baconian Ideal and Ante-bellum American Religious Thought* (Chapel Hill: University of North Carolina Press, 1977); and Herbert Hovenkamp, *Science and Religion in America, 1800–1860* (Philadelphia: University of Pennsylvania Press, 1978).

19. Principal's Report, July 1867, Principals and Presidents Reports, Folder 1, MHCA, pp. 5–6.

20. A course titled "Gray's Botany" replaces its predecessor "Wood's Botany" for the first time in the 1865–1866 catalogue. See: *Twenty-Ninth Annual Catalogue of the Mount Holyoke Female Seminary in South Hadley, Mass., 1865–66* (Northampton, Mass.: Bridgman & Childs, 1865), pp. 19–20.

21. See n. 11 and Cole, 157.

22. See Rossiter, *Women Scientists*, pp. 78–79 and n. 11; Shea, "Mount Holyoke College," pp. 84–86, 97–98; Cole, *A Hundred Years*, p. 156.

23. Cole, *Ibid.*

24. Rossiter, *Women Scientists*, pp. 12–13.

25. List of Trustees. See the Mount Holyoke catalogue for the academic year 1872–1873:

Andrew W. Porter, Esq. (1836–1877); Monson
Rev. E. Y. Swift (1847–1874); Secretary 1848–1859; Northampton
Rev. Edward N. Kirk, D.D. (1856–1874/died); President 1858–1874; Boston
Abner Kingman, Esq. (1856–1880/died); Boston
Austin Rice, Esq. (1858–1880/died); Conway
Rev. Hiram Mead (1858–1873); Secretary 1859–1869; South Hadley
Rev. William S. Tyler, D.D., L.L.D. (1862–1897/died); President 1874–1894; Amherst
Sidney E. Bridgman, Esq. (1865–1906/died); Secretary 1901–1904; Northampton
Rev. John M. Greene (1866–1875); Secretary 1869–1874; Lowell
Henry F. Durant, Esq. (1867–1879); Boston
A. Lyman Williston, M.A., L.L.D. (1867–1915/died); Treasurer 1873–1915; Northampton
Nathaniel G. Clark, D.D., L.L.D. (1868–1896/died); Boston
Hon. William Claflin (1869–1894); Boston
Edward Hitchcock [Jr.], M.A., M.D., L.L.D. (1869–1911); Secretary 1874–1880; Amherst
Rev. Julius H. Seelye, D.D., L.L.D. (1872–1896/died); Amherst

26. Cole, *A Hundred Years*, pp. 161–163.

27. William S. Tyler, "The Higher Education of Women," *Address Delivered at Mount Holyoke Seminary*, 3 July 1873 (Northampton: 1874). Quoted in Cole, *A Hundred Years*, p. 162.

28. See principal's reports, 1870 and 1871, Office of the President, Reports, Folder 1 (1867–1874), MHCA, pp. 159–160.

29. See MHS annual catalogues, 1867–1876.

30. See Daniel Kevles's biography of Rowland in *The Dictionary of Scientific Biography*, ed. Charles Coulston Gillispie (New York: Charles Scribner's Sons, 1976), pp. 577–579. Hereafter DSB. For information on his attitude toward women, see Rossiter, *Women Scientists*, pp. 45–46.

31. See photo taken at the 1874 Priestley Centennial, reprinted in Rossiter, *Women Scientists*, p. 79 [plate 12].

32. Principal's Report, 1867, p. 3; Principal's Report, 1868, p. 8; Principal's Report, 1869, p. 5. Office of the President, Reports, Folder 1 (1867–1874), MHCA. See also Cole, *A Hundred Years*, p. 155.

33. Principal's reports, 1870 and 1871, Office of the President, Reports, Folder 1 (1867–1874), MHCA.

34. See Rossiter, *Women Scientists*, pp. 83–86.

35. Veysey, *Emergence of the American University*, p. 60. See his discussion of utility in *ibid.*, pp. 57–120; see also Kevles' distinction between "abstract" and "practical" science in "The Physics, Mathematics, and Chemistry Communities: A Comparative Analysis," in *The Organization of Knowledge in Modern America, 1860–1920*, eds. Alexandra Oleson and John Voss (Baltimore: Johns Hopkins University Press, 1979), pp. 140–141.

36. Nicholas Murray Butler. Quoted in Veysey, *Emergence of the American University*, p. 68.

37. Quoted in Cole, *A Hundred Years*, p. 163 and n. 36. See Shea, "Mount Holyoke College," for a study of the long and painful transition period. The role of the science faculty is not discussed here, save as references to the activities of particular individuals; however, a personal communication from Dr. Shea to the author indicated that the science faculty had played a significant part in the transition. Also see Cole, chaps. 8 and 9.

38. Principal's Report, July 1873, Folder 1, MHCA, pp. 12–14. A study of the phenomenon of women's college founding in the second half of the nineteenth century is sorely needed. Of use are Roberta Frankfort, *Collegiate Women: Domesticity and Career in Turn-of-the-Century America* (New York: New York University Press, 1977); Horowitz, *Alma Mater*; Rossiter, *Women Scientists*, esp. chap. 1; Thomas Woody, *A History of Women's Education in the United States* (New York and Lancaster, Penn.: The Science Press, 1929).

39. Shattuck to Harriet M. Dowd, July 1875, Lydia W. Shattuck Papers, Box 1, Series A, Folder 1, MHCA.

40. Jane Maienschein, ed., *Defining Biology: Lectures from the 1890s* (Cambridge, Mass.: Harvard University Press, 1986), pp. 4–5; Edward Lurie, *A Life in Science*, pp. 379–381, and *idem, Nature and the American Mind*, pp. 25–45.

41. Joan N. Burstyn, "Early Women in Education: The Role of the Anderson School of Natural History," *Boston University Journal of Education* 159 (1977): pp. 51, 53–55.

42. *Ibid.*, pp. 53, 55–56.

43. See n. 8 above. For further biographical information on Lydia Shattuck, see Rossiter in *Women Scientists*, pp. 19, 78, 83–86; "Death of a Veteran Republican," *Springfield Republican*, 4 November 1889; Henrietta Hooker, "Miss Shattuck as a Student and Teacher of Science," in *Memorial of Lydia W. Shattuck*, p. 38.

44. Shea, "Mount Holyoke College," pp. 106–107, 111–112, 121; Cole, *A Hundred Years*, pp. 167, 208.

45. Shea, "Mount Holyoke College," p. 97; Maienschein, *Defining Biology*, pp. 4–5; Lurie, *Life in Science*, pp. 379–381; and *idem, Nature in the American Mind*, pp. 25–45. For women at the Anderson School, see Rossiter, *Women Scientists*, p. 86.

46. Rossiter, *ibid.*

47. Burstyn, "The Anderson School," pp. 50, 54, 59.

48. Maienschein, *Defining Biology*, pp. 4–5.

49. Ann Haven Morgan, "Notes Taken," p. 4.

50. The term "Penikesian" was used by Morgan herself in her biography of Clapp. See Morgan's manuscript, Cornelia M. Clapp Papers, Box 2, Series C, Folder 4, MHCA, p. 31. On the role of the Anderson School in introducing distinctions between amateurs and professionals, see Rossiter, *Women Scientists*, pp. 87–88; Sally Gregory Kohlstedt, "The Nineteenth Century Amateur Tradition: The Case of the Boston Society of Natural History," in *Science and Its Public: The Changing Relationship*, eds. Gerald Holton and William A. Blanpied (Boston: D. Reidel, 1976), pp. 183–84.

51. *Dictionary of Scientific Biography*, vol. vii (1973), pp. 169–170. Jordan's autobiography, however, reveals that he played down or recalled these relationships in less egalitarian or more gendered terms. Jordan, *Days of a Man*, pp. 111–112, 116–117, 165, 185, 411, 421–422, 452.

52. See Ernst Mayr's biography of Charles Otis Whitman in *The Dictionary of Scientific Biography*, vol. xiv, ed. Charles Coulston Gillispie, pp. 313–15. Morgan, "Notes Taken," p. 3.

53. Morgan, *Ibid.*, pp. 4–5.

54. *Ibid.*, p. 5.

55. See Elizabeth Noble Shor's biography of Jordan in *The Dictionary of Scientific Biography*, vol. vii (1973), pp. 169–70.

56. Burstyn, "The Anderson School," p. 58.

57. Sally Gregory Kohlstedt, "Curiosities and Cabinets: Natural History Museums and Education on the Antebellum Campus," *Isis* 79, A Special Issue on Artifact and Experiment (Sept. 1988): pp. 405–26.

58. Rossiter, *Women Scientists*, p. 61 and n. 25.

59. Morgan, "Notes Taken," pp. 5–6.

60. MHS Catalogue, 1882–1883. This description is based on photographs reproduced in the catalogue. The collection was destroyed by fire in 1917. For the origins of these campus museums, see Kohlstedt, "Curiosities and Cabinets."

61. Williams's collections, housed in Jackson Hall by 1855, were comprised primarily of specimens collected by student members of the Lyceum Society, founded in 1835. Professors Albert Hopkins and Paul Chadbourne (both of whom lectured at MHS) led society expeditions that voyaged as far away as South America (1867) and Honduras (1871) in this period. Williams College Science Center web site: http://www.williams.edu/resources/sciencecenter/center/HistSci00/chapter2.html; W. M. Smallwood, "The Williams Lyceum of Natural History 1835–1888," *New England Quarterly*, vol. 10, no. 3, Sept. 1937: pp. 553–557.

62. See Clapp's comments in Morgan, "Notes Taken," n.p.; Also see Larry Owens, "Pure and Sound Government: Laboratories, Playing Fields, and Gymnasia in the Nineteenth-Century Search for Order," *Isis* 76 (June 1985): pp. 182–194, and 183 n. 3.

63. Thomas Le Duc, *Piety and Intellect at Amherst College* (New York: Columbia Universtiy Press, 1946), chaps. 3 and 4 passim.

64. *Ibid.*, pp. 45–47.

65. Veysey, *Emergence of the American University*, pp. 41–42, 49–50.

66. Morgan, "Notes Taken," pp. 8–9.

67. See Shea on faculty strategies, "Mount Holyoke College," Chaps. 4 and 5 passim. Also see Principal's Report, 1882–1883, Principal's and President's Reports, Folder 3, MHCA, p. 6.

68. Veysey, *Emergence of the American University;* Frederick Rudolph, *The American College and University, A History* (New York: Alfred A. Knopf, 1962); Geiger, *To Advance Knowledge*, pp. 2–7, and *idem*, "Era of Multipurpose Colleges," pp. 129–130; Robert E. Kohler, "The Ph.D. Machine: Building on the Collegiate Base," *Isis* 81 (Dec. 1990): pp. 646–650.

69. Principal's Reports, 1880–1883.

70. Shea, "Mount Holyoke College," pp. 157–158; and Mariana Holbrook, *The Mount Holyoke of Today* (Boston, 1888), pp. 3–4.

71. On claims for science at Holyoke, see Shea, "Mount Holyoke College," pp. 108–109, 155, 157; and Patricia Palmieri, *In Adamless Eden: The Community of Women Faculty at Wellesley* (New Haven, Conn.: Yale University Press, 1995), pp. 173–174, 176.

72. *Report of Franklin Carter, President of Williams College, of the Third Year of His Administration* (Williamstown, Mass.: 1884), p. 7.

73. Edmund B. Wilson, "Aspects of Modern Zoological Research," January and February, 1884, printed syllabus, Williams College Archives and Special Collections (WCASC), Williamstown, Mass.

74. Geiger, *To Advance Knowledge*, p. 7.

75. Luke E. Steiner, "Science at Oberlin," *The Oberlin Alumni Magazine* 57 no. 8 (Dec. 1961).

76. Le Duc, *Piety and Intellect*, pp. 84–85.

77. *Report of Franklin Carter*, p. 7. (see n. 72 above).

78. "Catalogue of the Offices and Students of Williams College for the Year 1883–84" (1883), WCASC, p. 22.

79. See Garland Allen's biography of Edmund Beecher Wilson in *The Dictionary of Scientific Biography*, vol. xiv (1976), pp. 423–436.

80. Hugh Hawkins, "University Identity: The Teaching and Research Functions," in *Organization of Knowledge*, pp. 285–291.

81. *Ibid.*, pp. 287, 289.

82. See comments in MH Principal's Report, 1883, p. 3, on decision to eschew courses of lectures in chemistry that year in order to concentrate on laboratory courses. Also see MHS catalogue 1880–1881.

83. Shea, "Mount Holyoke College," p. 137 and 138, n. 15; Rudolph, *American College and University*, chap. 13; Veysey, *Emergence of the American University*, chap. 3.

84. Shea, "Mount Holyoke College," p. 105.

85. On the Christian variety of character building, see: Veysey, *Emergence of the American University*, pp. 9, 22–26, 35; Rudolph, *American College and University*, pp. 183–185, 193–194; Kevles, "Comparative Analysis," pp. 141–142. See also Owens, "Pure and Sound Gov-

ernment," pp. 182–183, indicates sports took up some of this slack as well—although he does not treat any women's colleges.

86. MHS, "Annual Catalogue, 1887–88," p. 19.

87. See for example, Thompson's Journal Letter, 17 March 1870, quoted in Shea, "Mount Holyoke College," p. 117.

88. *Ibid.*, pp. 47–53.

89. *Ibid.*, pp. 50, 154–155.

90. Morgan, "Notes Taken," p. 8.

91. Shea, "Mount Holyoke College," pp. 144–161; Cole, *A Hundred Years*, pp. 183, 187–194.

92. Shea, "Mount Holyoke College," p. 86.

93. Morgan, "Notes Taken," p. 11.

94. Quoted in Shea, "Mount Holyoke College," p. 151.

95. Cited in *ibid.*, p. 156 and n. 46. The quote is from Holbrook, *Mount Holyoke of Today*, pp. 3–4. Also see the comment by Clapp in Morgan, "Notes Taken," p. 11, on the issue of credentials.

96. Palmieri, *Adamless Eden*, p. 13.

97. Shea, "Mount Holyoke College," pp. 151–152, 162–163.

98. Quoted in Stow, *History of Mount Holyoke*, p. 70.

99. See Rossiter, *Women Scientists*, chap. 3 *passim*, who discusses changes in the market that opened new forms of work for people with scientific training at the end of the nineteenth century.

4. Redefining Scientific Labor in the Age of Specialization (1889–1900) (pp. 101–128)

1. "List of Attendees," *Marine Biological Laboratory Annual Report*, 1890 (Boston: 1891).

2. "Address of C. O. Whitman," *First Annual Report, Marine Biological Laboratory Reports, 1888–1912* (Boston: 1913), pp. 10–31.

3. *Ibid.*, see esp. pp. 11, 14–15, 23–25.

4. Many years later when she looked back on this period, Clapp in fact copied a section on specialization and organization from a published summary of Whitman's talk into a notebook. Woods Hole Reports, Cornelia M. Clapp Papers, Box 2, Series C, Folder 4, MHCA, p. 7.

5. Robert H. Wiebe, *The Search for Order, 1877–1920* (New York: Hill and Wang, 1967), p. 113.

6. Geiger, *To Advance Knowledge*, p. v.

7. John Barnard, *From Evangelicalism to Progressivism at Oberlin College, 1866–1917* (Columbus: Ohio State University Press, 1969), pp. 82–83; Le Duc, *Piety and Intellect*, pp. 110–112; Veysey, *Emergence of the American University*, p. 53.

8. Barnard, *Oberlin College*, p. 82.

9. *Ibid.*, chap. 1; Geiger, *To Advance Knowledge*, p. 12.

10. Geiger, *To Advance Knowledge*, p. 13.

11. *Ibid.*, p. 9.

12. Rudolph, *Curriculum*, pp. 178–180.

13. Burke, *Collegiate Populations*, p. 187; Rudolph, *Curriculum*, p. 107; Veysey, *American University*, p. 343 and n. 1.

14. Geiger, *To Advance Knowledge*, p. 8.

15. Jane Maienschein, *Transforming Traditions in American Biology, 1880–1915* (Baltimore: Johns Hopkins University Press, 1991); Frank R. Lillie, *The Woods Hole Marine Biological Laboratory* (Chicago: University of Chicago Press, 1944), pp. 34–61.

16. Lillie, *Woods Hole*, pp. 34–49. Whitman's ideas were presented in "Address of C. O. Whitman," pp. 24–31, and in his lecture on specialization published in *Biological Lectures Delivered at the Marine Biological Laboratory of Wood's Holl in the Summer Session of 1890* (Boston: Ginn & Co., 1891), pp. 1–26.

17. Barnard, *Oberlin College*, p. 42.

18. Catalogue of Williams College, 1892–1893, Williams College Archives and Special Collections, p. 34.

19. *Ibid.*

20. See catalogues of Oberlin and Western Reserve Colleges for the years 1890–1899.

21. C. O. Whitman, *Report of the Director, 1894–95, Marine Biological Laboratory Reports 1–15, 1888–1912* (Boston: 1913), p. 45.

22. *Ibid.*, p. 27.

23. President's Report, 1891, Office of the President, Reports, Folder 4, MHCA, pp. 1, 11.

24. See Hawkins, "Teaching and Research," in *Organization of Knowledge*, pp. 293–294.

25. Rossiter, *Women Scientists*, pp. 53–54 and n. 6.

26. "MHC Annual Catalogue, 1899–1900," MHCA, pp. 46, 42.

27. For a survey of chemistry at Mount Holyoke, see Shmurak and Hadler, "'Castle of Science.'"

28. For her position on religion, see Mary Frances Leach to Sarah D. Stow, 5 August 1886, Sarah D. Locke Stow Papers, MHCA.

29. "In Memorium, Mary Frances Leach, Ph.D., 1858–1939," booklet, Mary Frances Leach, Faculty and Staff Biographical File, MHCA. She held the position until 1900 but spent the last three years studying in Europe. I am grateful to Professor Pamela Mack for sharing her unpublished manuscript material on Leach and Goldthwaite with me.

30. Mary Frances Leach to Nellie Goldthwaite, 5 June 1897, Chemistry Department Records, Series C, Sub-series 1, Folder 1, MHCA.

31. Nellie Goldthwaite, Faculty and Staff Biographical File, Folder 1, MHCA.

32. *The Mount Holyoke*, May 1902, p. 446.

33. See Hawkins, "Teaching and Research," in *Organization of Knowledge*, pp. 294–295.

34. "MHC Annual Catalogue, 1899–1900," MHCA, pp. 15, 64, 82.

35. For information on these graduates, see: individual MHC faculty files; MHC

annual catalogues; individual entries in *One Hundred Year Biographical Directory* (South Hadley, Mass.: Alumnae Association of Mount Holyoke College, 1937).

36. "Annual of Mount Holyoke Seminary and College in South Hadley, Mass., 1891–92," MHCA, p. 13.

37. "Annual of Mount Holyoke Seminary and College in South Hadley, Mass., 1892–93," MHCA, pp. 12–13.

38. See Cole, *A Hundred Years*, p. 185; Stow, *History of Mount Holyoke*, p. 171.

39. President's Reports, December 1895, MIT Archives, pp. 66–68.

40. Clara Amity Bliss was one of seven Mount Holyoke graduates who attended MIT. She attended MIT in 1890–1891 and 1904–1905 before going on to earn an M.A. at Columbia University. On Bliss and the others see, Marilyn Bever, "The Women of M.I.T., 1871–1941: Who They Were, What They Achieved," MIT Department of Humanities, B.S. Thesis, 1976; *One Hundred Year Biographical Directory*, p. 174.

41. See correspondence between Bardwell and Charles Young, Elisabeth M. Bardwell, Faculty and Staff Biographical File, Folder 3, MHCA.

42. President's Report, 1892–1893, Office of the President, Reports, Folder 4 (1891–1893/94), MHCA, p. 18.

43. See the biography of Mead by Mary Sumner Benson in *Notable American Women* vol. III (1971), pp. 519–520.

44. See Oberlin College Catalogue, 1882–83, Oberlin College Archives, p. 63. Labs were offered in Qualitative and Quantitative Analysis, Mineralogy, Chrystallography, and Chemical Classification. Organic Chemistry was added in 1891. A description of the chemistry laboratory provides some sense of what the Mount Holyoke facilities must have been like in the following decade: At Oberlin there were well-equipped work tables, spigots for water and gas, and balances and apparatus for analytical work.

45. See Barnard, *Oberlin College*, pp. 42–43; Steiner, "Science at Oberlin," n.p.

46. See MHC catalogues and MBL annual reports from 1888 through the 1890s.

47. Whitman, "Report of the Director," *Marine Biological Laboratory 8th Annual Report, 1895* (Boston: 1896), p. 25.

48. Cornelia Clapp, "Some Recollections of the First Summer at Woods Hole, 1888," *The Collecting Net* 2 (1927): 3–10, quote on p. 10.

49. MHC Annual Report, 1892–93, MHCA, p.18.

50. On the Naples Table Association, see Rossiter, *Women Scientists*, pp. 47–48, 87, 122–23, 261, 306–7, 333–34, 396.

51. Quoted in Cole, *A Hundred Years*, p. 208 and n. 9.

52. See "List of Teachers with Their Salaries for 1889–90," Trustees Minutes, 1836–1890, MHCA, p. 265.

53. See Goldthwaite and Turner Faculty and Staff Biographical Files, MHCA.

54. Rossiter, *Women Scientists*, pp. 86–88.

55. See MHC Annual Catalogue, 1899–1900, MHCA, p. 55.

56. Horowitz, *Alma Mater*, p. 74.

57. Cole, *A Hundred Years*, pp. 231, 247–248.

58. Quoted in Anne Carey Edmonds, *A Memory Book: Mount Holyoke College, 1837–1987* (South Hadley, Mass.: Mount Holyoke College, 1988), p. 75.

59. Cole, *A Hundred Years*, pp. 231, 247–248.

60. Veysey, *Emergence of the American University*, pp. 180–251 passim; Shea, "Mount Holyoke College," p. 115.

61. More courses and a new curriculum were proposed to "permit a wider range of elective studies, and at the same time, insure discipline of mind and generous culture." President's Report, 1893–1894, Office of the President, Records, Box 2, Series C, Folder 4 (1891–1893/94), MHCA, p. 9.

62. See Edmonds, *Memory Book*, pp. 76–77; and Cole, *A Hundred Years*, pp. 228–229. On Biology Club, see MHC Annual Catalogue, 1892–93, MHCA, p. 13.

63. *Laboratory Life*, especially chapter 2.

64. Mary F. Leach, "On the Chemistry of Bacillus Coli Communis," *Journal of Biological Chemistry* vol. 1, no. 6 (June 1906): 463–502. [P. Mack, unpublished ms.]

65. Rossiter, *Women Scientists*, p. 28, n. 61; President's Report, 1904–05, MHCA, p. 5, notes that she resigned intending to devote herself to the science of household research. One can only deduce that Mount Holyoke did not consider this appropriate research. Goldthwaite's dissertation had been in traditional organic chemistry: Goldthwaite went on to successful research in her new field. After working at the Rockefeller Institute for Medical Research she held a number of jobs in home economics, ending as an associate professor in the home economics section of the Experimental Station at Colorado State Agricultural College (1919–25). She made significant contributions to scientific home economics, including the discovery of pectin. Goldthwaite file, MHCA. [P. Mack, unpublished ms.]

66. See Rossiter, *Women Scientists*, pp. 46–50.

67. On political activities of women scientists at this time and a bit earlier, see Sally Gregory Kohlstedt, "Maria Mitchell and the Advancement of Women in Science," *Uneasy Careers and Intimate Lives: Women in Science 1789–1979*, eds. Penina Abir-Am and Dorinda Outram (New Brunswick: Rutgers University Press, 1987), pp. 139–146; and Rossiter, *Women in American Science*, p. 100.

68. Rossiter, *Women Scientists*, chap. 3 *passim*.

69. *Ibid.*, pp. 53–54.

5. Apogee and Defeat of the Female Science Mission (1901–1937) (pp. 129–151)

1. Mary Woolley, "Inaugural Address," *The Mount Holyoke*, Inauguration Number, 15 May (1901): 12.

2. See Tidball and Kistiakowsky, "Baccalaureate Origins."

3. Rosalind Rosenberg, *Beyond Separate Spheres: Intellectual Roots of Modern Feminism* (New Haven, Conn.: Yale University Press, 1982); Anne Fausto-Sterling, *Myths of Gender: Biologi-*

cal Theories About Women and Men (New York: Basic Books, 1985); Jill G. Morawski, *Practicing Feminisms, Reconstructing Psychology: Notes on a Liminal Science* (Ann Arbor, Mich.: University of Michigan Press, 1994); Rossiter, *Women Scientists*, p. 13.

4. H. T. Woolley, *The Mental Traits of Sex: An Experimental Investigation of the Normal Mind in Men and Women* (Chicago: University of Chicago Press: 1903); *idem*, "The Validity of Standard of Mental Measurement in Young Childhood," *School and Society* 21(1925): 476–482. For biographical information on Woolley, see also Rosenberg, *Beyond Separate Spheres*, pp. 55–57, 68–83, 110–113; Elizabeth Scarborough and Laurel Furumoto, *Untold Lives: The First Generation of American Women Psychologists* (New York: Columbia University Press, 1987), pp. 134, 146, 199–201; M. W. Zapoleon and L. M. Stolz, "Woolley, Helen Bradford Thompson," in James et al., eds., *Notable American Women*. See the references found in the bibliography of Tidball and Kistiakowsky, "Baccalaureate Origins." See also http://www.webster.edu/~woolflm/wooley.html

5. Linda M. Perkins, " The African American Female Elite: The Early History of African American Women in the Seven Sister Colleges, 1880–1960," *Harvard Educational Review* 67 (Winter 1997): pp. 731–733.

6. Cole, *A Hundred Years*, p. 272.

7. "Episodes in the History of Physiology at Mount Holyoke," *The Mount Holyoke Alumnae Quarterly* 24 (May 1940), p. 8.

8. Ann Haven Morgan, *Field Book of Ponds and Streams: An Introduction to the Life of Fresh Water* (New York: G. P. Putnam's Sons, 1930), p. v; see also Zoology Department Annual Report, 1930–31, Zoology Department Records, Folder 1, MHCA, pp. 1–2.

9. Zoology Department Annual Report, 1933–1934, Zoology Department Records, Folder 1, MHCA, p. 2.

10. *Mount Holyoke College: The Seventy-Fifth Anniversary*, compiled by Bertha E. Blakely (South Hadley, Mass.: The College [*sic*], 1912), pp. 197–198, 204.

11. Schmurak and Handler, "'Castle of Science,'" Table 2, pp. 324–325.

12. Smith College Catalogue, 1925–26, p. 62; Amherst College Catalogue 1925–26, n.p.; Williams College Catalogue, 1925–26, p. 192.

13. Rossiter, *Women Scientists*, p. 170.

14. Memorandum, c. 1935–36, Philosophy and Psychology Department Records, General Material, Folder 1, MHCA, n.p.

15. *Ibid.*

16. Schmurak and Handler, "'Castle of Science,'" table 4, p. 330.

17. Letter to Mary Woolley, 12 July 1938, Mary Emma Woolley Papers General Correspondence, Box 10, Folder 12. MHCA.

18. Cole, *A Hundred Years*, chap. 11 passim.

19. Rossiter, *Women Scientists*, p. 150.

20. C. Clapp to D.S. Jordan, 14 June 1912, Stanford University Archives (SUA).

21. C. Clapp to D.S. Jordan, 7 December 1903, SUA; C. Clapp to D.S. Jordan, 18 December 1907, SUA.

22. C. Clapp to D.S. Jordan, 12 April 1912, SUA.

23. C. Clapp to D.S. Jordan, 2 January 1923, SUA.

24. C. Drinker to A. Turner, 10 August 1926, Abby H. Turner Papers, MHCA.

25. Zoology Department Annual Report, 1933–34, Zoology Department Annual Reports, Folder 1, MHCA, p. 20.

26. *Ibid.*, pp. 9, 20.

27. See Elizabeth Shor biography of Davenport, *DSB* vol. III (1971), pp. 589–591.

28. Alumnae Biographical Files, MHCA.

29. Alumnae Biographical files, MHCA. Also see Ida B. Scudder Papers, Schlesinger Library, Harvard University.

30. Ann Haven Morgan, *Laboratory Studies in General Zoology* (Ann Arbor, Mich.: Edwards Brothers, 1936).

31. Christianna Smith, Faculty and Staff Biographical Records, MHCA.

32. Gladys McCosh, Alumnae Biographical Files, MHCA.

33. Woolley, "Inaugural Address," p. 14. (See n. 1 above.)

34. Keller, *Feeling for the Organism*, chap. I.

35. See Biographical Information, Abby Howe Turner Papers, Box 3, Series 5, Folder 13, MHCA. One example is "An Appreciation," no author, typescript dated 28 July 1958.

36. "College Traditions and Religion," *Mount Holyoke Alumnae Quarterly* 32 (Feb. 1949): 175.

37. Kenneth R. Manning, *Black Apollo of Science: The Life of Ernest Everett Just* (New York: Oxford University Press, 1983).

38. See, for example, Abby Turner, "Respiratory and Circulatory Tests of Physical Fitness in Healthy Young Women" (Ph.D. diss., Harvard University, 1926).

39. "Heredity," in notebook "Heredity," Class notes of Lorna E. Stockdale (1923), Zoology Department Records, Box 3, Folder 8, MHCA.

40. Amy Sue Bix, "Experience and Voices of Eugenics Field-Workers: 'Women's Work' in Biology," *Social Studies of Science* 27 (1997): 625–668. A number of Mount Holyoke students took courses, including eugenics, at the Brooklyn Institute, later The Biological Laboratory at Cold Spring Harbor Long Island, New York, both of which Davenport headed. Professor Christiana Smith did summer research on human blood rhythms there, assisted by Margaret Harland, also from Mount Holyoke. See Brooklyn Institute yearbooks, 1902, 1912–1913, and 1914; The Biological Laboratory, Annual Announcements and Annual Reports, 1924, 1928, 1929, 1930–1931, 1932.

41. Geography and Geology Department Records, MHCA.

42. F. G. Benedict to Abby Turner, 10 Aug. 1925, Abby Howe Turner Papers, Box 3, Series 2, Folder 5, MHCA.

43. For example, Turner arranged for the school to participate in the Rockefeller Foundation sponsored training courses for nurses during World War I. See newsclip, April 1920, source unknown, Abby Turner Papers, Box 3, Series 5, Folder 13, MHCA. Also see Cole, *A Hundred Years*, p. 261.

44. See Mount Holyoke College catalogues for the 1920s and the class notes of Lorna E. Stockdale n. 39 above.

45. Daniel Kevles, *In the Name of Eugenics: Genetics and the Uses of Human Heredity* (New York: Knopf, 1985), p. 20, refers to the role of the colleges in disseminating eugenics theories. From the Mount Holyoke record it appears that the faculty members were inter-

ested in heredity, but were careful to make it clear that social and physical environment were both important factors in creating differences among humans.

46. Zoology Department Annual Report, 1932–33, Zoology Department Records, Folder 1, MHCA, pp. 3–10. See n. 9 above.

47. On Carr see Emmy Carr to Glenola Behling Rose, 2 February 1927, Attachment to Glenola Behling Rose to Pennington, O'Brien, Carr and Woodford, 22 October 1926, Carr Papers, Series A, MHCA [P. Mack, unpublished manuscript]. Student's comment is: Cleora Church, Faculty and Staff Biographical Records, MHCA.

48. Shmurak and Handler, "'Castle of Science,'" pp. 335–339.

49. See n. 46.

50. Gould, Alumnae Biographical Files, MHCA.

51. Letter from B. F. Kingsbury to Mary Woolley, 12 January 1921 in, Christianna Smith, Alumnae Biographical File, Folder 2, MHCA.

52. Ernest L. Merritt to the Appointment Committee of Mount Holyoke College, dated 8 March 1914, Maud H. Ingalls, Alumnae Biographical File, Folder 2, MHCA. Words that appear in italics were underlined in the original letter.

53. Christine Brougham, Alumnae Biographical File, MHCA.

54. On Smedley, see Lois S. (Smedley) Simpson to Isabelle Sprague, 10 September 1983, "Letters to Isabelle Sprague Concerning Death of Christianna Smith," Christianna Smith, Faculty and Staff Biographical Records, Folder 4, MHCA. On Fullerton, see correspondence from Vorhee's Appointment Bureau in Ruth Fullerton, Alumnae Biographical File, Folder 1, MHCA.

55. See Horowitz, *Alma Mater,* pp. 284–292.

56. Cole, *A Hundred Years,* p. 333.

57. Physiology Department Report, 1937–38, Physiology Department Records, Series B, Folder 1, MHCA, pp. 3–4.

58. Edna Linsley, *The Mount Holyoke* (March 1902), p. 363.

59. Cole, *A Hundred Years,* pp. 342–43; Rossiter, *Women Scientists,* p. 366, n. 31.

60. Department Report, 1933–34, Zoology Department Records, Folder 1, MHCA, p. 11.

61. See letter from Emma Perry Carr arguing for hiring of women over men during the depression because they were willing to work for lower pay! Emma Perry Carr Records, Correspondence, MHCA. This was a return to the reasoning of Mary Lyon but in circumstances where opportunity was shrinking rather than growing.

62. Lois Scharf, *To Work and To Wed: Female Employment, Feminism, and the Great Depression* (Westport, Conn.: Greenwood Press, 1980).

63. The work of Mary E. Cookingham on work and marriage patterns of women college graduates in the Gilded era and through the first three and a half decades of the twentieth century are important here. See "Bluestockings, Spinsters and Pedagogues: Women College Graduates, 1865–1910," *Population Studies:* 38 (1984), 349–364; "Working after Childbearing in Modern America," *Journal of Interdisciplinary History* 14 (Spring 1984): 773–792; "Combining Marriage, Motherhood, and Jobs before World War II: Women

College Graduates, Classes of 1905–1935," *Journal of Family History,* 9 (1984): 178–195. Judging from appointment bureau information in alumnae files in the MHCA, although graduates often went back to work or did serious volunteer work after marriage and childbearing, the great majority did not return to the fields in which they had originally been trained. As for those who went into medicine, their numbers increased radically after rather than during the period in which Cookingham notes opportunities for them grew, despite the introduction of the premedical program in the 1890s.

    64. See A. Elizabeth Adams, Circular Letter, 5 November 1935, Presidential Succession Documents, Folder 7, MHCA; Ann Haven Morgan, "Mount Holyoke's Next President," *Mount Holyoke Alumnae Quarterly,* vol. 19, no. 1 (1 May 1935), pp. 28–29. Carr's radio address is reprinted in *The Mount Holyoke Alumnae Quarterly,* vol. 20, no. 3 (November 1936), pp. 135–138.

    65. President's Report, 1955–56, (South Hadley, Mass.: Mount Holyoke College, 1956), p. 7.

    66. President's Report, 1956–57 (South Hadley, Mass.: Mount Holyoke College, 1957), p. 13.

6. Conclusion (pp. 152–166)

    1. Information in this chapter is partially based on an article published by the author: Miriam R. Levin, "Sex, Science and Religion: Mount Holyoke College and the Development of Professional Science (1837–1996)," in Sigrid Metz-Göckel and Felicitas Steck, eds., Frauenuniversitäten: *Initiativen und Reformprojekte im internationalen Vergleich* (Opladen: Leske and Budrich, 1997), pp. 235–243.

    2. On the history of the American colleges, see chapter 1. Also, see Veysey, *The Emergence of the American University;* Rudolph, *The American College and University;* Rudolph, *Curriculum: A History of the American Undergraduate Course of Study Since 1636;* Hugh Hawkins, *Between Harvard and America: The Educational Leadership of Charles W. Eliot* (New York: Oxford University Press, 1973); Woody, *A History of Women's Education in the United States;* Horowitz, *Alma Mater.* R. Freeman Butts and Lawrence Cremin, *A History of Education in American Culture* (New York: Holt, 1953) is somewhat useful.

    3. See chapter 1 and Veysey, *The Emergence of the American University;* Rudolph, *The American College and University;* Bruce, *The Launching of Modern American Science;* Guralnick, *Science and the Ante-bellum American College;* and Rossiter, *Women Scientists in America,* who does not consider the role religion played in founding and setting the goals of the women's colleges and seminaries.

    4. David Kaiser, "Cold War requisitions, scientific manpower, and the production of American physicists after World War II," *Historical Studies in the Physical Sciences* 33 (2002): 131–159; Peter Galison and Bruce Hevly, eds. *Big Science: The Growth of Large Scale Research* (Stanford, Calif.: Stanford University Press, 1992).

    5. Sam C. Carrier and David Davis-Van Atta, *Maintaining America's Scientific Productiv-*

ity: The Necessity of the Liberal Arts Colleges (Oberlin, Ohio: Offices of the Provost and Institutional Research, Oberlin College [1987]).

6. The National Science Foundation Advance Program was inaugurated in 2001 for this purpose. Information on the program can be found at http://www.nsf.gov/pubsys/ods/getpub.cfm?nsf02121. Also see Sue V. Rosser, "Twenty-Five Years of NWSA: Have We Built the Two-Way Streets between Women's Studies and Women in Science and Technology?," *NWSA Journal* 14 (2002): 103–123.

7. See for example, *Catalogue of Mount Holyoke College, 1995–96*, pp. 1–2.

8. See Tidball and Kistiakowski, "Baccalaureate Origins," pp. 646–652.

9. Data from the NSF R&D Expenditures Survey. Total separately budgeted R&D expenditures in the sciences and engineering, by field: selected years (dollars in thousands), http://caspar.nsf.gov/cgibin/WebIC.exe?template=/profiles/esshtm.wi&which=E002192

10. The Five Colleges, Inc., was founded in the 1970s. It includes Amherst, Smith, Hampshire, and Mount Holyoke colleges and the University of Massachusetts. Among the programs and centers it sponsors that are supported by the consortium members and outside grants is the Five College Women's Studies Center. This center is located on the Mount Holyoke campus. It provides office space and facilities for visiting scholars, as well as offering a vigorous program of weekly seminars by and for women which are open to the public and serving as a meeting place for women's studies courses and committees.

11. "A report, at the request of the conference committee, from the ad hoc committee on principles of the College," Typescript, 27 September 1971, Origins and Governance Records, Box 6, Series 8, Folder 3, MHCA.

12. "Awards Times Four: Decatur, Fink, Gill, and Peterson," *Mount Holyoke College Street Journal* 14 (26) (April 27, 2001), http://www.mtholyoke.edu/offices/comm/csj/042701/awards.shtml.

13. http://www.mtholyoke.edu/acad/misc/profile/names/mdyar.shtml, accessed February 13, 2004.

14. Student testimonial, MHC Web Page, Engineering Program.

15. Elizabeth Fox-Genovese, *Feminism without Illusions: A Critique of Individualism* (Chapel Hill: University of North Carolina Press, 1991), pp. 139–140.

16. Sandra Harding, *The Science Question in Feminism* (Ithaca, N.Y.: Cornell University Press, 1986), esp. pp. 15–57.

Bibliography

Allmendinger, David, Jr. "Mount Holyoke Students Encounter the Need for Life-Planning, 1837–1850." *History of Education Quarterly* 19 (Spring 1979): 27–46.

——. *Paupers and Scholars: The Transformation of Student Life in Nineteenth-Century New England.* New York: St. Martin's Press, 1975.

Barnard, John. *From Evangelicalism to Progressivism at Oberlin College, 1866–1917.* Columbus: Ohio State University Press, 1969.

Bledstein, Burton J. *The Culture of Professionalism: The Middle Class and the Development of Higher Education in America.* New York: W. W. Norton and Co., Inc., 1976.

Bolzau, Emma Lydia. *Almira Hart Lincoln Phelps: Her Life and Work.* Lancaster, Penn.: Science Press Printing Company, 1936.

Boorstin, Daniel J. *The Americans: The National Experience.* New York: Random House, 1965.

Boyer, Ernest L. *College: The Undergraduate Experience in America.* New York: Harper and Row, 1987.

Bozeman, Theodore Dwight. *Protestants in an Age of Science: The Baconian Ideal and Ante-Bellum American Religious Thought.* Chapel Hill: University of North Carolina Press, 1977.

Brereton, Virginia Lieson. *From Sin to Salvation: Stories of Women's Conversions, 1800 to the Present.* Bloomington: Indiana University Press, 1991.

Bruce, Robert V. *The Launching of Modern American Science, 1846–1876.* New York: Alfred A. Knopf, 1987.

Burke, Colin B. *American Collegiate Populations: A Test of the Traditional View.* New York: New York University Press, 1982.

Butts, R. Freeman, and Lawrence A. Cremin. *A History of Education in American Culture.* New York: Holt Publishers, 1953.

Cole, Arthur C. *A Hundred Years of Mount Holyoke College: The Evolution of an Educational Ideal.* New Haven, Conn.: Yale University Press, 1940.

Conway, Jill Ker, Susan C. Bourque, and Joan W. Scott, eds. *Learning about Women: Gender, Politics and Power.* Ann Arbor: University of Michigan Press, 1989.

Cookingham, Mary E. "Bluestockings, Spinsters and Pedagogues: Women College Graduates, 1865–1910." *Population Studies* 38 (1984): 349–364.

——. "Combining Marriage, Motherhood, and Jobs before World War II: Women College Graduates, Classes of 1905–1935." *Journal of Family History* 9 (1984): 178–195.

————. "Working after Childbearing in Modern America." *Journal of Interdisciplinary History* 14 (Spring 1984): 773–792.

Daniels, George H. *American Science in the Age of Jackson.* New York: Columbia University Press, 1968.

————. "The Process of Professionalization in American Science: The Emergent Period, 1820–1860." *Isis* 58 (Summer 1967): 150–166.

Degler, Carl. *At Odds: Women and the Family in America from the Revolution to the Present.* New York: Oxford University Press, 1980.

Dennis, Michael Aaron. "Historiography of Science: An American Perspective." In *Science in the Twentieth Century,* edited by John Krige and Dominique Pestre, 1–26. Amsterdam: Harwood Academic Press, 1997.

Drakeman, Lisa Natale. "Seminary Sisters: Mount Holyoke's First Students, 1837–1849." Ph.D. diss., Princeton University, 1988.

Dupree, A. Hunter. *Asa Gray, American Botanist, Friend of Darwin.* Baltimore: Johns Hopkins University Press, 1988.

Edmonds, Anne Carey. *A Memory Book: Mount Holyoke College, 1837–1987.* Meriden, Conn.: Stinehour Press, 1988.

Fausto-Sterling, Anne. *Myths of Gender: Biological Theories About Women and Men.* New York: Basic Books, 1985.

Fox-Genovese, Elizabeth. *Feminism without Illusions: A Critique of Individualism.* Chapel Hill: University of North Carolina Press, 1991.

Frankfort, Roberta. *Collegiate Women: Domesticity and Career in Turn-of-the-Century America.* New York: New York University Press, 1977.

Galison, Peter, and Bruce Hevly, eds. *Big Science: The Growth of Large Scale Research.* Stanford, Calif.: Stanford University Press, 1992.

Geiger, Roger L. "The Crisis of the Old Order: The Colleges in the 1890s." In *The American College in the Nineteenth Century,* edited by Roger Geiger, 264–276. Nashville: Vanderbilt University Press, 2000.

————. "The Era of Multipurpose Colleges in American Higher Education, 1850–1890." In *The American College in the Nineteenth Century,* 127–152.

————. "The 'Superior Instruction of Women,' 1836–1890." In *The American College in the Nineteenth Century,* 183–195.

Gilchrist, Beth Bradford. *The Life of Mary Lyon.* Boston: Houghton Mifflin, 1910.

Gillispie, Charles Coulston, ed. *The Dictionary of Scientific Biography,* 18 vols. New York: Charles Scribner's Sons, 1970–1990.

Green, Elizabeth Alden. *Mary Lyon and Mount Holyoke: Opening the Gates.* Hanover, N.H.: University Press of New England, 1979.

Guralnick, Stanley M. *Science and the Ante-bellum American College.* Philadelphia: American Philosophical Society, 1975.

————. "Geology and Religion before Darwin: The Case of Edward Hitchcock, Theologian and Geologist (1793–1864)." *Isis* 63 (Dec. 1972): 529–543.

Hall, Peter Dobkin. "Noah Porter Writ Large? Reflections on the Modernization of

American Higher Education and Its Critics, 1866–1916." In *The American College in the Nineteenth Century*, edited by Roger Geiger, 196–220. Nashville: Vanderbilt University Press, 2000.

Harding, Sandra. *The Science Question in Feminism*. Ithaca, N.Y.: Cornell University Press, 1986.

Hardy, Kenneth. "Social Origins of American Scientists and Scholars." *Science* 185 (9 Aug. 1974): 497–506.

Hawkins, Hugh. *Between Harvard and America: The Educational Leadership of Charles W. Eliot*. New York: Oxford University Press, 1972.

———. "University Identity: The Teaching and Research Functions." In *The Organization of Knowledge in Modern America, 1860–1920*, edited by Alexandra Oleson and John Voss, 285–312. Baltimore: Johns Hopkins University Press, 1979.

Hofstadter, Richard. *Academic Freedom in the Age of the College*. New York: Knopf, 1962.

Holbrook, Mariana. *The Mount Holyoke of Today*. Boston: 1888.

Horowitz, Helen Lefkowitz. *Alma Mater: Design and Experience in the Women's Colleges from Their Nineteenth-Century Beginnings to the 1930s*. New York: Knopf, 1984.

Hounshell, David. "Rethinking the Cold War; Rethinking Science and Technology in the Cold War; Rethinking the Social Study of Science and Technology." *Social Studies of Science* 31 (April 2001): 289–297.

Hovenkamp, Herbert. *Science and Religion in America, 1800–1860*. Philadelphia: University of Pennsylvania Press, 1978.

James, Edward T., Janet Wilson James, and Paul S. Boyer, eds. *Notable American Women, 1607–1950: A Biographical Dictionary*. 3 vols. Cambridge, Mass.: Belknap Press of Harvard University Press, 1971.

Jordan, David Starr. *The Days of a Man, Being Memories of a Naturalist, Teacher, and Minor Prophet of Democracy*. Yonkers-on-Hudson, N.Y.: World Book Co., 1922.

Juster, Susan. *Disorderly Women: Sexual Politics and Evangelicalism in Revolutionary New England*. Ithaca, N.Y.: Cornell University Press, 1994.

Kaiser, David. "Making Tools Travel: Pedagogy and the Transfer of Skills in Postwar Theoretical Physics." In *Pedagogy and the Practice of Science*, edited by David Kaiser. Cambridge, Mass.: MIT Press, forthcoming.

Kargon, Robert, and S. G. Knowles. "Knowledge for Use: Science, Higher Learning and America's New Industrial Heartland, 1880–1915." *Annals of Science* 59 (2002): 1–20.

Keller, Charles Roy. *The Second Great Awakening in Connecticut*. New Haven, Conn.: Yale University Press, 1942.

Keller, Evelyn Fox. *A Feeling for the Organism: The Life and Work of Barbara McClintock*. New York: W. H. Freeman, 1983.

Kevles, Daniel. *In The Name of Eugenics: Genetics and the Uses of Human Heredity*. New York: Knopf, 1985.

———. *The Physicists: The History of a Scientific Community in Modern America*. New York: Vintage Books, 1978.

———. "The Physics, Mathematics, and Chemistry Communities: A Comparative Analysis." In *The Organization of Knowledge in Modern America, 1860–1920*, edited by

Alexandra Oleson and John Voss, 139–172. Baltimore: Johns Hopkins University Press, 1979.

Kohler, Robert E. "The Ph.D. Machine: Building on the Collegiate Base." *Isis* 81 (Dec. 1990):638–662.

Kohlstedt, Sally Gregory. "Curiosities and Cabinets: Natural History Museums and Education on the Antebellum Campus." *Isis* 298 (Sept. 1988): 406–429.

————. *The Formation of the American Scientific Community: The American Association for the Advancement of Science, 1848–60.* Urbana: University of Illinois Press, 1976.

————. "The Geologists' Model for National Science, 1840–1847." *Proceedings of the American Philosophical Society* 118 (April 1974): 179–195.

————. "Maria Mitchell and the Advancement of Women in Science." In *Uneasy Careers and Intimate Lives: Women in Science 1789–1979*, edited by Penina Abir-Am and Dorinda Outram, 139–146. New Brunswick: Rutgers University Press, 1987.

————. "The Nineteenth Century Amateur Tradition: The Case of the Boston Society of Natural History." In *Science and Its Public: The Changing Relationship*, edited by Gerald Holton and William A. Blanpied, 173–190. Dordrecht, Holland: D. Reidel Pub. Co., 1976.

————. "Reassessing Science in Antebellum America." *American Quarterly* 29 (Fall 1977): 444–453.

Kuhn, Thomas. *The Structure of Scientific Revolutions.* Chicago: University of Chicago Press, 1962.

Larson, Magali S. "In the Matter of Experts and Professionals, or how impossible it is to leave nothing unsaid." In *The Formation of the Professions: Knowledge, State and Strategy*, edited by Rolf Torstendahl and Michael Burrage, 24–50. London: Sage Publishers, 1990.

————. *The Rise of Professionalism: A Sociological Analysis.* Berkeley: University of California Press, 1977.

Latour, Bruno. "On Recalling ANT." *Keynote Speech: "Actor Network and After" Workshop.* Keele University, July 1997. http://www.comp.lancs.ac.uk/sociology/stslatour1.html.

Latour, Bruno, and Steve Woolgar. *Laboratory Life: The Construction of Scientific Facts.* Beverly Hills, Calif.: Sage, 1979.

Lawrence, Philip J. "Edward Hitchcock: The Christian Geologist." *Proceedings of the American Philosophical Society* 116 (Feb. 1972): 21–34.

Le Duc, Thomas. *Piety and Intellect at Amherst College, 1865–1912.* New York: Columbia University Press, 1946.

Lehman, Hartman, and Gunther Roth, eds. *Weber's Protestant Ethic.* Cambridge: Cambridge University Press, 1993.

Leslie, Stuart, and Scott Knowles. "'Industrial Versailles': Eero Saarinen's Corporate Campuses for GM, IBM, and AT&T." *Isis* 92 (March 2001):1–33.

Levin, Miriam R. "Center and Periphery in the History of Science." In *Reconstructing History: The Emergence of a New Historical Society*, edited by Elisabeth Lasch-Quinn and Elizabeth Fox-Genovese, 322–346. New York: Routledge, 1999.

————. "Sex, Science and Religion: Mount Holyoke College and the Development of Professional Science (1837–1996)." In Frauenuniversitäten: *Initiativen und Reformprojekte im internationalen Vergleich,* edited by Sigrid Metz-Göckel and Felicitas Steck, 235–243. Opladen: Leske and Budrich, 1997.

Lillie, Frank R. *The Woods Hole Marine Biological Laboratory.* Chicago: University of Chicago Press, 1944.

Lurie, Edward. *Louis Agassiz: A Life in Science.* Chicago: University of Chicago Press, 1960.

————. *Nature and the American Mind: Louis Agassiz and the Culture of Science.* New York: Science History Publications, 1974.

Lynch, Margaret. "Darwinism at Mount Holyoke Seminary: An Educational Response." Thesis for degree of bachelor of arts with honors in history, Mount Holyoke College, 1981.

Maienschein, Jane. *Transforming Traditions in American Biology, 1880–1915.* Baltimore: Johns Hopkins University Press, 1991.

————, ed. *Defining Biology: Lectures from the 1890s.* Cambridge: Harvard University Press, 1986.

Manning, Kenneth R. *Black Apollo of Science: The Life of Ernest Everett Just.* New York: Oxford University Press, 1983.

Mathews, Donald G. "The Second Great Awakening as an Organizing Process, 1780–1830: An Hypothesis." *American Quarterly* 21 (Spring 1969): 23–43.

Mattingly, Paul H. *The Classless Profession: American Schoolmen in the Nineteenth Century.* New York: New York University Press, 1975.

Merton, Robert K. *Science, Technology and Society in Seventeenth Century England.* New York: Harper & Row, 1970.

Mitchell, Wilmott B. "A Remarkable Bowdoin Decade: 1820–1830." Paper read at Town and College Club, Brunswick, Maine, December 1950. Brunswick, Maine: Bowdoin College, 1952.

Morantz-Sanchez, Regina Markell. *Sympathy and Science: Women Physicians in American Medicine.* New York: Oxford University Press, 1985.

Morawski, Jill G. *Practicing Feminisms, Reconstructing Psychology: Notes on a Liminal Science.* Ann Arbor, Mich.: University of Michigan Press, 1994.

Morgan, Ann Haven. *Field Book of Ponds and Streams: An Introduction to the Life of Fresh Water.* New York: G. P. Putnam's Sons, 1930.

Nash, Margaret A. "A Salutary Rivalry." In *The American College in the Nineteenth Century,* edited by Roger Geiger, 169–182. Nashville: Vanderbilt University Press, 2000.

Noble, David F. *A World Without Women: The Christian Clerical Culture of Western Science.* New York: Alfred A. Knopf, 1992.

Owens, Larry. "Pure and Sound Government: Laboratories, Playing Fields, and Gymnasia in the Nineteenth-Century Search for Order." *Isis* 76 (June 1985): 182–194.

Palimieri, Patricia Ann. *In Adamless Eden: The Community of Women Faculty at Wellesley.* New Haven, Conn.: Yale University Press, 1995.

Perkins, Linda M. "The African American Female Elite: The Early History of African American Women in the Seven Sister Colleges, 1880–1960." *Harvard Educational Review* 67 (Winter 1997): 718–756.

Porterfield, Amanda. *Mary Lyon and the Mount Holyoke Missionaries.* New York: Oxford University Press, 1997.

Prude, Jonathan. *The Coming of Industrial Order: Town and Factory Life in Rural Massachusetts, 1810–1860.* Cambridge: Cambridge University Press, 1983.

Rosenberg, Charles. "Science in American Society: A Generation of Historical Debates, with Headnote and Afterword." In *The Scientific Enterprise in America: Readings from Isis,* edited by Ronald Numbers and Charles Rosenberg, 2–21. Chicago: University of Chicago Press, 1996.

Rosenberg, Rosalind. *Beyond Separate Spheres: Intellectual Roots of Modern Feminism.* New Haven, Conn.: Yale University Press, 1982.

Rossiter, Margaret. *Women Scientists in America: Struggles and Strategies to 1940.* Baltimore: Johns Hopkins University Press, 1982.

———. "Women's Work in Science, 1880–1910." In *The Scientific Enterprise in America: Readings from Isis,* edited by Ronald Numbers and Charles Rosenberg, 123–140. Chicago: University of Chicago Press, 1996.

Rothenberg, Winifred Barr. *From Market-places to a Market Economy: The Transformation of Rural Massachusetts, 1750–1850.* Chicago: University of Chicago Press, 1992.

Rudolph, Frederick. *The American College and University, A History.* New York: Knopf, 1962.

———. *Curriculum: A History of the American Undergraduate Course of Study Since 1636.* San Francisco: Jossey-Bass, 1977.

Sarton, George. "Remarks Concerning the History of Twentieth Century Science." *Isis* 26 (Dec. 1936): 53–62.

Scarborough, Elizabeth, and Laurel Furumoto. *Untold Lives: The First Generation of American Women Psychologists.* New York: Columbia University Press, 1987.

Scharf, Lois. *To Work and To Wed: Female Employment, Feminism, and the Great Depression.* Westport, Conn.: Greenwood Press, 1980.

Sellers, Charles. *The Market Revolution: Jacksonian America, 1815–1846.* New York: Oxford University Press, 1991.

Shea, Charlotte King. "Mount Holyoke College, 1875–1910: The Passing of the Old Order." Ph.D. diss., Cornell University, 1983.

Shmurak, Carole B., and Bonnie S. Hadler. "'Castle of Science': Mount Holyoke College and the Preparation of Women in Chemistry, 1837–1941." *History of Education Quarterly* 32 (Fall 1992): 315–342.

Sklar, Kathryn Kish. "The Founding of Mount Holyoke Female Seminary: A Case Study in Educational Change." In *Women of America: A History,* edited by Carol Ruth Berkin and Mary Beth Norton, 177–197. Boston: Houghton Mifflin Co., 1979.

Solomon, Barbara Miller. *In the Company of Educated Women: A History of Women and Higher Education in America.* New Haven, Conn.: Yale University Press, 1985.

Steiner, Luke E. "Science at Oberlin." *The Oberlin Alumni Magazine* 57 no. 8 (Dec. 1961): n.p.

Stow, Sarah D. (Locke). *History of Mount Holyoke Seminary, South Hadley, Mass., During Its First Half Century, 1837–1887.* South Hadley, Mass., 1887.

Sweet, Leonard I. *Health and Medicine in the Evangelical Tradition: Not by Might nor Power.* Valley Forge, Penn.: Trinity Press International, 1994.

———. *The Minister's Wife: Her Role in Nineteenth-Century American Evangelicalism.* Philadelphia: Temple University Press, 1983.

Tidball, Elizabeth M., and Vera Kistiakowsky. "Baccalaureate Origins of American Scientists and Scholars." *Science* 193 (20 Aug. 1976): 646–52.

Veysey, Laurence R. *The Emergence of the American University.* Chicago: University of Chicago Press, 1965.

Warner, Deborah Jean. "Commodities for the Classroom: Apparatus for Science and Education in Antebellum America." *Annals of Science* 45 (July 1988): 387–397.

Warner, Frances Lester. *On a New England Campus.* Boston and New York: Houghton Mifflin Co., 1937.

Wauzzinski, Robert A. *Between God and Gold: Protestant Evangelicalism and the Industrial Revolution, 1820–1914.* Rutherford, N.J.: Fairleigh Dickinson University Press, 1993.

Weber, Max. *The Protestant Ethic and the Spirit of Capitalism.* Second Roxbury Edition. Los Angeles, Calif.: Roxbury Publishing Company, 1998.

Wiebe, Robert H. *The Search for Order, 1877–1920.* New York: Hill and Wang, 1967.

Wilkie, Richard W., and Jack Tager. *Historical Atlas of Massachusetts.* Amherst: University of Massachusetts Press, 1991.

Woody, Thomas. *A History of Women's Education in the United States.* 2 vols. New York and Lancaster, Penn.: Science Press, 1929.

Index

Page numbers in italics indicate illustrations.